PALETTE
mini
MULTICOLOUR

Published and distributed by
viction:workshop ltd.

viction:ary™

viction:workshop ltd.
Unit C, 7/F, Seabright Plaza, 9-23 Shell Street,
North Point, Hong Kong SAR
Url: victionary.com
Email: we@victionary.com
@victionworkshop
@victionworkshop
@victionary
@victionary

Edited and produced by viction:ary

Creative direction by Victor Cheung
Book design by viction:workshop ltd.
Typeset in NB International Pro from Neubau

Fourth Edition

ISBN 978-988-79034-8-2
Printed and bound in China

2

PREFACE

According to the Cambridge Dictionary, the word 'palette' may refer to the range of colours that an artist usually paints with on a canvas. Today, however, more than just the primary means of creative expression for wielders of the physical brush, its role has expanded to include that of an important digital tool for crafting meaningful solutions in design. On top of manifesting pure works of the imagination as it has always done, the palette has become a purveyor of infinite visual possibilities with the power to bridge art and commerce. Since the release of its first edition in 2012, viction:ary's PALETTE colour-themed series has become one of the most successful and sought-after graphic design reference collections for students and working professionals around the world; showcasing a thoughtful curation of compelling ideas and concepts revolving around the palette featured. In keeping with the needs and wants of the savvy modern reader, the all-new PALETTE mini Series has been reconfigured and rejuvenated with fresh content, for all intents and purposes, to serve as the intriguing, instrumental, and timeless source of inspiration that its predecessor was, in a more convenient size.

INTRO

Colours have the power to not only express the intentions of the artist or designer applying them, but also affect the emotions of their audiences on a visceral level; eliciting sensations and responses on a variety of canvases without the need for words. Although one's preference for colour seems to be driven primarily by taste, there are many reasons as to why colour theory continues to be relevant especially in the field of design today, even though it has been years since the colour wheel was invented by Sir Isaac Newton, enhanced with psychological research findings by Johann Wolfgang Goethe, and refined into its current form by the Bauhaus's Johannes Itten.

On an elemental level, colours can instantly capture and convey a feeling or mood. For Hey's Let It Blow 2019 project in collaboration with digital artist Andrés Reisinger on page 276, blown streamers in bright but messy gradients were digitally recreated in 3D against a black backdrop to set a celebratory tone for posters sent to the former's clients. Rather than take photographs of actual streamers, the studio decided to play and experiment with different techniques to come up with imagery that they could own, adding a twist to their yearly New Year tradition. Similarly, Andstudio created 200 multicoloured pictograms to form a versatile graphic system for SMK Lithuania as part of the university's refreshed brand experience. The resulting visual identity across online and on-ground platforms as seen on page 198 mirrors the exuberance and unique personalities of the students that go there.

A colourful palette can also surprise viewers depending on the context it is used within. Resort Studio's editorial project on page 328 follows this line of thought through the neon gradient chosen for the cover of their book, 'I'm An Office Worker'. The juxtaposition of fluorescent tones with the latter's contents comprising everyday poetry, satire, and tragedy in the workplace – tied together by simple graphics that look like they were generated by a generic word processor – are a clever take on dark humour. On page 182, Post Projects' artwork for The Hope Slide's eponymous album illustrates the theme of 'perseverance triumphing over adverse circumstances' perfectly through cut-outs that hint at an outburst of colours behind a slate of dull grey. To get to the actual vinyl, listeners would have to slide it out and, in doing so, inadvertently reveal the colourful layer and demonstrate the dichotomy between pain and joy.

When working with multiple colours, the ability to mix and match them appropriately requires a certain level of instinct and understanding. It is a skill not unlike mastering new vocabulary for different situations or environments, and can be used to compelling effect. To emphasise the expertise of PIGMENTPOL® as one of the best digital printing companies in Germany, ATMO Designstudio and FELD embedded the idea of individuality and possibilities into its visual identity through a coherent combination of shades and shapes derived from a hexagon. As seen on page 122, the at-times unexpected pairings exemplify the company's appetite for personalisation and innovation through the striking composite of details. On the other hand, Carl Nas Associates' subtle fusion of warm and delicate hues for Tangent's organic soap packaging design on page 432 merge seamlessly to speak volumes about the environmentally-friendly brand.

Ultimately, colours are practical tools that can simplify ideas, catch the eye, and establish the deepest connections. Upon determining a project's communications objectives and creative direction, it is up to the designer to balance visual impact and substance with a suitable approach to tell stories that make lasting impressions.

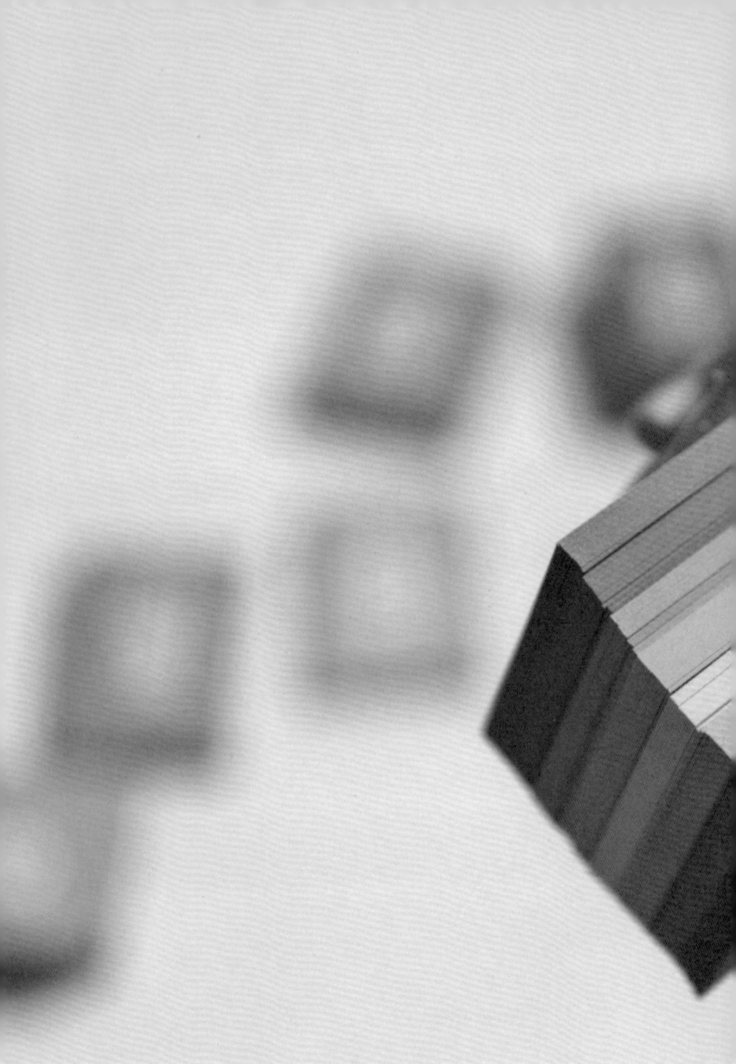

ChariTea arabian mint
ChariTea wild fruit
ChariTea chamomile
Kamillentee aus Ägypten, aus biologischem Anbau und fairem Handel
5–8 Min / 100°C
ChariTea oriental nights
Gewürztee-Mischung, verfeinert mit Feige und Orange, aus biologischem Anbau und Zutaten aus fairem Handel
5–8 Min / 100°C
ChariTea red rooibos
Rooibos-Tee aus Südafrika, aus biologischem Anbau und fairem Handel
5–8 Minuten / 90°C
ChariTea black darjeeling
Schwarzer Tee aus dem indischen Darjeeling, aus biologischem Anbau und fairem Handel
4–6 Minuten / 90°C
BIO

ChariTea wild fruit
ChariTea masala chai
ChariTea ginger lemon
ChariTea oriental nights
Gewürztee-Mischung, verfeinert mit Feige und Orange, aus biologischem Anbau und Zutaten aus fairem Handel
5–8 Min | 100°C
BIO
ChariTea arabian mint
BIO
ChariTea ceylon breakfast
Schwarztee-Mischung aus Sri Lanka,
Ruanda und dem indischen Assam, aus
biologischem Anbau und fairem Handel
BIO

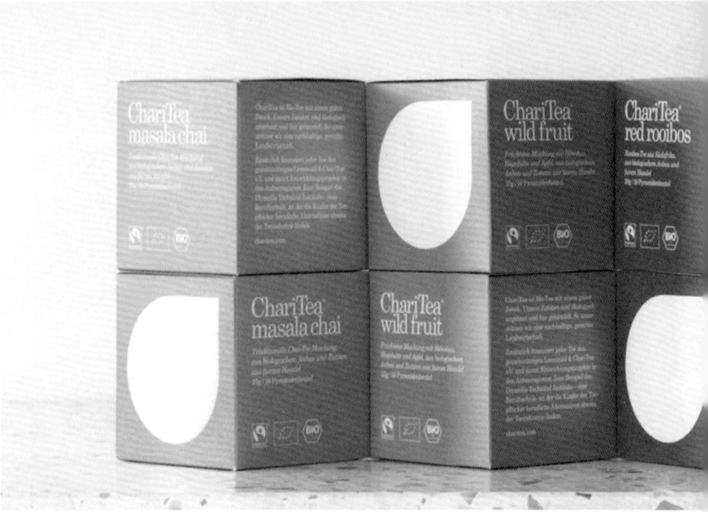
ChariTea masala chai
ChariTea wild fruit
ChariTea red rooibos
ChariTea masala chai
ChariTea wild fruit

ChariTea green rooibos
ChariTea green himalaya
ChariTea
ChariTea green rooibos
ChariTea green himalaya

ChariTea
oriental
nights
ChariTea
african
summer
ChariTea
oriental
nights
ChariTea
african
summer

ChariTea
arabian mint
ChariTea
mate boost
ChariTea
arabian mint
ChariTea
mate boost

ChariTea
green
ChariTea
black
Black tea with lemon. Organic and freshly brewed.
ChariTea
red
Rooibos tea with passion fruit. Organic and freshly brewed.

ChariTea
oriental
nights
ChariTea
wild fruit
ChariTea
chamomile
BIO

18.3 oz
toocatti
airtight stainless steel container.
37.2 oz
toocatti
airtight stainless steel container.
64.2 oz
toocatti
airtight stainless steel container.
91.3 oz
toocatti
airtight stainless steel container.

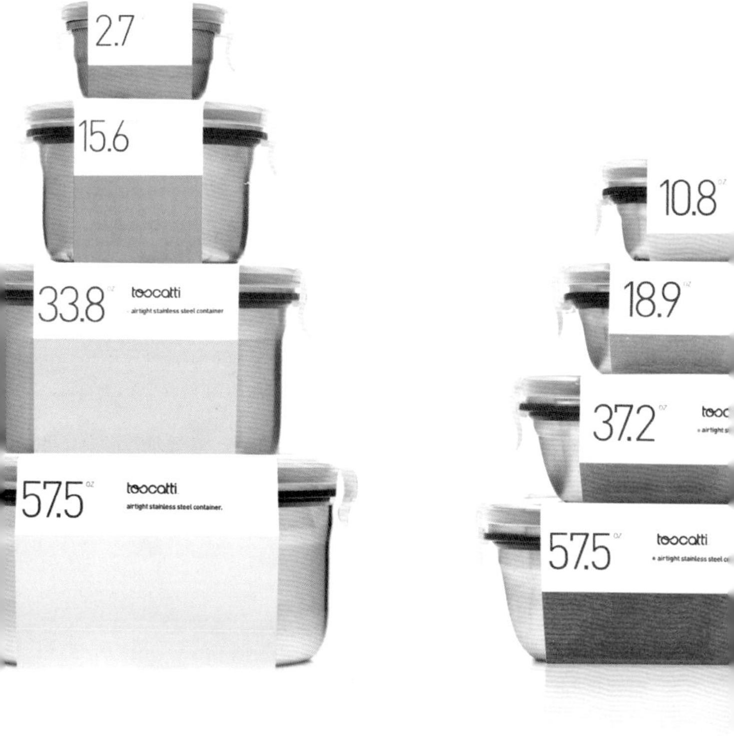
2.7
15.6
33.8
toocatti
airtight stainless steel container
57.5
toocatti.
airtight stainless steel container.
10.8
18.9
37.2
57.5
toocatti

57.5 oz
toocatti
airtight stainless steel co
toocatti
37.2 / 1.1
37.2 oz
toocatti
airtight stainless steel container.
toocatti
18.9 / 560
18.9 oz
toocatti
airtight stainless steel container.

toocatti
91.3 oz
toocatti
• airtight stainless steel container.
33.8 / 1.0
33.8 oz
toocatti
• airtight stainless steel container.
toocatti
64.2 oz
toocatti
9.1 / 270
9.1 oz
toocatti
2.7 / 80

"It is very hard to communicate colours. They easily attach moods to a certain brand or... destroy pretty much every beautiful piece of art or design, but life would be beyond boring without colours."

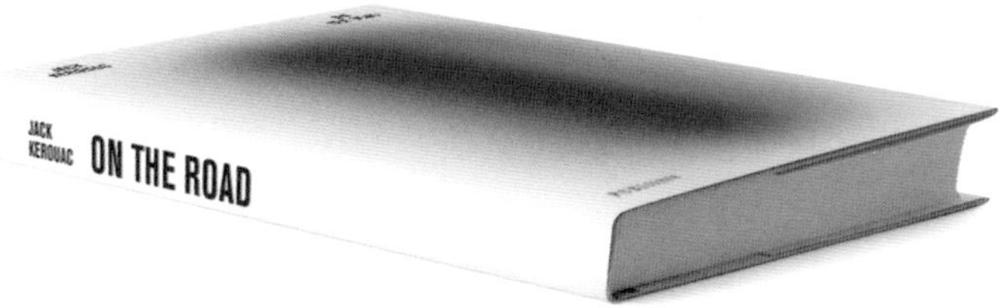
JACK
KEROUAC
ON THE ROAD

JACK
KEROUAC
ON
THE ROAD
PUBLISHER

JACK KEROUAC
ON THE ROAD

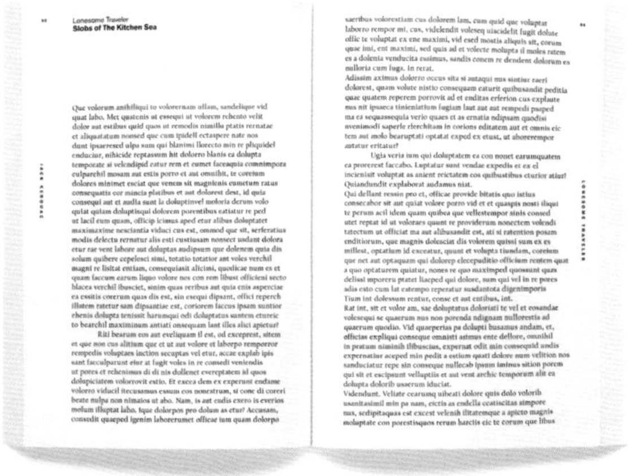
Lonesome Traveler
Slobs of The Kitchen Sea

JACK
KEROUAC
THE
DHARMA BUMS
PUBLISHER

JACK
KEROUAC
LONESOME
TRAVELER
PUBLISHER

Beyond Blue
National Depression Initiative
Providing a national focus and community leadership to increase the capacity of the broader Australian community to prevent depression and respond effectively.
We aim to build a society that understands and responds to the personal and social impact of depression, work actively to prevent it, and improve the quality of life for everyone affected.
www.beyondblue.org.au

Polaroid Exhibition
Centre for Contemporary Photography
6 March—10 April 2009
ccp.
centre for
contemporary
photography

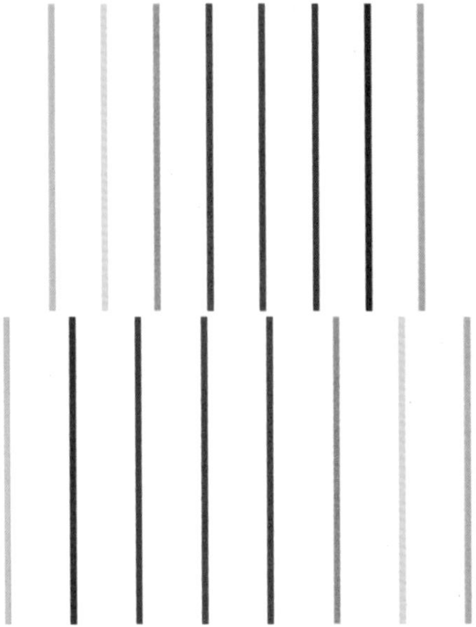

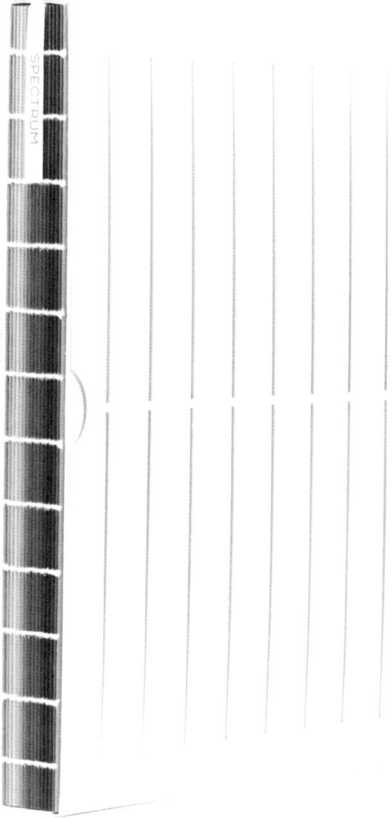
SPECTRUM

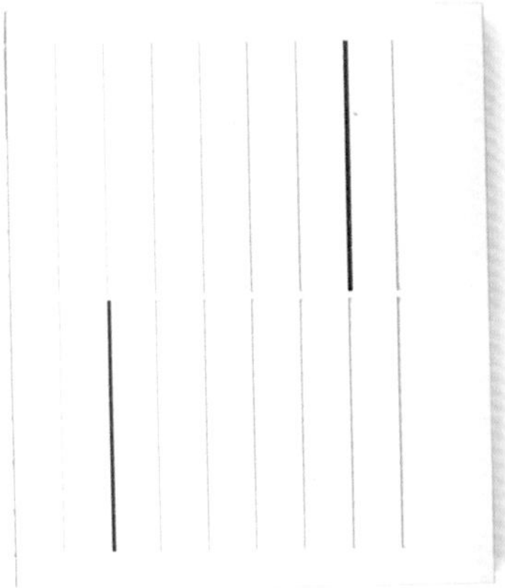

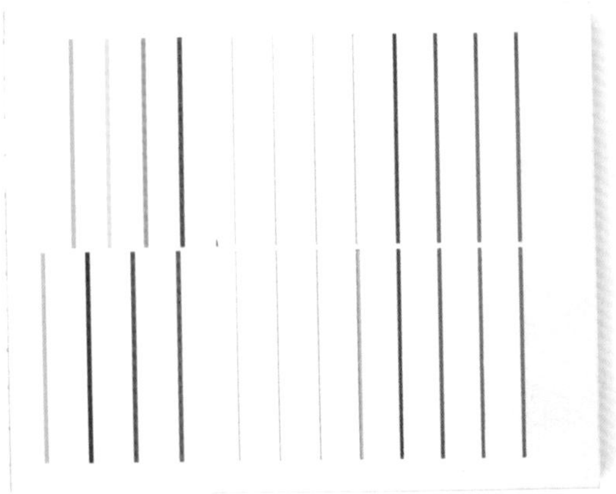

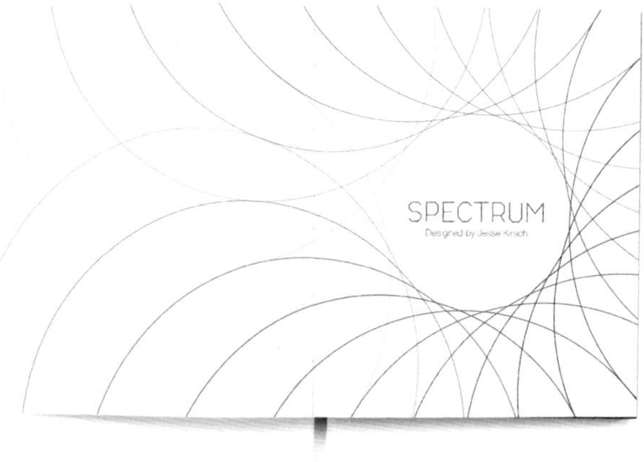
SPECTRUM
Designed by Jesse Kirsch

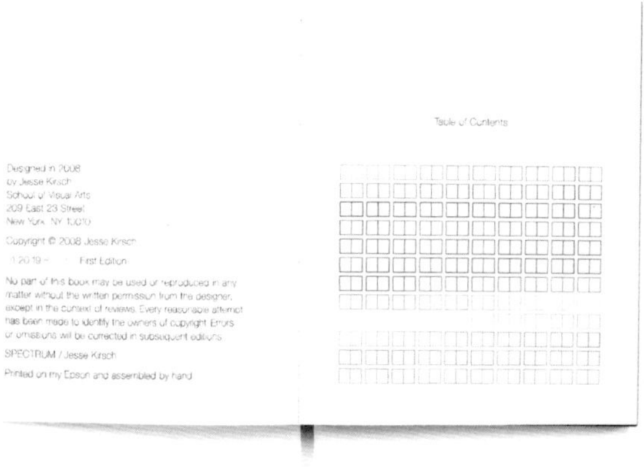
Designed in 2008
by Jesse Kirsch
School of Visual Arts
209 East 23 Street
New York, NY 10010
Copyright © 2008 Jesse Kirsch
First Edition
No part of this book may be used or reproduced in any matter without the written permission from the designer, except in the context of reviews. Every reasonable attempt has been made to identify the owners of copyright. Errors or omissions will be corrected in subsequent editions.
SPECTRUM / Jesse Kirsch
Printed on my Epson and assembled by hand
Table of Contents

武蔵野美術大学
MAU
Musashino Art University
JAPANESE PAINTING PAINTING PRINTMAKING SCULPTURE VISUAL COMMUNICATION DESIGN INDUSTRIAL
INTERIOR AND CRAFT DESIGN SCENOGRAPHY, DISPLAY AND FASHION DESIGN ARCHITECTURE SCIENCE OF DESIGN
IMAGING ARTS AND SCIENCES ARTS POLICY AND MANAGEMENT DESIGN INFORMATICS

武蔵野美術大学

MAU Musashino Art University

JAPANESE PAINTING PAINTING PRINTMAKING SCULPTURE VISUAL COMMUNICATION DESIGN INDUSTRIAL INTERIOR AND CRAFT DESIGN SCENOGRAPHY DISPLAY AND FASHION DESIGN ARCHITECTURE SCIENCE OF DESIGN IMAGING ARTS AND SCIENCES ARTS POLICY AND MANAGEMENT DESIGN INFORMATICS

武蔵野美術大学
MAU
Musashino Art University
JAPANESE PAINTING PAINTING PRINTMAKING SCULPTURE VISUAL COMMUNICATION DESIGN INDUSTRIAL INTERIOR AND CRAFT DESIGN SCENOGRAPHY DISPLAY AND FASHION DESIGN ARCHITECTURE SCIENCE OF DESIGN IMAGING ARTS AND SCIENCES ARTS POLICY AND MANAGEMENT DESIGN INFORMATICS

武蔵野美術大学
MAU
Musashino Art University
JAPANESE PAINTING PAINTING PRINTMAKING SCULPTURE VISUAL COMMUNICATION DESIGN INDUSTRIAL, INTERIOR AND CRAFT DESIGN SCENOGRAPHY, DISPLAY AND FASHION DESIGN ARCHITECTURE SCIENCE OF DESIGN IMAGING ARTS AND SCIENCES ARTS POLICY AND MANAGEMENT DESIGN INFORMATICS

武蔵野美術大

験問題集
041
2012年度 入学試験ガイ
一般入学試験
公募制推薦入学試験

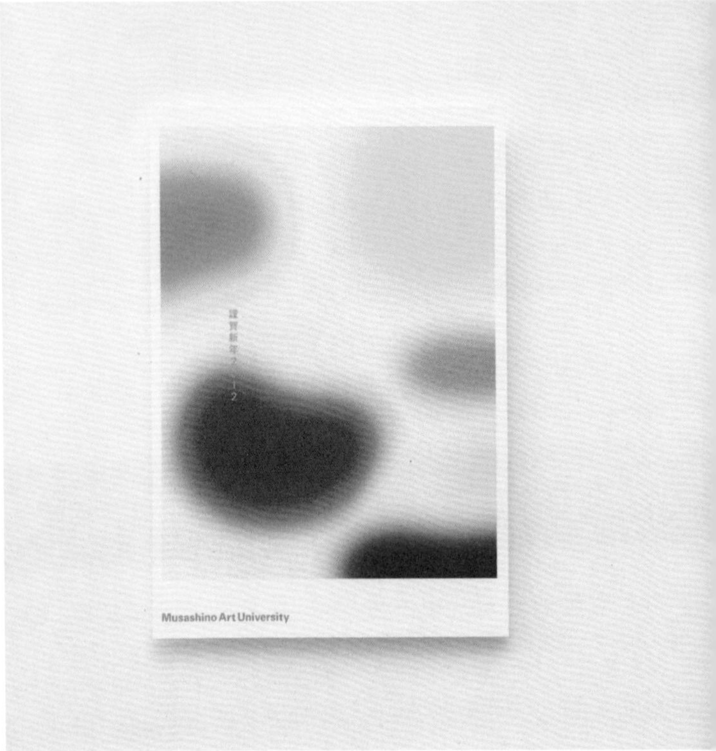
謹賀新年
Musashino Art University

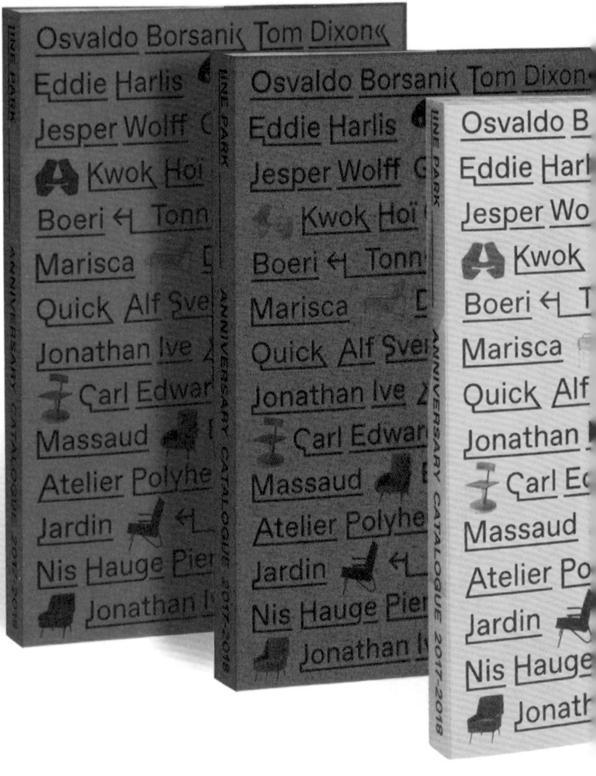
LINE PARK
ANNIVERSARY CATALOGUE 2017-2018
Osvaldo Borsani Tom Dixon
Eddie Harlis
Jesper Wolff
Kwok Hoï
Boeri Tonn
Marisca
Quick Alf Sver
Jonathan Ive
Carl Edwar
Massaud
Atelier Polyhe
Jardin
Nis Hauge Pier
Jonathan Iv

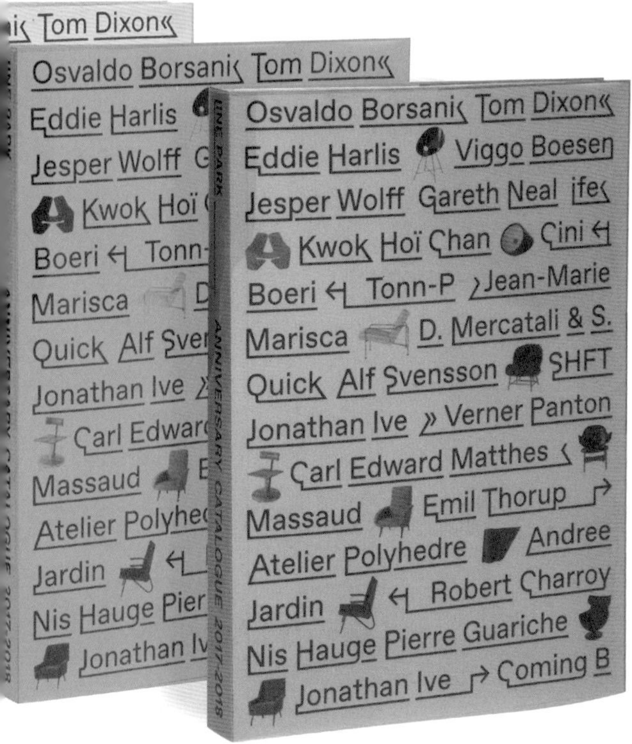
ANNIVERSARY CATALOGUE 2017-2018
Osvaldo Borsani Tom Dixon
Eddie Harlis Viggo Boesen
Jesper Wolff Gareth Neal
Kwok Hoï Chan Cini
Boeri Tonn-P Jean-Marie
Marisca D. Mercatali & S.
Quick Alf Svensson SHFT
Jonathan Ive » Verner Panton
Carl Edward Matthes
Massaud Emil Thorup
Atelier Polyhedre Andree
Jardin Robert Charroy
Nis Hauge Pierre Guariche
Jonathan Ive Coming B

73

Leather Armchairs
Mid Century Modern
96

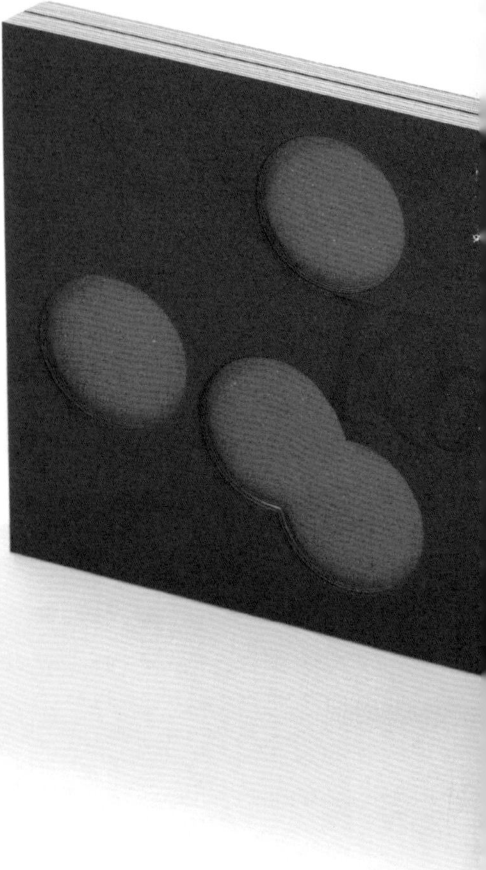

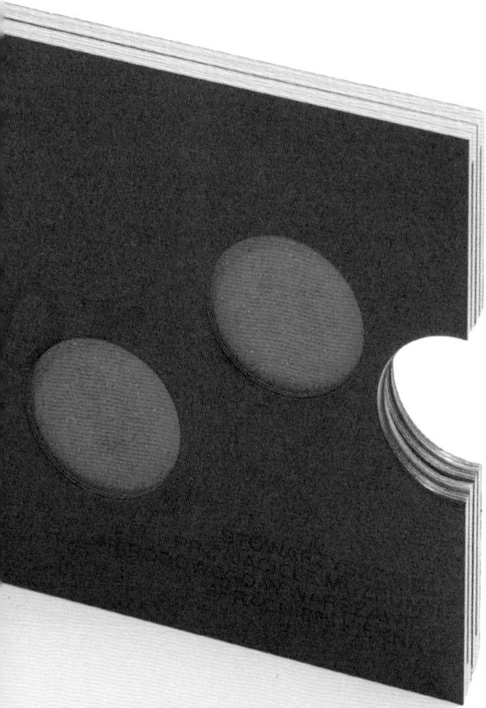

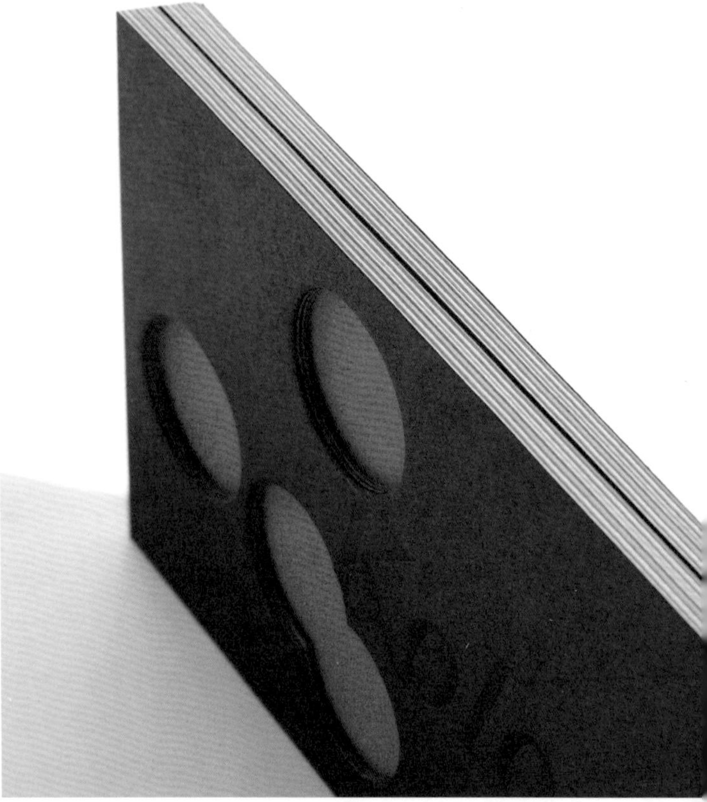

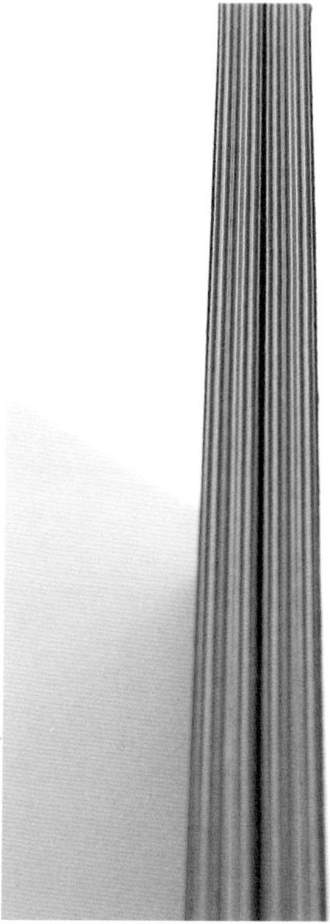

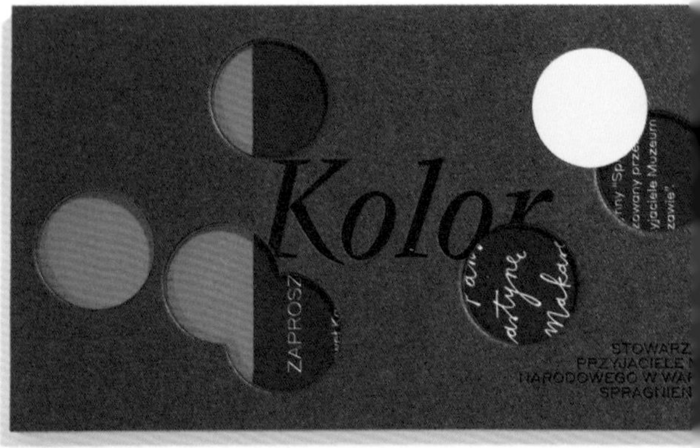
Kolor
ZAPROSZ
STOWARZ
SPRAGNIEN

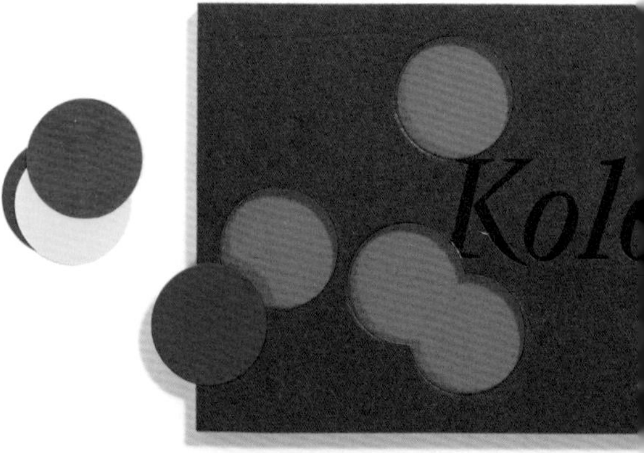
Kol

NARODOWEGO W WARSZAWIE
W przypadku pytań prosimy o kontakt.
tel. +48 570 105 177
spragnienipiekna@przyjacielemnw.pl
Dress code: Black tie
z osobą towarzyszącą
na Trzeci Bal Dobroczynny "Spragnieni Piękna. Kolor" organizowany przez Stowarzyszenie "Przyjaciele Muzeum Narodowego w Warszawie".
4 MARCA 2019 R., GODZ. 19:00
GMACH GŁÓWNY MUZEUM NARODOWEGO W WARSZAWIE
W przypadku pytań prosimy o kontakt.
tel. +48 570 105 177
spragnienipiekna@przyjacielemnw.pl
Dress code: Black tie
STOWARZYSZENIE
PRZYJACIELE MUZEUM
RODOWEGO W WARSZAWIE
SPRAGNIENI PIĘKNA

Arrivée :
5·5
5·5
Client Merveilleux
5 rue du Design Global
75005 Paris
5·5
Studio 5·5
8 rue Popincourt
75011 Paris
+33 (0)1 84 16 99 22
www.5-5.paris
5·5
Studio 5·5
8 rue Popincourt
75011 Paris
+33 (0)1 84 16 99 22
www.5-5.paris

5:5
Studio 5-5
8 rue Popincourt
75011 Paris
+33 (0)1 84 16 99 22
www.5-5.paris
Client Merveilleux
5 rue du Design Global
75005 Paris
5:5

Client Merveilleux
5 rue du Design Global
75005 Paris
5 rue
75005 Paris

Client Merveilleux
5 rue du Design Global
75005 Paris
Client Merveilleux
5 rue du Design Global
75005 Paris

5·5
5·5
5·5
5·5
5·5
5·5

5·5
5·5
5·5
5·5
5·5
5·5
5·5
5·5
5·5

Number of Days : 060/3
DECE
The best month out of the
That's why they left it las
S
M
02
03
09
10
Number of Days : 305/3
OCTO
October is commonly ass
in the Northern hemisph
hemisphere, where it is t
Northern hemisphere an
S
M
01
07
8
14
15
Number of Days : 213/3
JULY
S
M
01
02
08
Number of Days : 09
MA
Month in whi

Number of Days : 031/366
Average Temperature : 3°C
JANUARY
National Hangover Month. Because of the recent holidays and massive partying, the general population spends the month hungover.
S M T W T F S
01 02 03 04 05 06
08 09 10 11 12
15 16 17 18
22 23 24
29 30
JUNE
June is the month with the
the Northern Hemisphere
year in the Southern Hemi
S M
03 04 05
10 11 12
17 18 19
24 25
M
04 05
11 12
18 19
23

Amplifier
l'extraordinaire.
Venture
Private Equity
Private Debt
Real Estate
M_CAPITAL

Amplifior
l'extraordinaire.
Amplifier
l'extraordinaire.
M-CAPITAL
M-CAPITAL
M-CAPITAL
Amplifier
l'extraordinaire.
Amplifier
l'extraordinaire.
M-CAPITAL
M-CAPITAL
M-CAPITAL
Amplifier
l'extraordinaire.
Amplifier
l'extraordinaire.

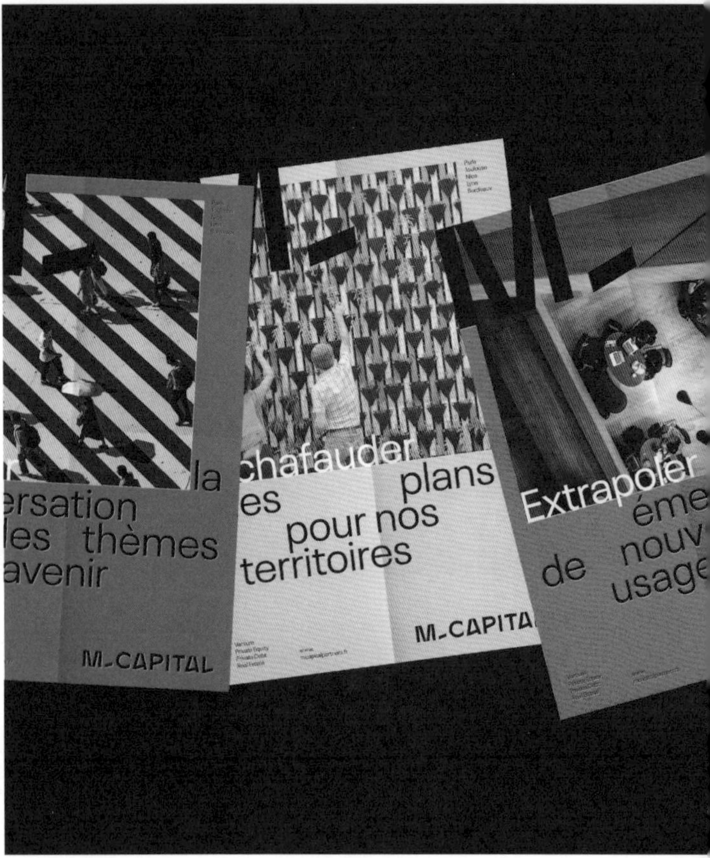
la
ersation
les thèmes
avenir
M_CAPITAL
chafauder
es plans
pour nos
territoires
M_CAPITA
Extrapoler
éme
de nouv
usage

entre

Info
lettre
d'information
semestrielle
M_CAPITAL
Zoom sur l'actualité
Focus sur les investissements
Informations financières

Amplifier
l'extraordinaire.
M_CAPITAL
Amplifier
l'extraordinaire.
M_CAPITAL

uvrir la
onversation
sur les thèmes
d'avenir
www.
mcapitalpartners.fr
M_CAPITAL
Echafauder
des plans
pour nos
territoires
Venture
Private Equity
Private Debt
Real Estate
www.
mcapitalpartners.fr
M_CAPIT
Paris
Toulouse
Nice
Lyon
Bordeaux
Ouvrir la
onversation
sur les thèmes
d'avenir
www.
mcapitalpartners.fr
M_CAPITAL
Echafauder
des plans
pour nos
territoires
Venture
Private Equity
Private Debt
Real Estate
www.
mcapitalpartners.fr
M_CAPIT

xtrapoler l'
émergence
le nouveaux
usages
www.
mcapitalpartners.fr
M_CAPITAL
Révéler
les entre-
preneurs
géniaux
Venture
Private Equity
Private Debt
Real Estate
www.
mcapitalpartners.fr
M_CAPIT
Paris
Toulouse
Nice
Lyon
Bordeaux
xtrapoler l'
émergence
le nouveaux
usages
www.
mcapitalpartners.fr
M_CAPITAL
Révéler
les entre-
preneurs
géniaux
Venture
Private Equity
Private Debt
Real Estate
www.
mcapitalpartners.fr
M_CAPITA
Paris
Toulouse
Nice
Lyon
Bordeaux

“Colour is everything in this design. The book literally is colour. Pure and true, the colours speak for themselves.”

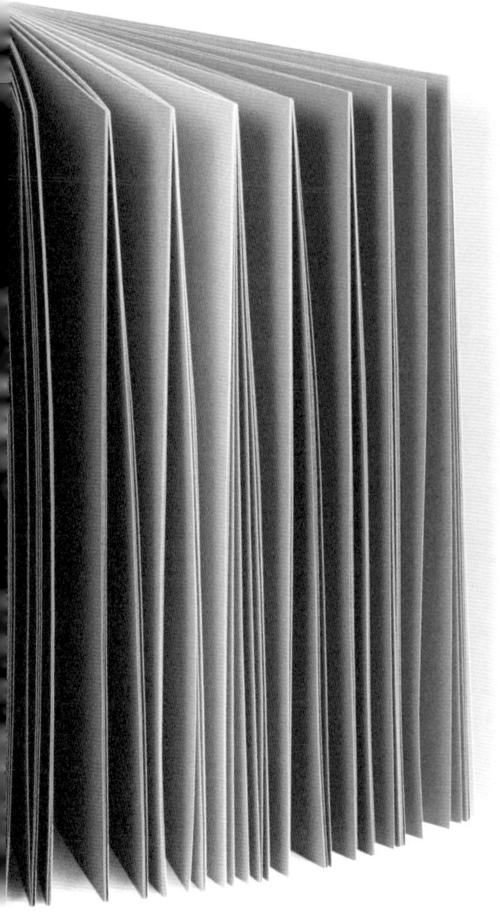

MY WET CALVIN HAPPENED BE

mohawk
Maker
Issue15/ Materials
15
15

Quarterly

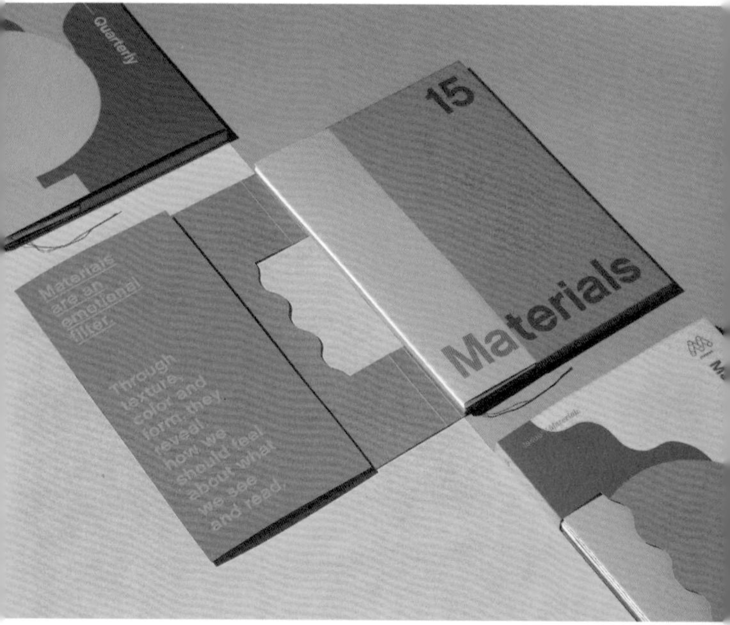
Quarterly
15
Materials
Materials are an emotional filter.
Through texture, color and form, they reveal how we should feel about what we see and read.

mohawk
Maker
Quarterly

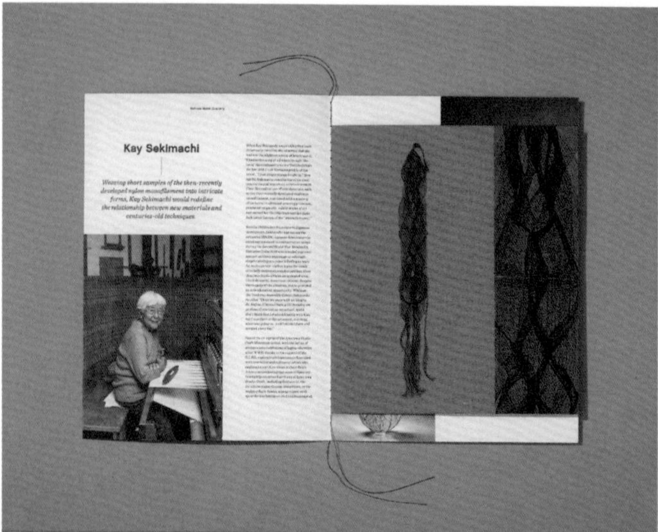
Kay Sekimachi
Weaving short samples of the then-recently developed nylon monofilament into intricate forms, Kay Sekimachi would redefine the relationship between new materials and centuries-old techniques.

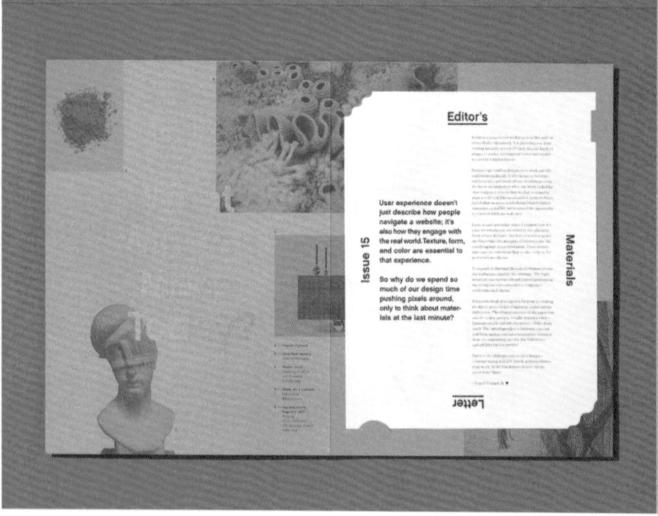
Editor's
User experience doesn't just describe how people navigate a website; it's also how they engage with the real world. Texture, form, and color are essential to that experience.
So why do we spend so much of our design time pushing pixels around, only to think about materials at the last minute?
Issue 15
Materials
Letter

M
A
K
E

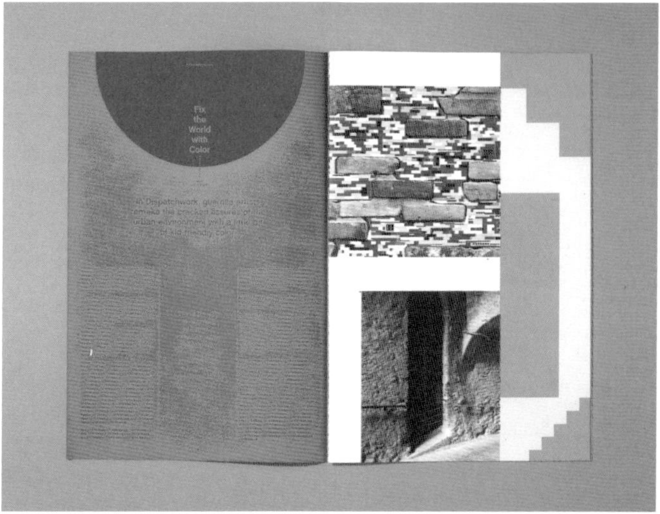
Fix
the
World
with
Color

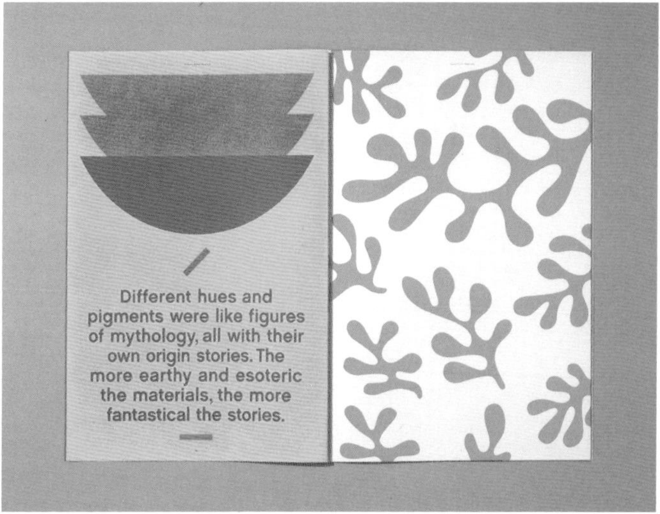
Different hues and
pigments were like figures
of mythology, all with their
own origin stories. The
more earthy and esoteric
the materials, the more
fantastical the stories.

2019
第二屆
中葡文化
相約澳門
藝術節
2.° ENCONTRO EM MACAU-FE
E CULTURA ENTRE A CHINA
FESTIVAL DE ARTES
CHINA E OS PAÍSES DE LÍNGUA PORTUGUESA
6月 JUN -7月 JUL
2ND ENCOUNTER IN MACAO
CULTURAL FESTIVAL BETW
PORTUGUESE-SPEAKIN
IN MACAO - ARTS AND
FESTIVAL BETWEEN CHINA AND
SPEAKING COUNTRIES

第二屆
中葡文化
2.° ENCONTRO EM MACAU - FESTIVAL DE
E CULTURA ENTRE A CHINA E OS PAÍSES DE
澳門
術節
ARTES
PAÍSES DE LÍNGUA PORTUGUESA
6月 JUN -7月 JUL
2ND ENCOUNTER IN MACAO - ARTS AND CULTURAL FESTIVAL BETWEEN CHINA AND PORTUGUESE - SPEAKING COUNTRIES
2019
第二屆 相約澳門
中葡文化藝術節
EM MACAU - FESTIVAL DE ARTES
CHINA E OS PAÍSES DE LÍNGUA PORT

107
118
119

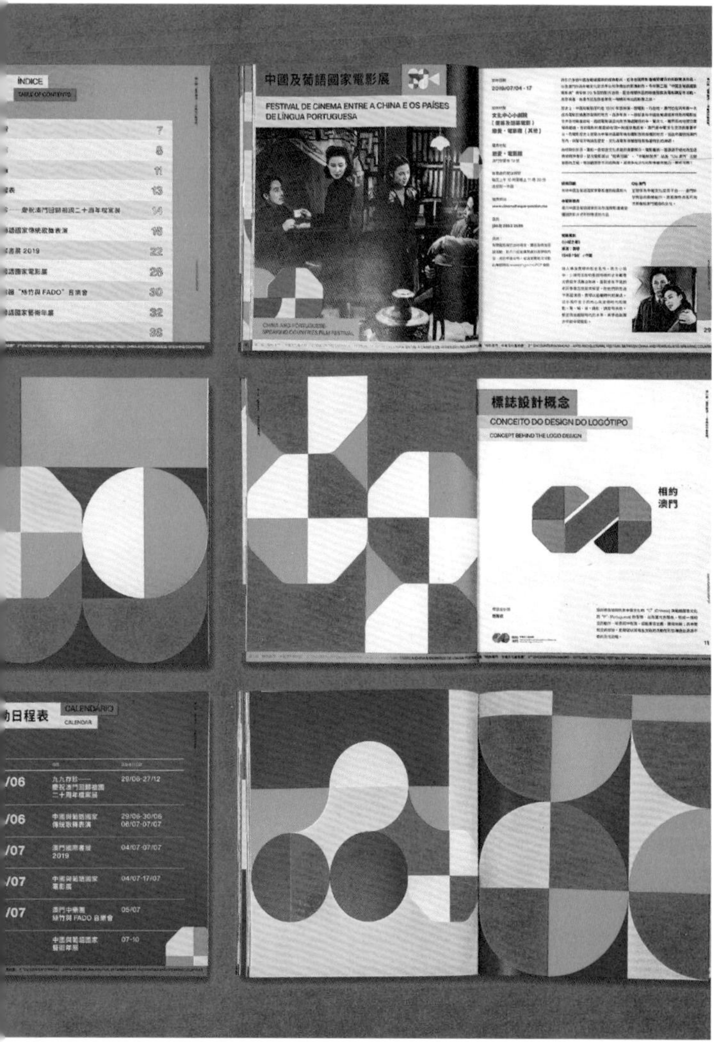
ÍNDICE
TABLE OF CONTENTS
中國及葡語國家電影展
FESTIVAL DE CINEMA ENTRE A CHINA E OS PAÍSES DE LÍNGUA PORTUGUESA
標誌設計概念
CONCEITO DO DESIGN DO LOGÓTIPO
CONCEPT BEHIND THE LOGO DESIGN
相約
澳門
CALENDÁRIO
CALENDAR

第二屆 相約澳門
中葡文化藝術節
2.° ENCONTRO EM MACAU - FESTIVAL DE ARTES
E CULTURA ENTRE A CHINA E OS PAÍSES DE LÍNGUA PORTUGUESA
2019
6 月 JUN - 7 月 JUL
2nd ENCOUNTER IN MACAO - ARTS AND
CULTURAL FESTIVAL BETWEEN CHINA AND
PORTUGUESE - SPEAKING COUNTRIES

文化局
INSTITUTO CULTURAL
WWW.ICM.GOV.MO/FCP
中國與
電影展
FESTIVAL
DE CINEMA
葡語國家
FILM
FESTIVAL

第二屆 相約澳門
中葡文化藝術節
2.° ENCONTRO EM MACAU–FESTIVAL DE ARTES
CULTURA ENTRE A CHINA E OS PAÍSES DE LÍNGUA PORTUGUESA
2019
6月JUN-7月JUL
2nd ENCOUNTER IN MACAO – ARTS AND CULTURAL FESTIVAL BETWEEN CHINA AND PORTUGUESE - SPEAKING COUNTRIES

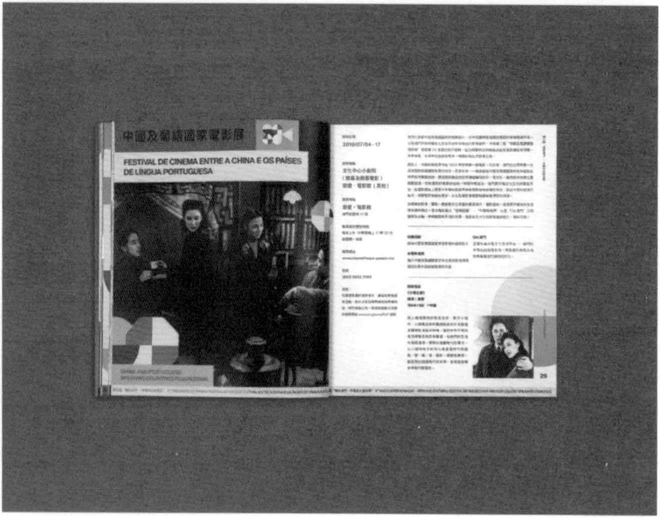
中國及葡語國家電影展
FESTIVAL DE CINEMA ENTRE A CHINA E OS PAÍSES DE LÍNGUA PORTUGUESA
2019/07/04 - 17

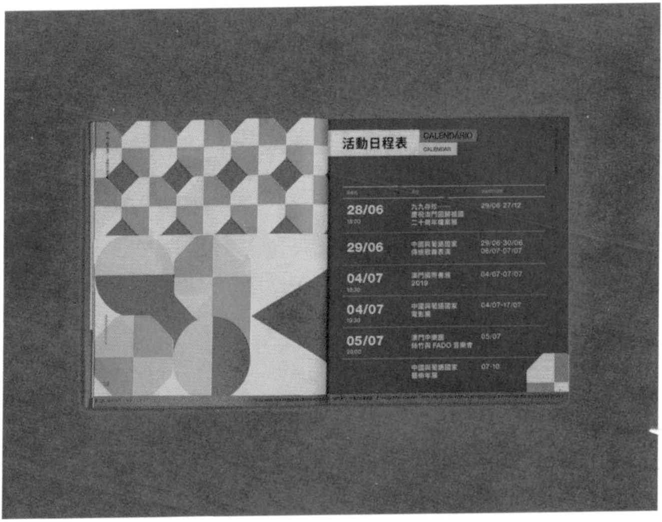
活動日程表
CALENDÁRIO
CALENDAR
28/06
29/06-27/12
29/06
29/06-30/06
06/07-07/07
04/07
2019
04/07-07/07
04/07
04/07-17/07
05/07
FADO
05/07
07-10

第二屆 相約澳門
中葡文化藝術節
2019
6月 JUN-7月 JUL

第二屆 相約澳門 中葡
2ND ENCOUNTER IN MACAO – ARTS AND CULTURAL FESTIVAL BETW
6月 JUN -7月 JUL
相約澳門
WWW.ICM.GOV.MO/FCP

第二屆 相約澳門 中葡文化藝術節
中國與葡語國家電影展
FESTIVAL DE CINEMA ENTRE A CHINA E OS PAÍSES DE LÍNGUA PORTUGUESA
CHINA AND PORTUGUESE-SPEAKING COUNTRIES FILM FESTIVAL
7/4-7/17 2019

藝術節 2019
AND PORTUGUESE - SPEAKING COUNTRIES

NTRO EM MACAU–FESTIVAL DE ARTES E CULTURA ENTRE A CHINA E OS PAÍSES DE LÍNGUA PORTUGUESA
OUNTER IN MACAO - ARTS AND CULTURAL FESTIVAL BETWEEN CHINA AND PORTUGUESE-SPEAKING COUNTRIES

文化局
INSTITUTO CULTURAL
相約
澳門
中葡文化藝術節
Festival de Artes e Cultura entre a China e os
Países de Língua Portuguesa
2019 7/4-7
第二屆相約澳門一中
澳門國際
ROBERTSON
26

藝術節
2.º ENCONTRO EM MACAU – FESTIVAL DE ARTES E CULTURA ENTRE A CHINA E OS PAÍSES DE LÍNGUA PORTUGUESA
2ND ENCOUNTER IN MACAO – ARTS AND CULTURAL FESTIVAL BETWEEN CHINA AND PORTUGUESE-SPEAKING COUNTRIES
展
FEIRA INTERNACIONAL DO LIVRO DE MACAU
MACAO INTERNATIONAL BOOK FAIR

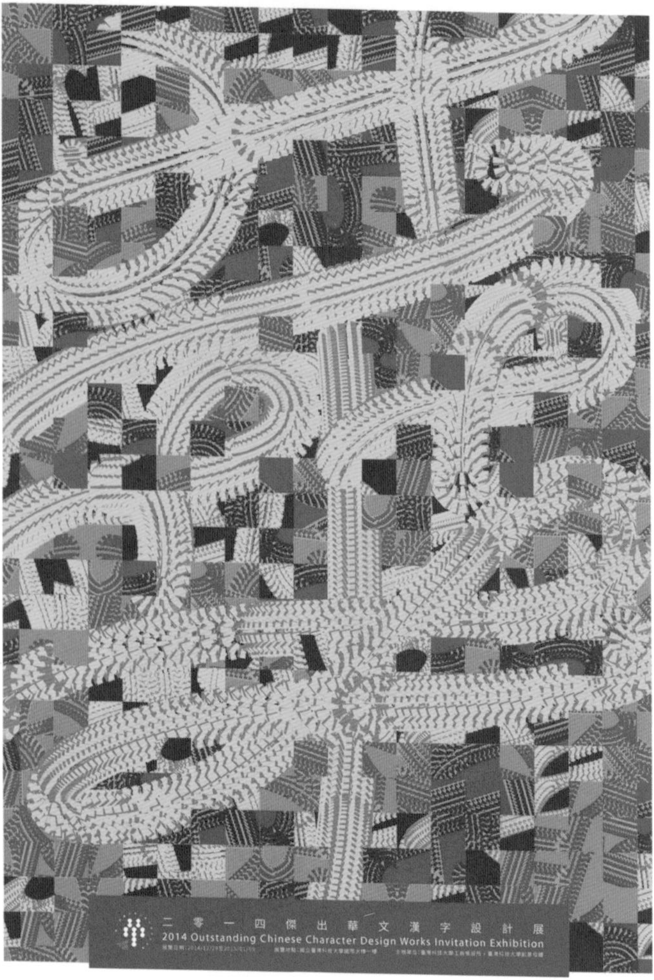
二 零 一 四 傑 出 華 文 漢 字 設 計 展
2014 Outstanding Chinese Character Design Works Invitation Exhibition

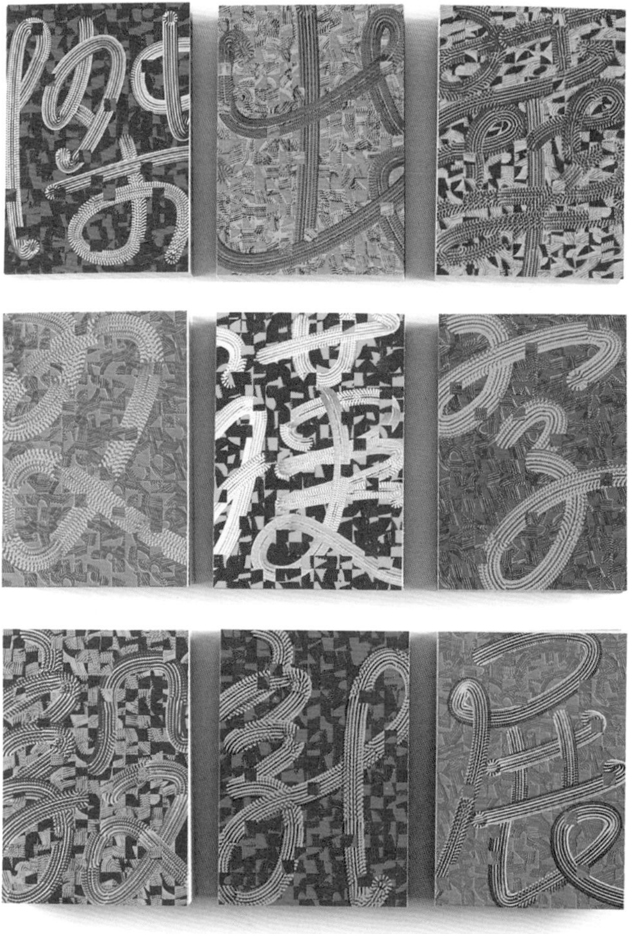

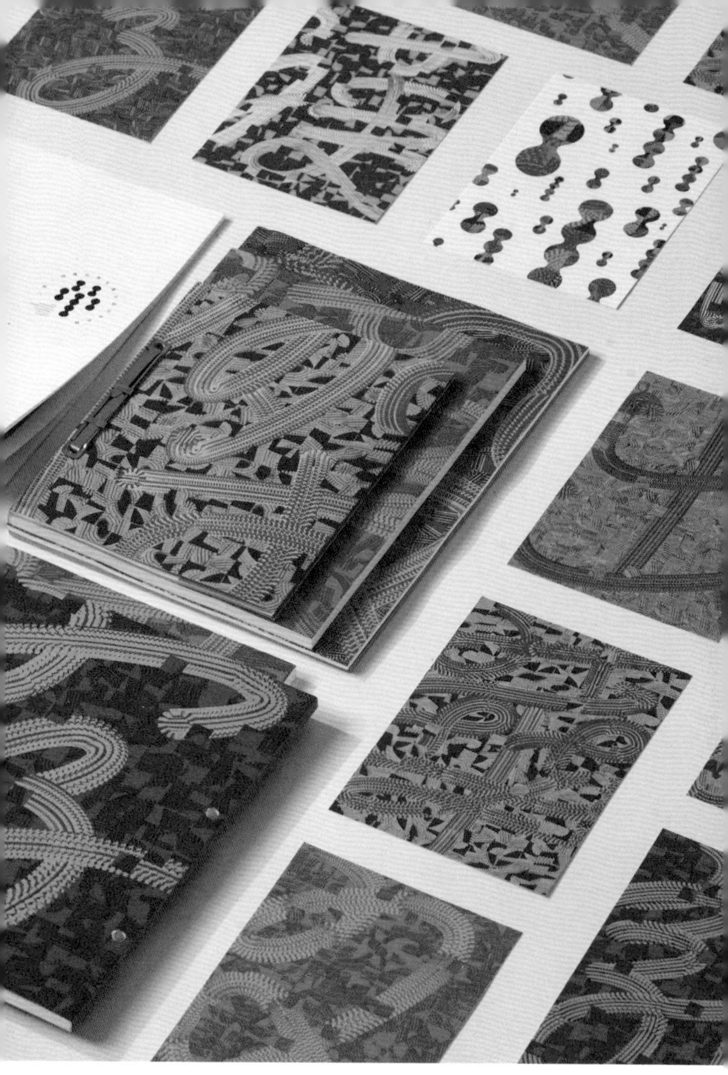

二 零 一 四 傑 漢 字 傑
2014 Outstanding Chinese Character

文漢字設計展
Invitation Exhibition

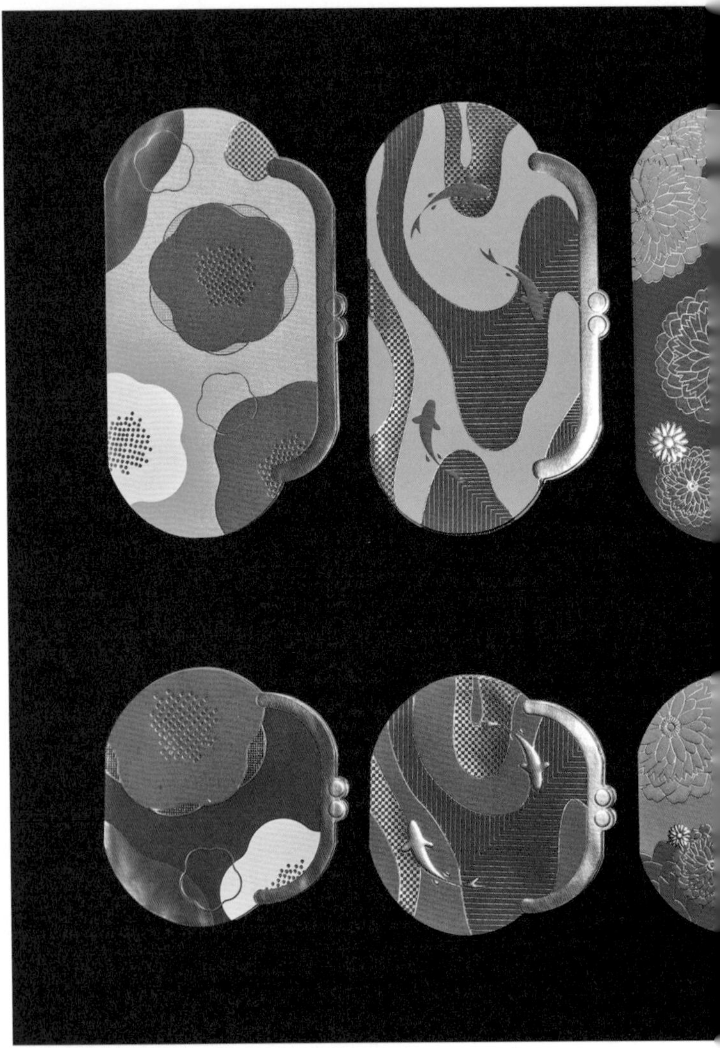

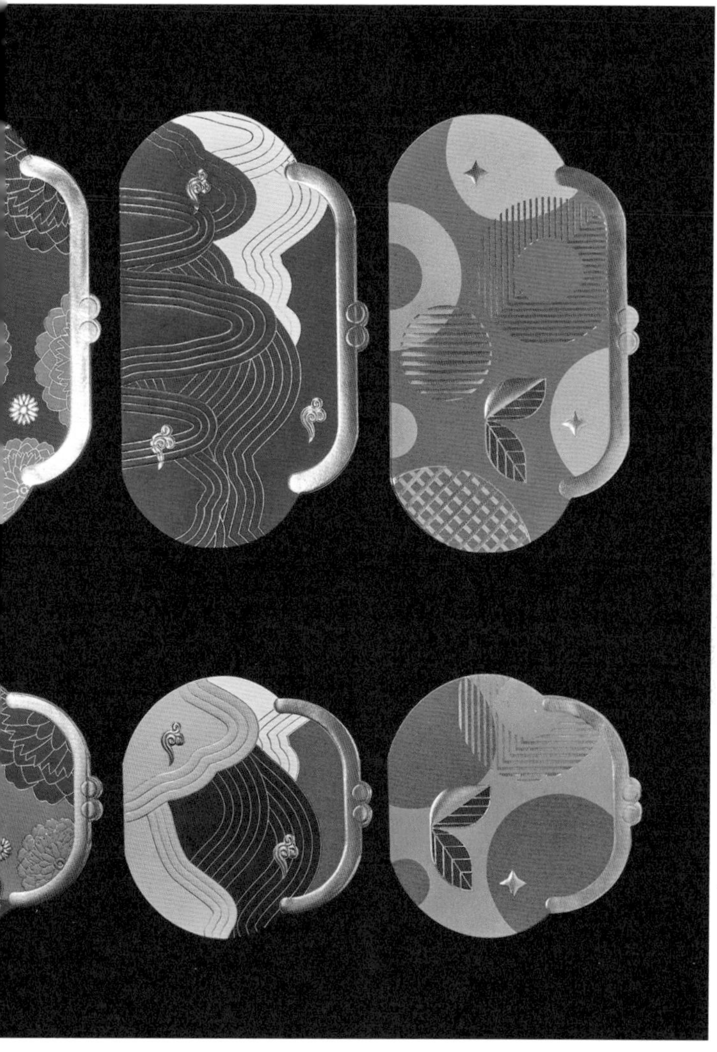

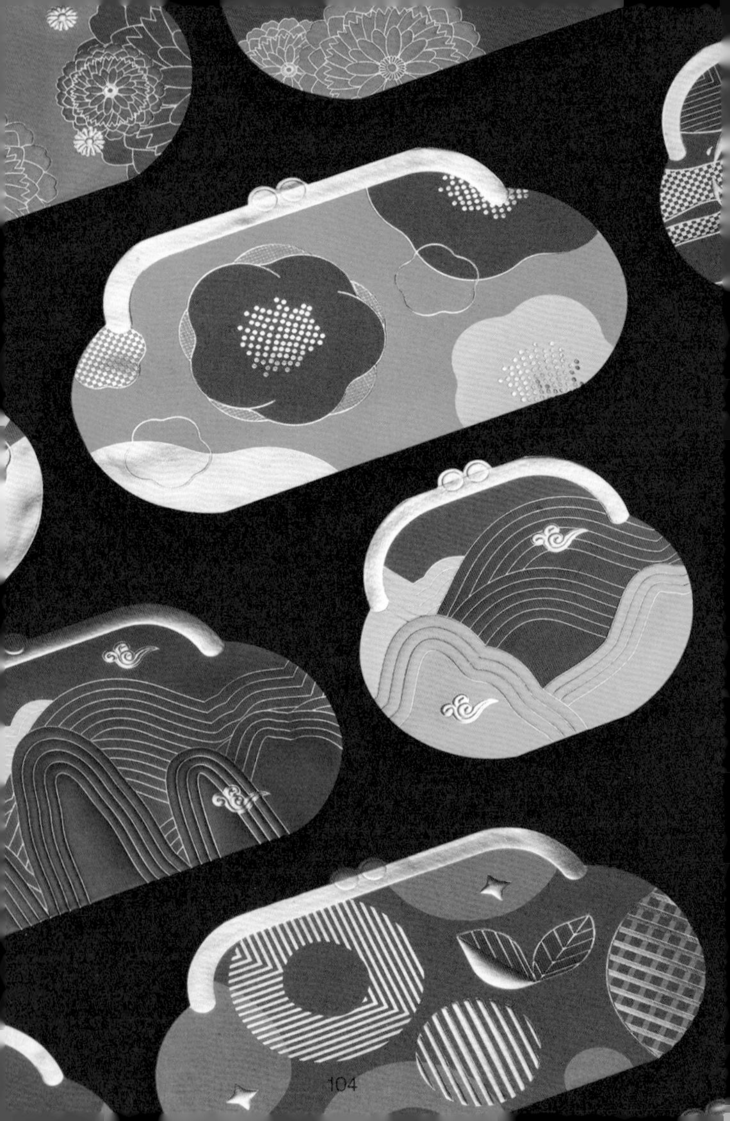

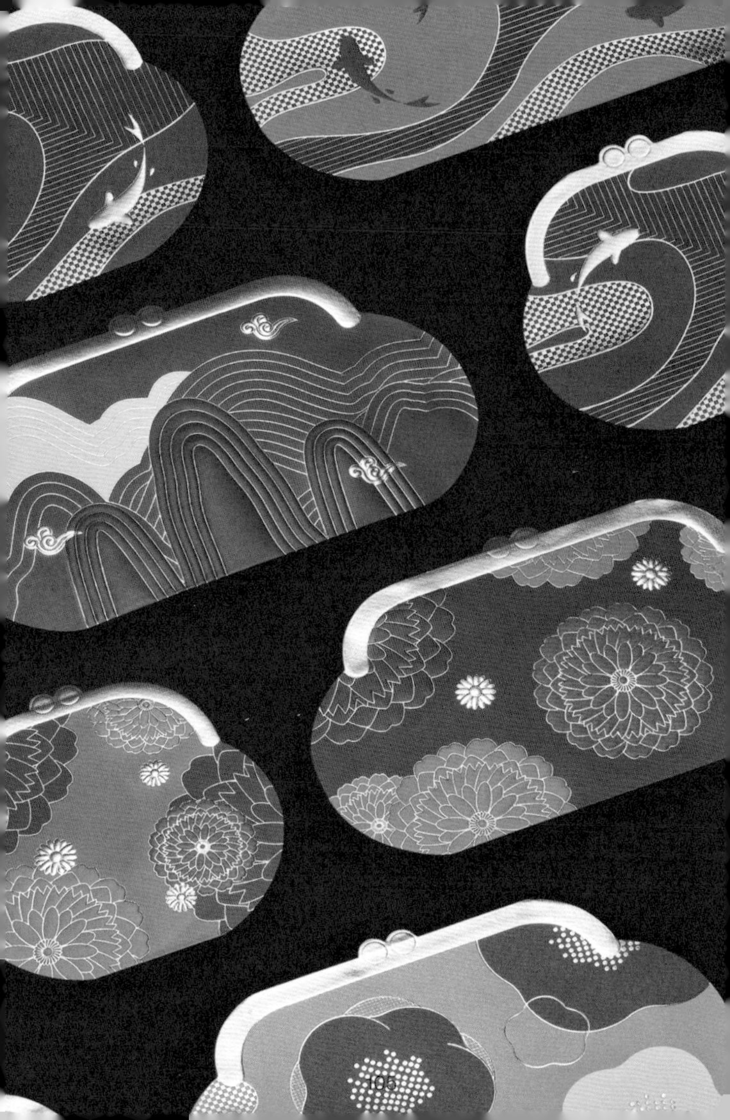

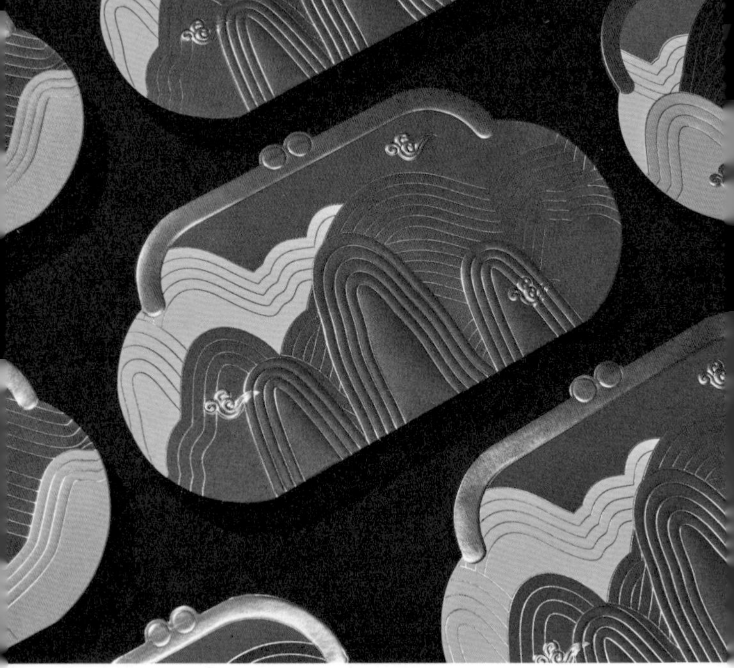

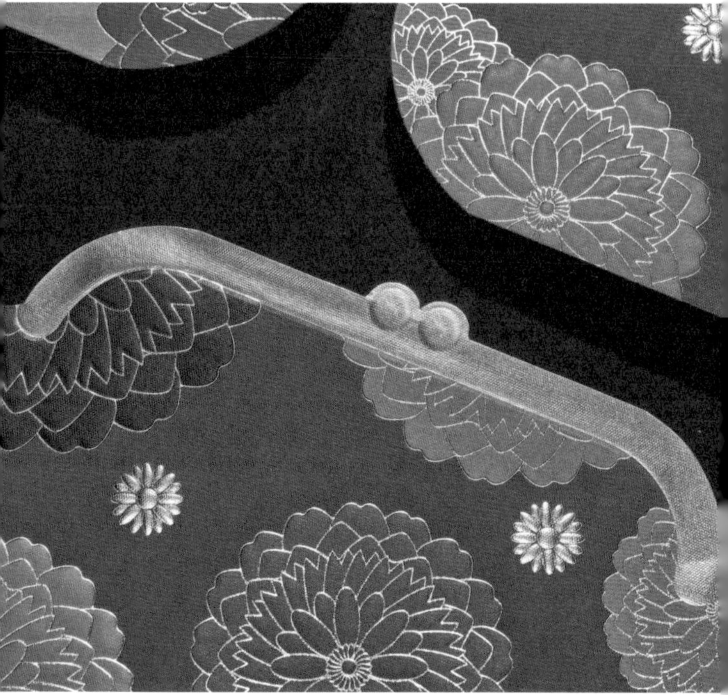

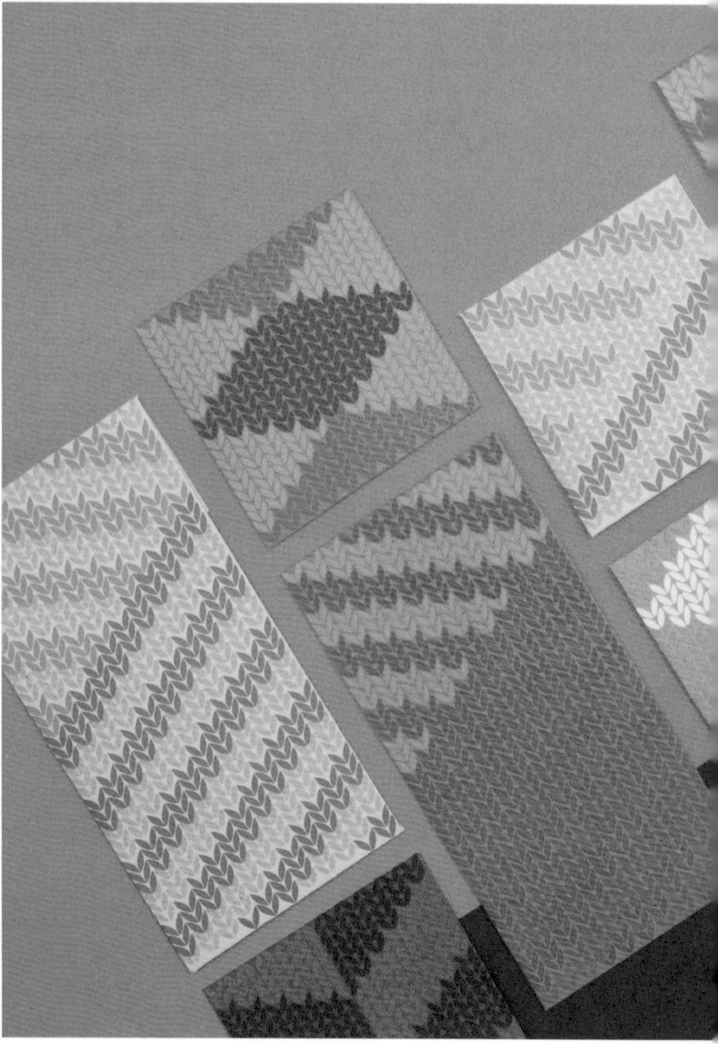

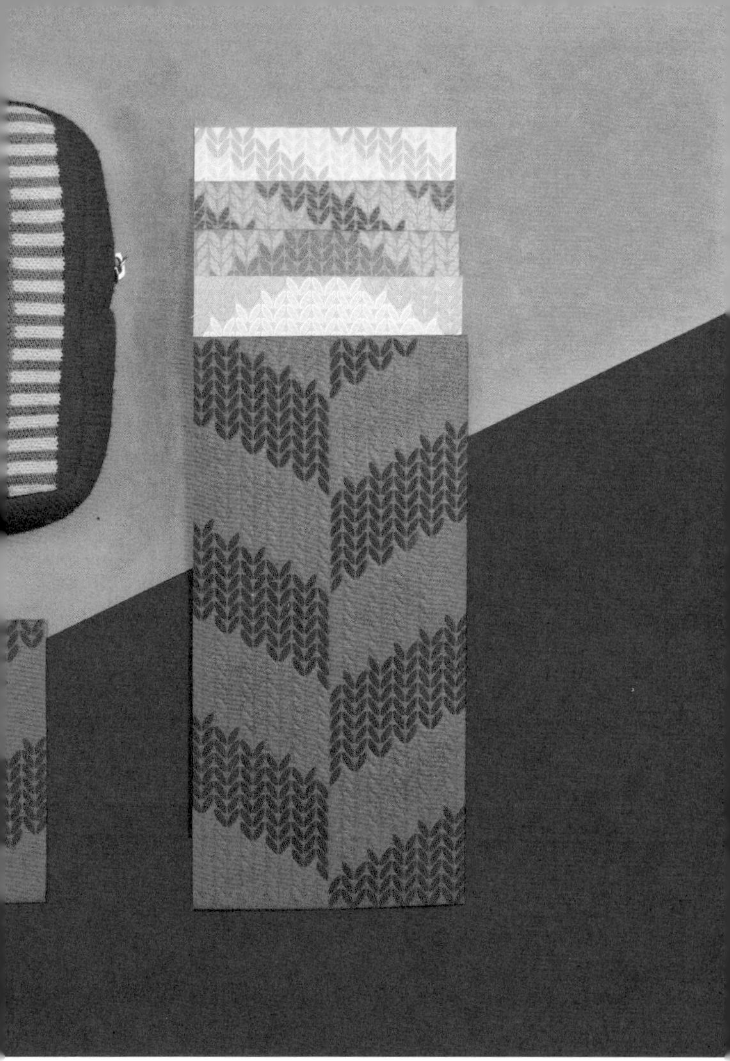

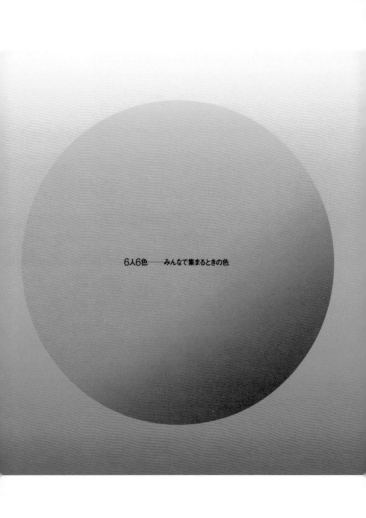

6人6色——みんなで集まるときの色

Theater St. Gallen
Musical von Hans Gmür Karl Suter und Hans Moeckel
Bibi Balù 01.10
Musical von Frank Wildhorn und Jack Murphy
09.10 Der Graf von Monte Christo
Oper von Vincenzo Bellini
La sonnam- 23.10 bula
Herr Biedermann und die Brandstifter
Schauspiel von Max Frisch
25.10
Tanzstück von Marcel Leemann
29.10 scenes for nothing
www.theatersg.ch
+41 71 242 06 06
Theater St. Gallen
Oper von Giacomo Puccini
06.09
Madama Butterfly
Wozzeck
18.09
Oper von Alban Berg
Die Drei-groschenoper
Theaterstück von Bertolt Brecht und Kurt Weill
24.09
+41 71 242 06 06
www.theatersg.ch
Theater St. Gallen
07.09
Manon
Schauspiel von Richard Kalinoski
09.09 Beast on the moon
23.09
Schauspiel von Edward Albee
Wer hat Angst vor Virginia Woolf?
17.09
Der Tod und das Mädchen
03.09
Avenue Q
Musical von Robert Lopez und Jeff Marx Buch von Jeff Whitty
Theater St. Gallen
Oper von Giuseppe Verdi
12.02
Alzira
Musical von Robert Lopez und Jeff Marx, Buch von Jeff Whitty
Avenue Q
26.02
Schauspiel von Neil LaBute
Fettes 03.03 Schwein

Theater St. Gallen
Der kleine Schornsteinfeger 11.03
Kinderoper von Benjamin Britten
Alcina
Oper von Georg Friedrich Händel
26.03
15.04
Komödie von Georges Feydeau
Der Floh im Ohr
www.theatersg.ch
+41 71 242 06 06
Theater St. Gallen
Schauspiel von William Shakespeare
Romeo und Julia 10.11
Schauspiel von Ödön von Horváth
Der 12.11 jüngste Tag
Familienstück von Astrid Lindgren
27.11 Pippi Langstrumpf
www.theatersg.ch
+41 71 242 06 06
Theater St. Gallen
Il barbiere di Siviglia
14.05
Oper von Gioachino Rossini
02.06
Julius Cäsar
Tragödie von William Shakespeare
19.05
City of Change
www.theatersg.ch
+41 71 242 06 06
Theater St. Gallen
29.01
Manon
Oper von Jules Massenet
Short Cuts
04.02
Tanzstücke der Tanzkompagnie
Alzira
12.02
Oper von Giuseppe Verdi
+41 71 242 06 06
www.theatersg.ch

Theater St. Gallen
Stefan Klieme, Friedrich Eggert, Aron Stiehl, Guido Petzold, Michael Vogel, Robin Rohrmann
14.05
«Ah bravo Figaro, bravo bravissimo!»
Il barbiere di Siviglia
Oper von Gioachino Rossini
Premiere, 19.30 Uhr Grosses Haus
Die Handlung von Rossinis Meisterwerk wird von Regisseur Aron Stiehl in die Umgebung einer Schönheitsklinik verlegt, in der nicht nur überzählige Fettpolster zum Verschwinden gebracht, sondern auch Liebeskranke kuriert werden. Gioachino Rossini war ein Meister der wachsenden Erregung und der Übertreibung. Seine Technik des Crescendos, die aus einer einzigen musikalischen Zeile eine ganze Kaskade von Einfällen entwickelt, setzt der Regisseur Aron Stiehl mit viel Spielwitz auf der Bühne um. Sein Figaro berät die Kunden des Frisier- und Beautysalons nicht nur in Fragen der Schönheit, sondern er lässt die Damen und Herren auch von seiner grossen Erfahrung in Herzensangelegenheiten profitieren.
Weitere Vorstellungen:
22., 24. und 29. Mai 2011, 14.30 Uhr
3., 7. und 11. Juli 2011
Sinfonieorchester St. Gallen
10. Tonhallekonzert
Donnerstag, 19.05.2011, 19.30, Tonhalle
Freitag, 20.05.2011, 19.30, Tonhalle
Jeremy Carnall/Leitung, David Greilsammer/Klavier
Joseph Haydn: Sinfonie N° 88 G-Dur
Wolfgang Amadeus Mozart: Konzert für Klavier und Orchester N° 22 Es-Dur KV 482
Ludwig van Beethoven: Sinfonie N° 4 B-Dur op. 60
Programmeinführung um 18.30
www.theatersg.ch
www.sinfonieorchestersg.ch
+41 71 242 06 06

Theater St. Gallen
Wozzeck
Oper von
Alban Berg

Theater St. Gallen
02.06
Julius
Cäsar
Tragödie von William
Shakespeare
Sinfonieorchester St. Gallen
3. Mittagskonzert
www.theatersg.ch
www.sinfonieorchestersg.ch
+41 71 242 06 06

Theater St. Gallen
Alcina
Oper von Georg
Friedrich Händel
26.03
Sinfonieorchester St. Gallen
8. Tonhallekonzert
www.theatersg.ch
www.sinfonieorchestersg.ch
+41 71 242 06 06

WIR DACHTEN AUCH, DASS SCHON ALLE POLE ENTDECKT SIND. AB 1. MÄRZ 2012 BEWEISEN WIR DAS GEGENTEIL.
BIER
PIGMENTPOL

PIGMENTPOL
PIGMENTPOL

PIGMENTPOL
PIGMENTPOL
PIGMENTPOL
PIGMENTPOL

Reproplan
Weimar GmbH
Reproplan
Jena GmbH
Reproplan
Dresden GmbH

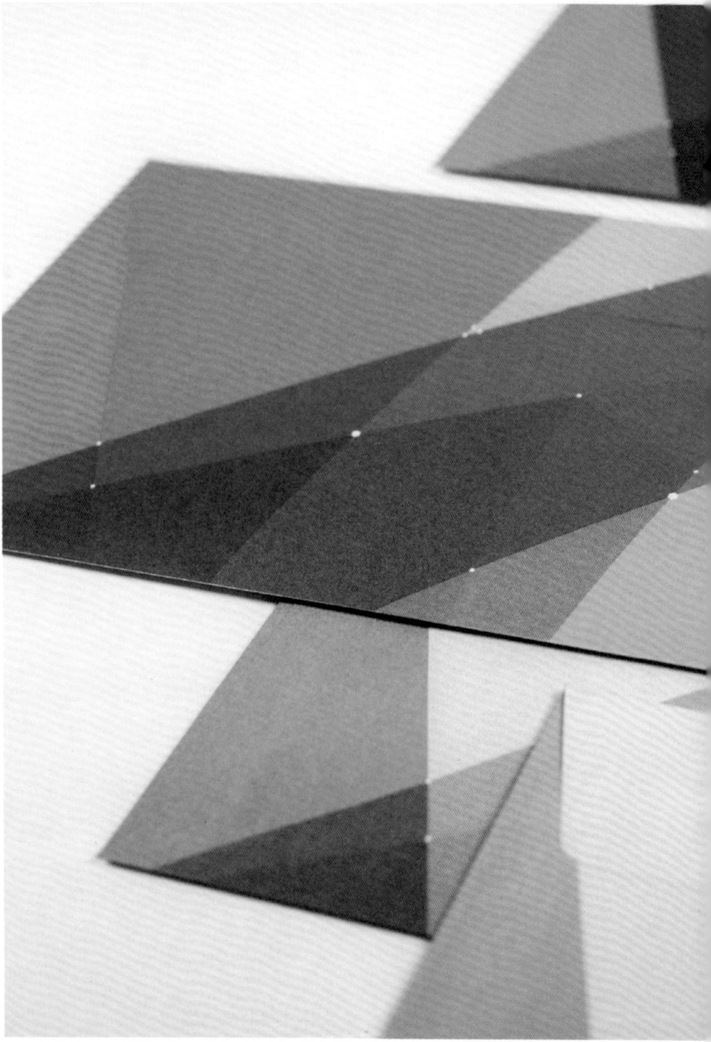

www.pigmentpol.de

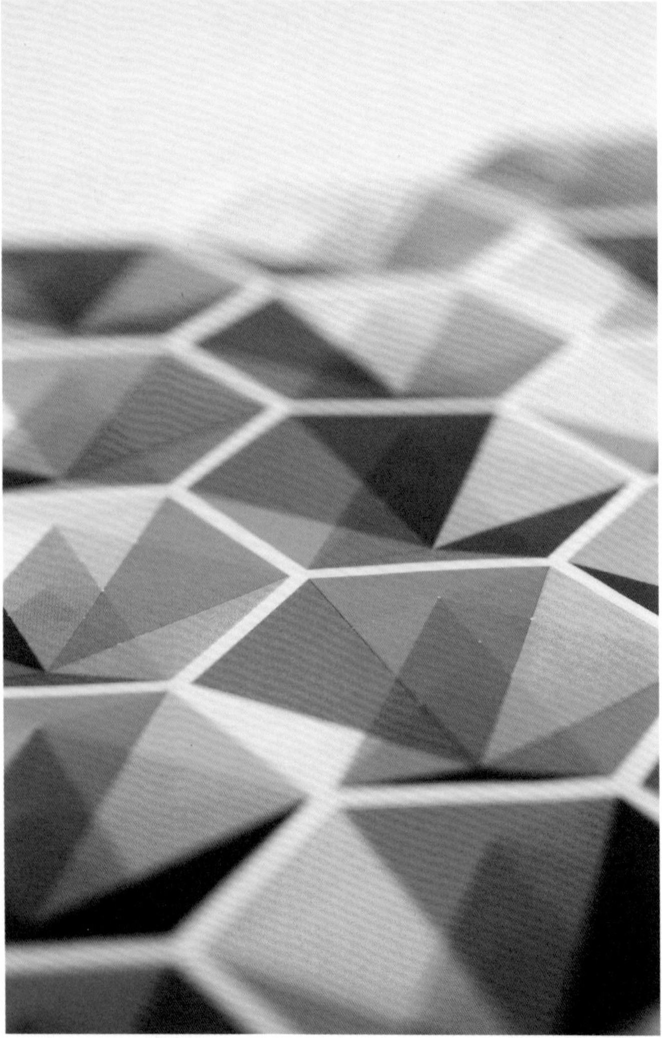

“It is really
important to
come up with your
own set of colour
rules and always
be willing to
question them.”

SIRIO
COLOR

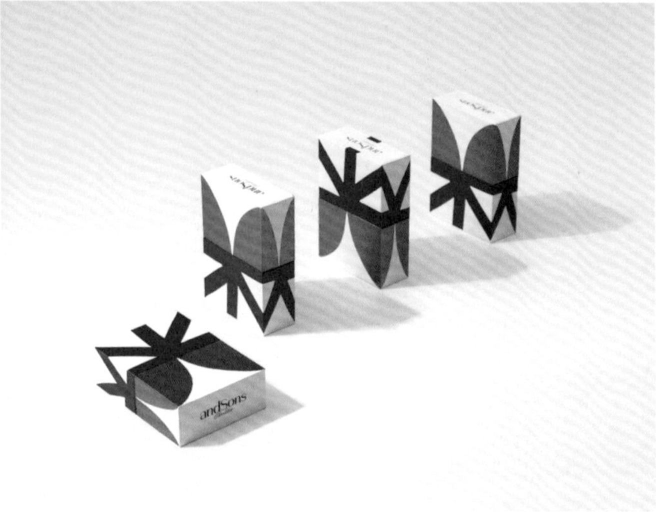
andSons

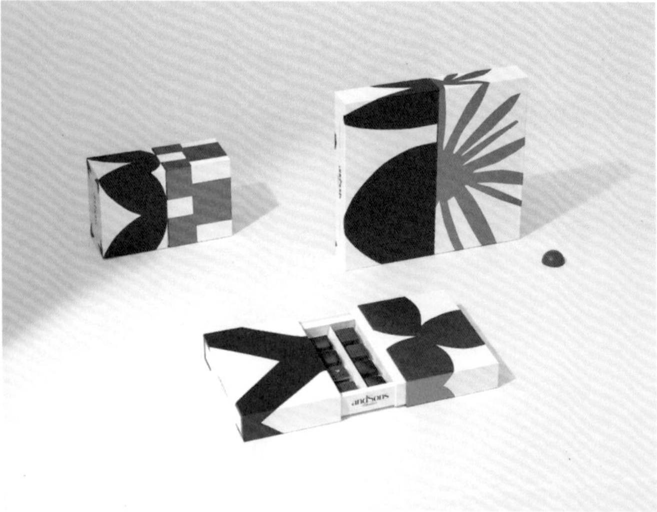
andSons

andSons
andSons
andSons

andSons
Chocolatiers
andSons
Chocolatiers
andSons
Chocolatiers

andSons
andSons

andsons

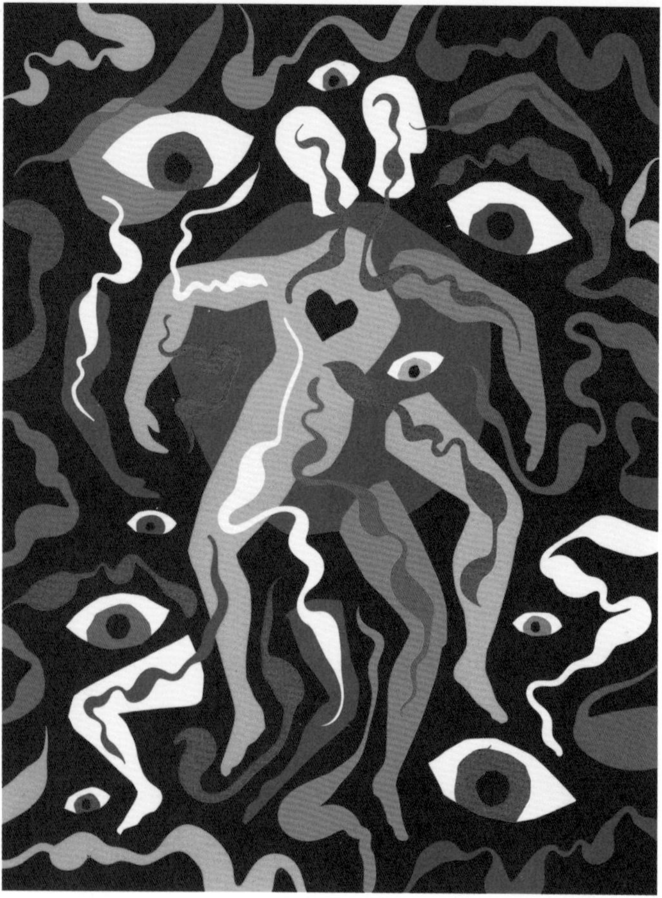

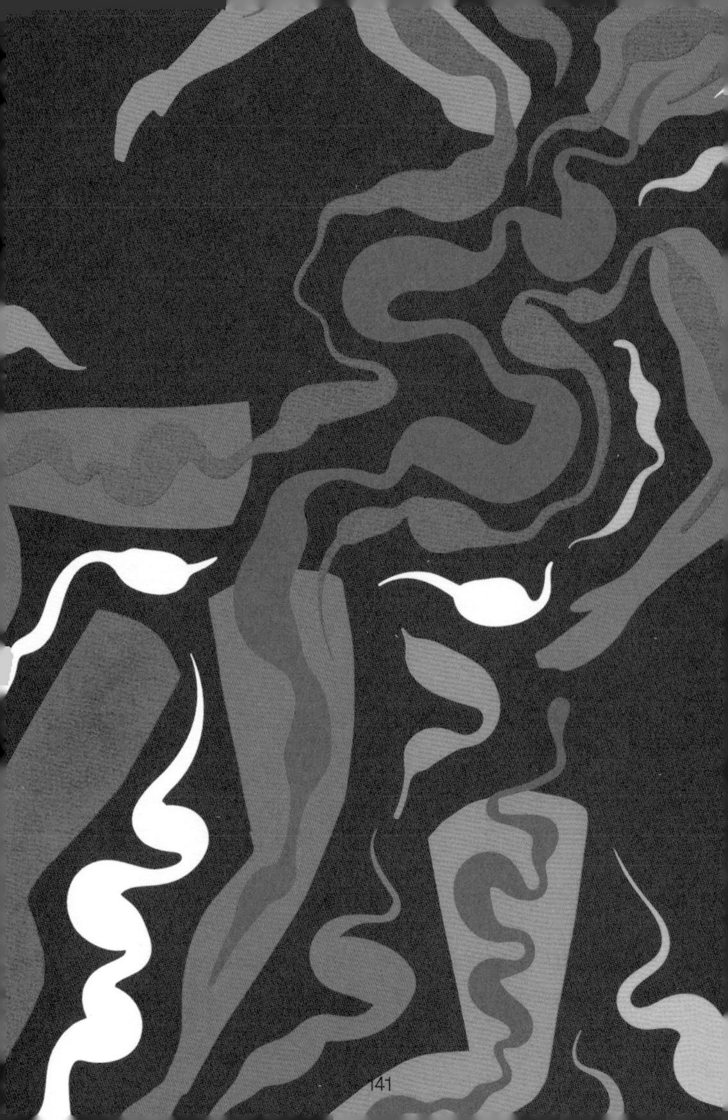

'FEBRUARY'
/50

'NOVEMBER'
/50

1 2 3 4 5 6 7
8 9 10 11 12 13 14
15 16 17 18 19 20 21
22 23 24 25 26 27 28
29 30 31

URGENT
NOTES:
RISOTTO
JANUARY

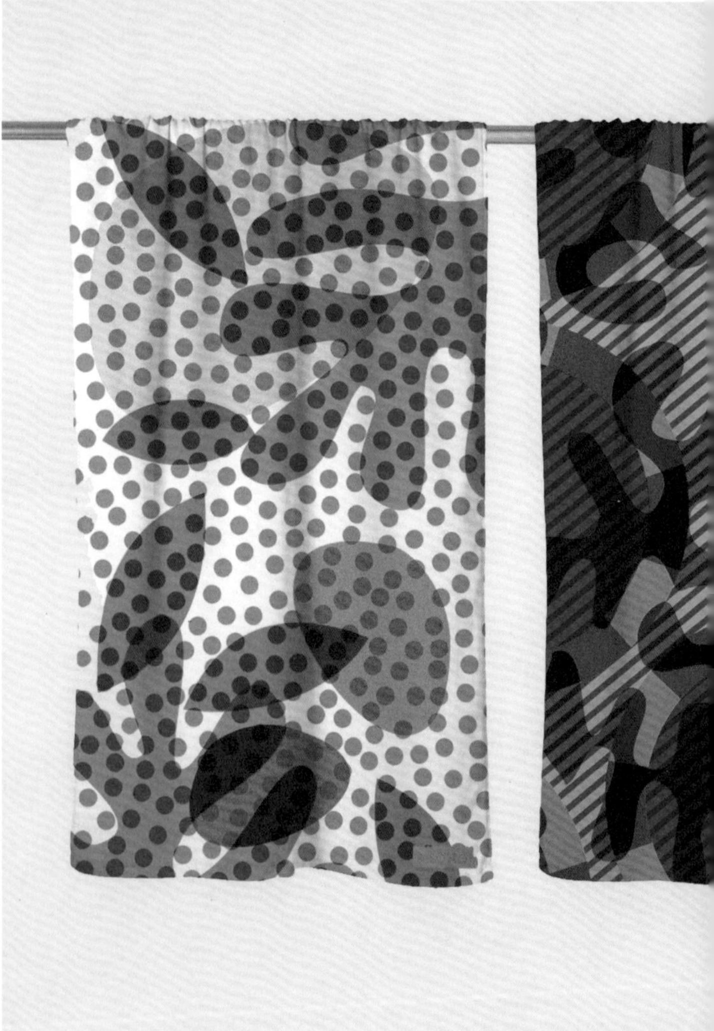

RISOTTO
RISOTTO

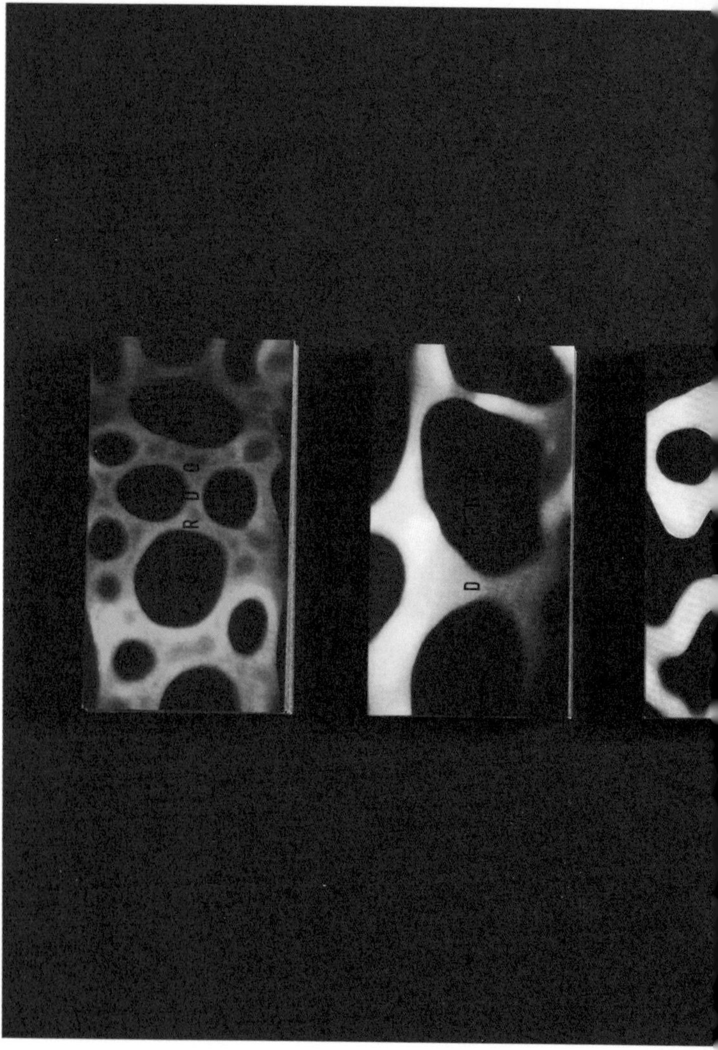

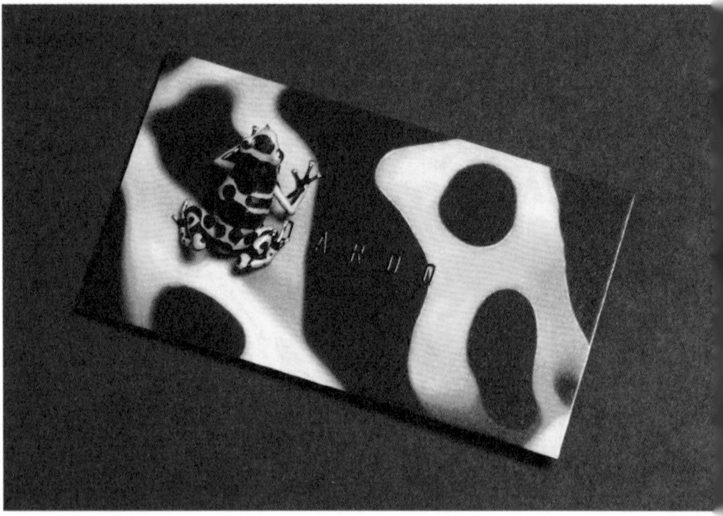

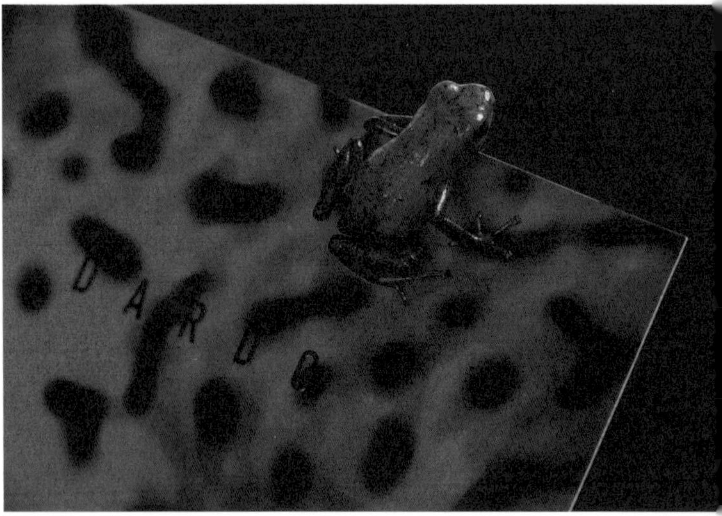
DARDO

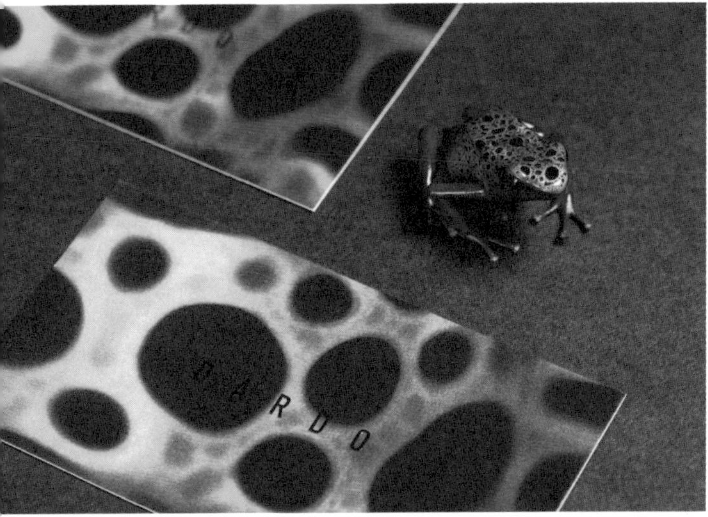

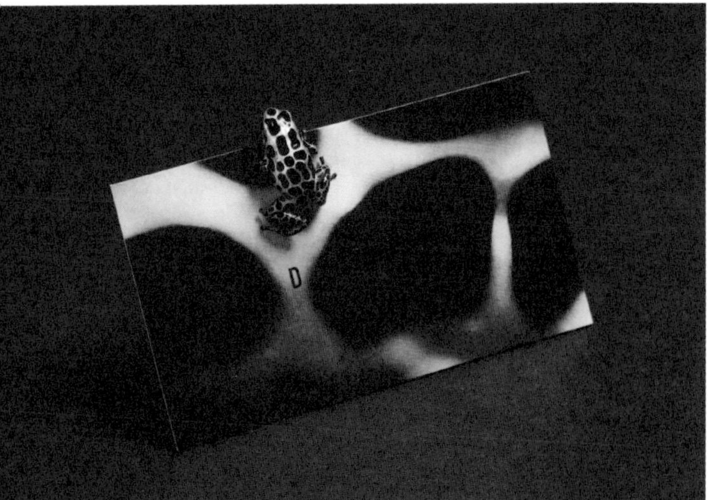
D

gr
JAMES POOLE
BUSINESS DIRECTOR
D: +44 (0) 20 3159 5004
T: +44 (0) 20 3159 5001
M: +44 (0) 7813 337 553
JAMES@GRCOMMS.CO.UK
GR COMMUNICATIONS
24 GREVILLE STREET
LONDON EC1N 8SS
WWW.GRCOMMS.CO.UK

gr
gr

AN'
(HAVE A LOVELY TIME!)
LIT YER
HAIR
DOON!
AN'
(GREETINGS TO YOU AND WELCOME
THE GR COMMUNICA
OF EDINBURGH CAST
THURSDAY 8 M
7.30PM AT THE
ORDER OF EV

ARRIVAL & DRINKS
DINNER SERVED 8.30
AFTER PARTY 10.30PM
BRAMMER
O A TIME!
(HAVE A LOVELY TIME!)
THE GR COMMUNICATIONS SIEGE
OF EDINBURGH CASTLE
THURSDAY 8 MARCH 2012
7.30PM AT THE JACOBITE ROOM
ORDER OF EVENT
ARRIVAL & DRINKS 7.30PM
DINNER SERVED 8.30PM
AFTER PARTY 10.30PM
LIT YE
HAIR
DOON!
(LET YOUR HAIR DOWN!)
THE GR COMMUNICATIONS SIEGE
OF EDINBURGH CASTLE

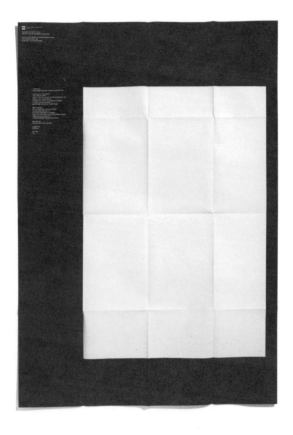

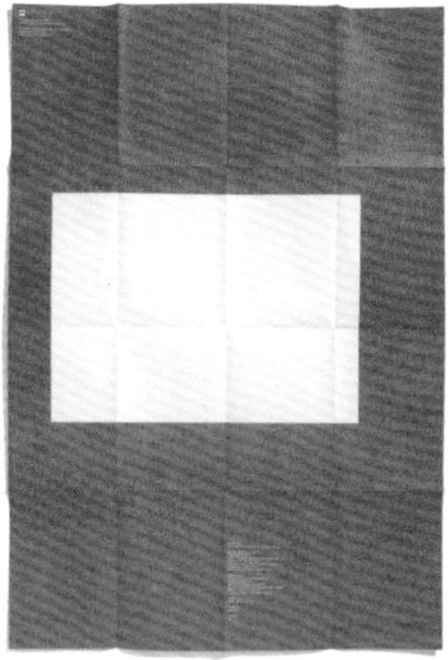

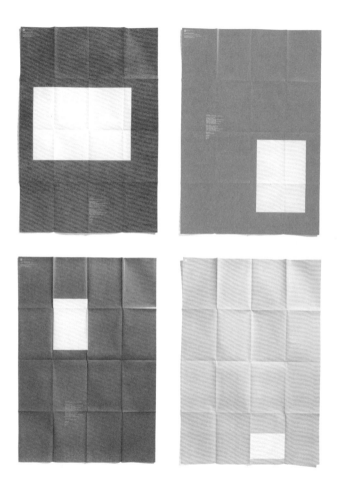

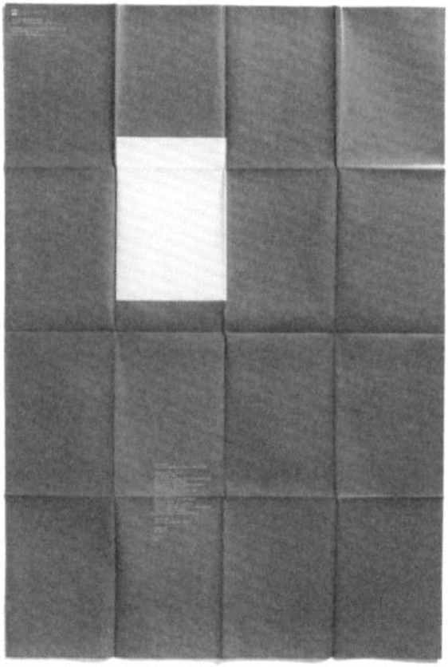

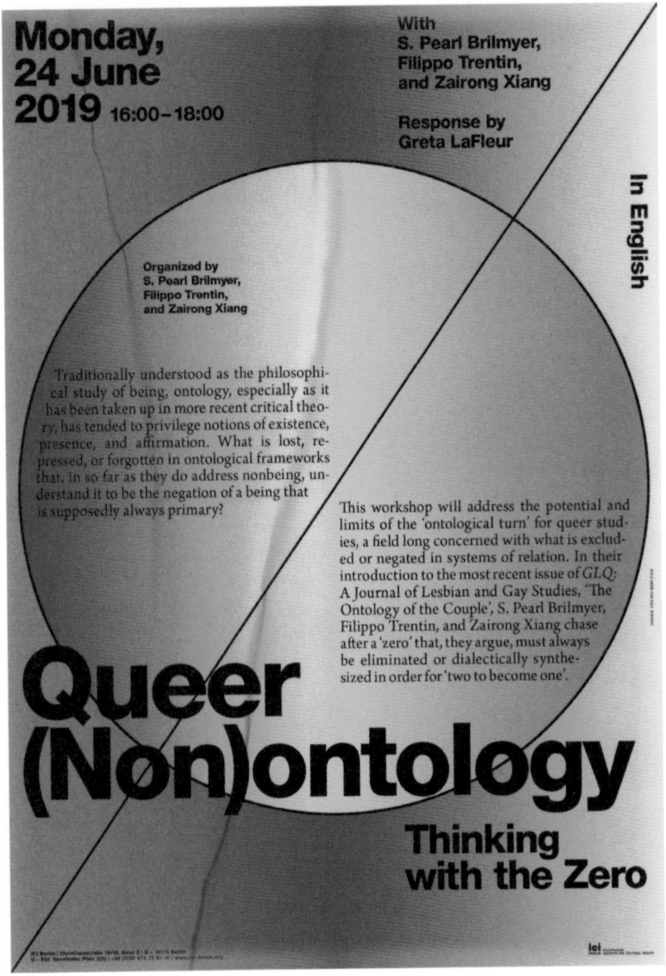
Monday, 24 June 2019 16:00–18:00
With S. Pearl Brilmyer, Filippo Trentin, and Zairong Xiang
Response by Greta LaFleur
In English
Organized by S. Pearl Brilmyer, Filippo Trentin, and Zairong Xiang
Traditionally understood as the philosophical study of being, ontology, especially as it has been taken up in more recent critical theory, has tended to privilege notions of existence, presence, and affirmation. What is lost, repressed, or forgotten in ontological frameworks that, in so far as they do address nonbeing, understand it to be the negation of a being that is supposedly always primary?
This workshop will address the potential and limits of the 'ontological turn' for queer studies, a field long concerned with what is excluded or negated in systems of relation. In their introduction to the most recent issue of GLQ: A Journal of Lesbian and Gay Studies, 'The Ontology of the Couple', S. Pearl Brilmyer, Filippo Trentin, and Zairong Xiang chase after a 'zero' that, they argue, must always be eliminated or dialectically synthesized in order for 'two to become one'.
Queer (Non)ontology
Thinking with the Zero
ici

Monday, 24 June 2019 16:00–18:00
With
S. Pearl Brilmyer,
Filippo Trentin,
and Zairong Xiang
Response by
Greta LaFleur
In English
Organized by
S. Pearl Brilmyer,
Filippo Trentin,
and Zairong Xiang
Traditionally understood as the philosophical study of being, ontology, especially as it has been taken up in more recent critical theory, has tended to privilege notions of existence, presence, and affirmation. What is lost, repressed, or forgotten in ontological frameworks that, in so far as they do address nonbeing, understand it to be the negation of a being that is supposedly always primary?
This workshop will address the potential and limits of the 'ontological turn' for queer studies, a field long concerned with what is excluded or negated in systems of relation. In their introduction to the most recent issue of GLQ: A Journal of Lesbian and Gay Studies, 'The Ontology of the Couple', S. Pearl Brilmyer, Filippo Trentin, and Zairong Xiang chase after a 'zero' that, they argue, must always be eliminated or dialectically synthesized in order for 'two to become one'.
Queer (Non)ontology
Thinking with the Zero
ici

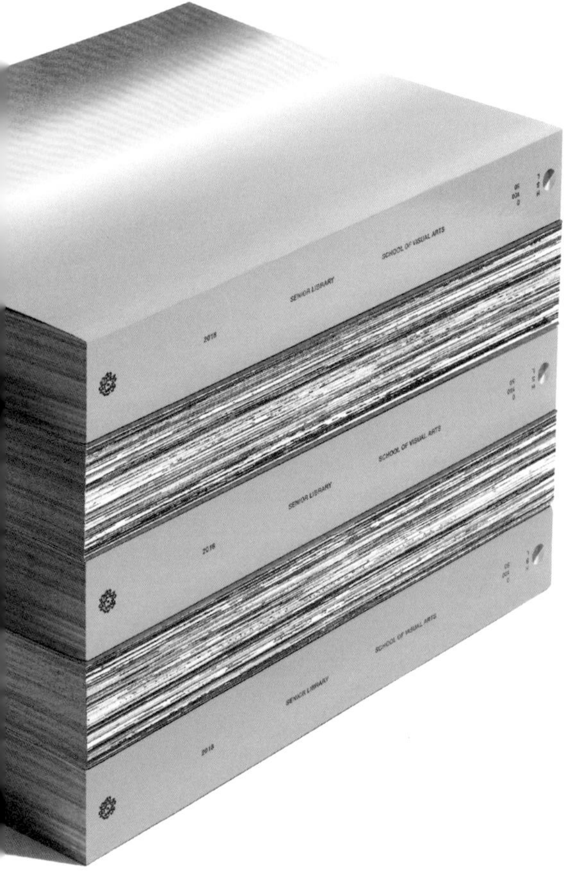
SENIOR LIBRARY
SCHOOL OF VISUAL ARTS

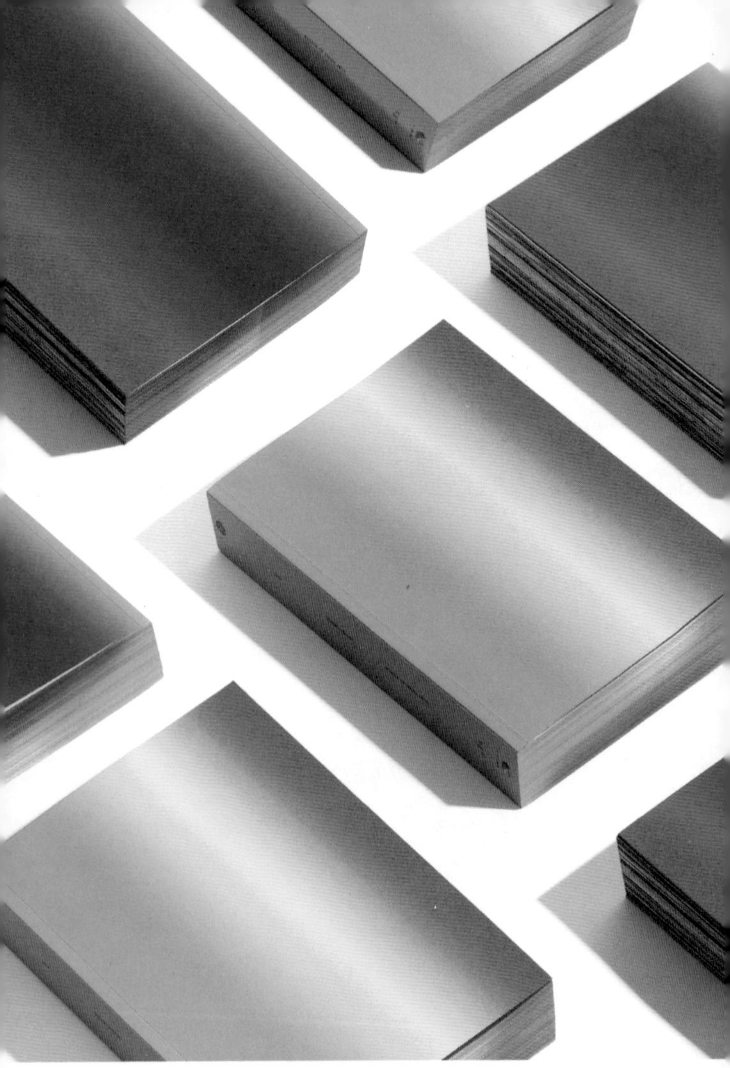

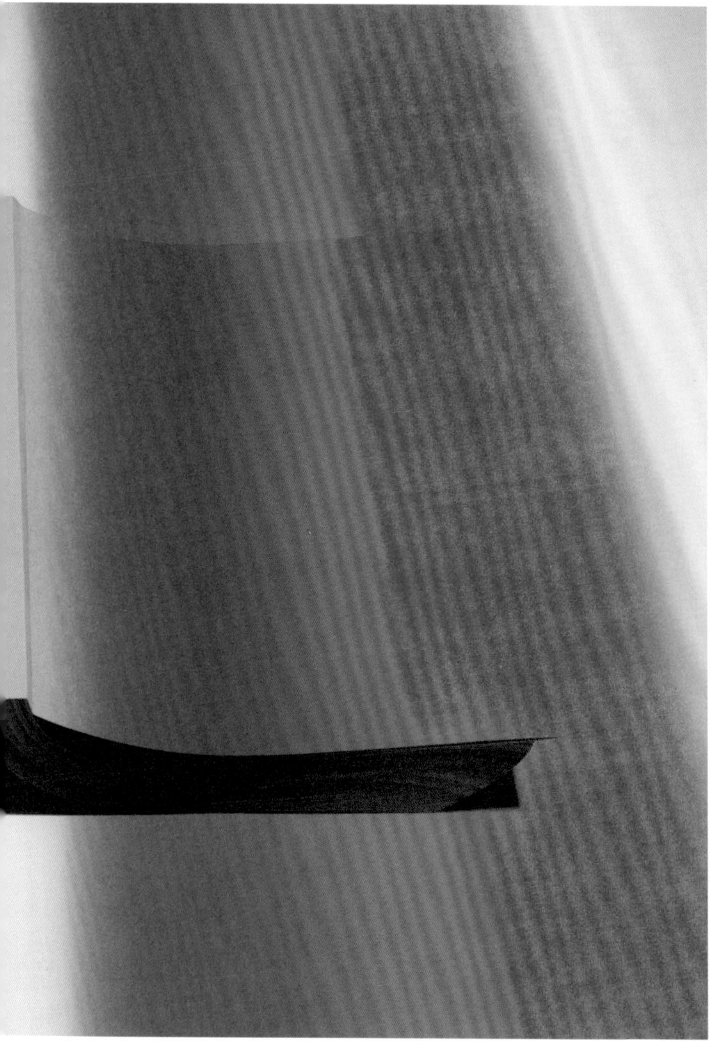

"Colour helps me brainstorm and focus on what I want to communicate when developing a design."

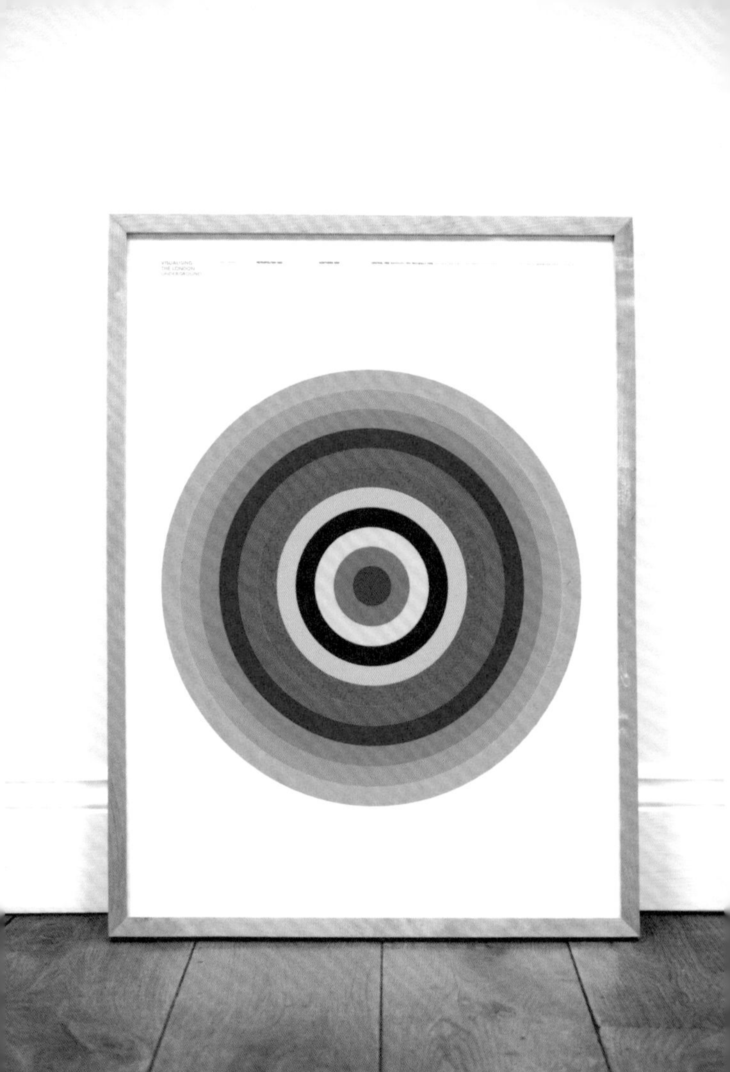
VISUALISING
THE LONDON
UNDERGROUND

VISUALISING
THE LONDON
UNDERGROUND

VISUALISING
THE LONDON
UNDERGROUND

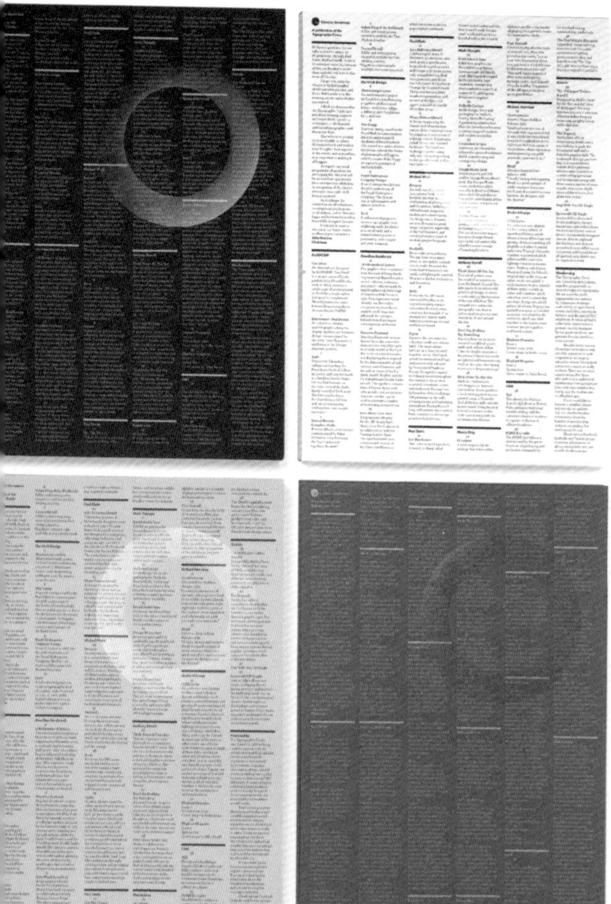

Samuel Beckett
Malone
Samuel Beckett
Molloy
and Other Plays
for Radio
and Screen
Samuel Beckett
Mercier
and other
Happy

Samuel Beckett
Seen Ill Said /
Worstward Ho
Stirrings Still
More Pricks
Kicks
The Unnam
able
The Expelled /
The Calmative /
The End
Selecte
Poems 1930-
1988
Texts for
Residua /

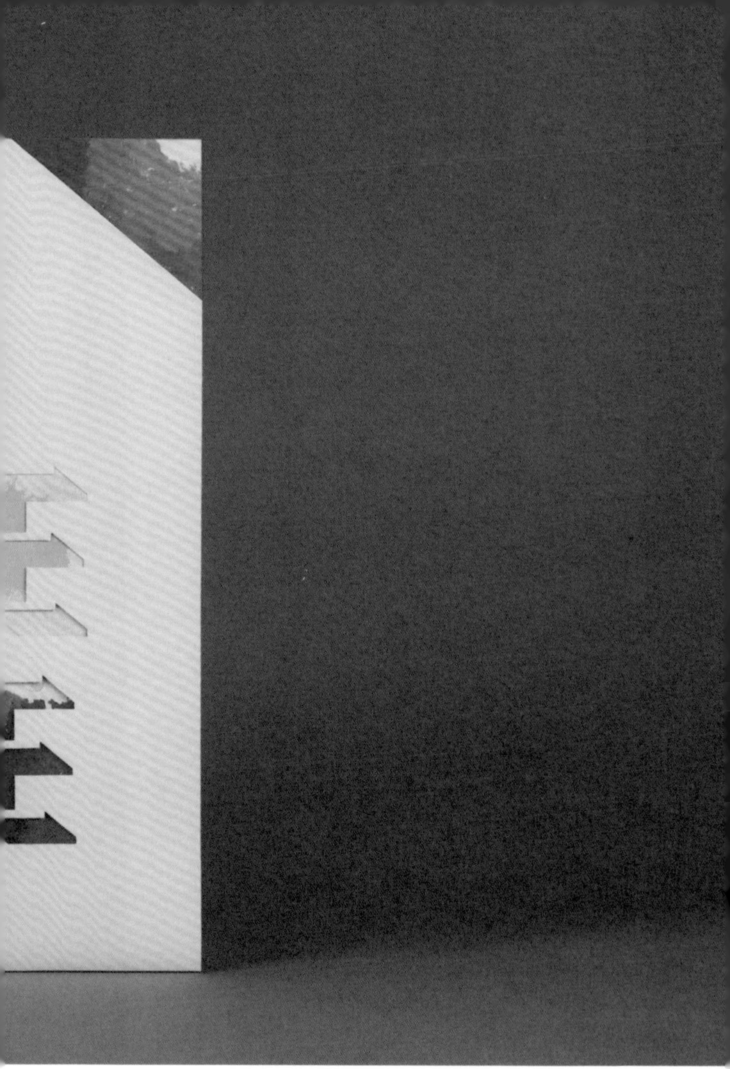

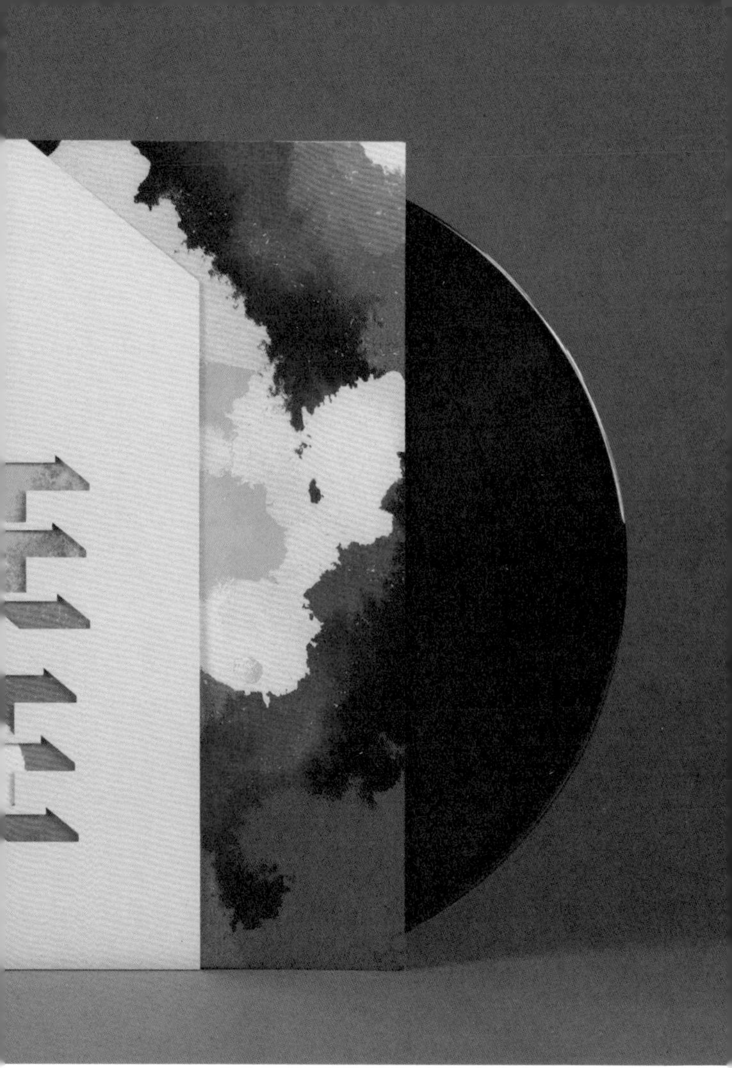

Laus
2010
40
adg
fad
laus.cat

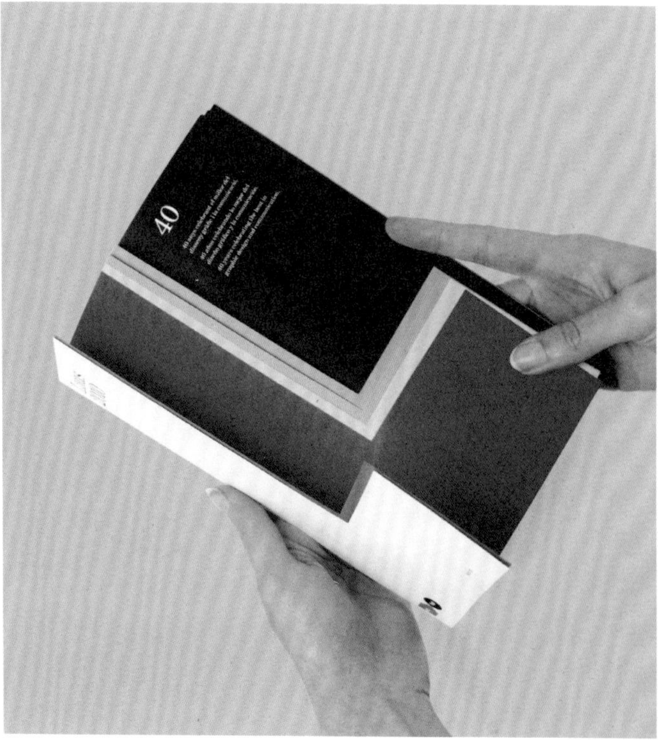
40

Laus 2010
Laus 2010
Laus 2010
Laus 2010
Laus 2010
Laus 2010
Laus 2010
40
Visual

40
Laus
2010
40

WHAT'S NEXT?
Spalio 18
ŠEŠTADIENIS
WHAT'S
NEXT?

SPEAKER
STAFF
PRESS

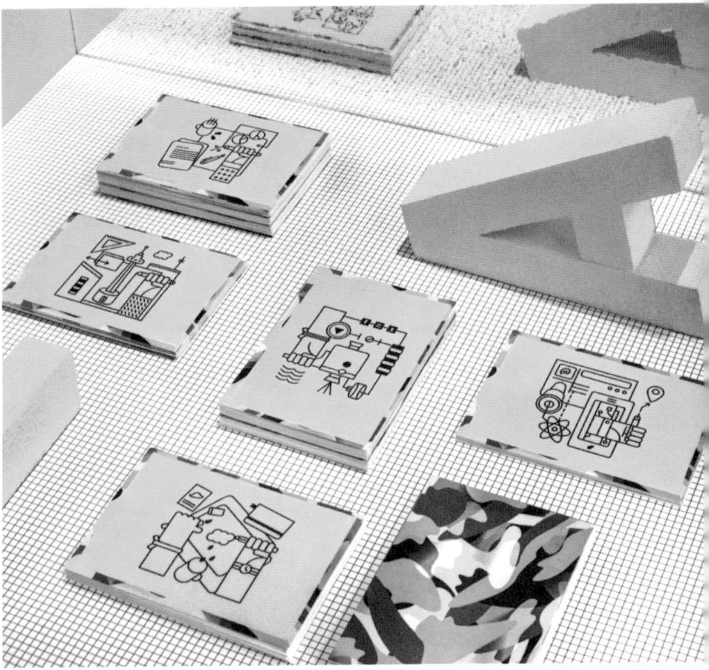

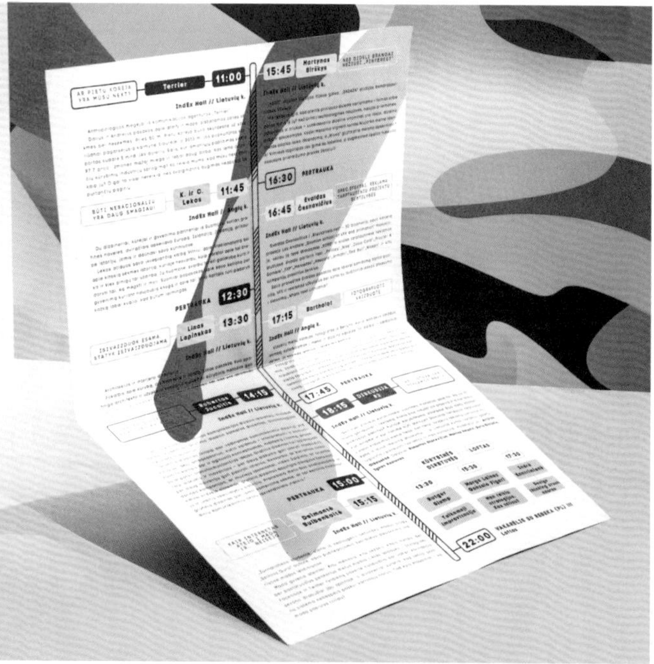
Terrier
11:00
IndEx Hall // Lietuvių k.
K. ir C. Lekos
11:45
12:30
PERTRAUKA
Linas Lapinskas
13:30
14:15
15:00
15:15
15:45
16:30
16:45
17:15
17:45
18:15
22:00

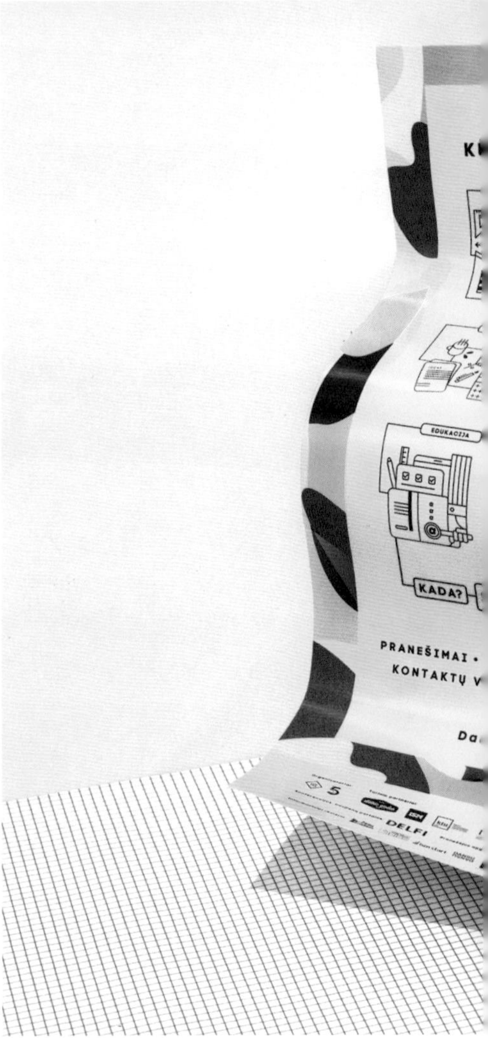
EDUKACIJA
KADA?
PRANEŠIMAI •
KONTAKTŲ
DELFI

IŲ INDUSTRIJŲ KONFERENCIJA
DIZAINAS
TECHNOLOGIJOS
VIDEO
ILIUSTRACIJA
WHAT'S NEXT?
FOTOGRAFIJA
MADA
MUZIKA
VERSLAS
O 17-18
LOF TAS
KUR?
OS • KŪRYBINĖS DIRBTUVĖS • VAKARĖLIS
DIZAINO MUGĖ (ĮĖJIMAS NEMOKAMAS)
ormacijos: whatsnext.lt
pallets
PENKI:SE
LIETUVOS PAŠTAS
Printagram
TICKETPRO

SMK
Hello,
SMK
Pagrindinės spalvos

SMK
SOCIALINIŲ MOKSLŲ KOLEGIJA
SOCIALINIŲ MOKSLŲ KOLEGIJA
PROFESINIO BAKALAURO
DIPLOMAS
SU PAGYRIMU
THE PROFESSIONAL BACHELOR DIPLOMA WITH HONORS
SMK DIREKTORĖ Gabija Skučaitė
John Lewis
CEO
J.Lewis@smk.lt
www.smk.lt
Kalvarijų g. 137E, LT-08221
370 600 000 00
Hello,
Regards,
SMK

Marketingas ir
eklamos kūrimas
SMK
9.
Mados ir
stiliaus vadyba
10.
Transporto ir
logistikos verslas
11.
Kompiuteriniai
žaidimai ir
animacija
14.
Programavimas ir
multimedija
(Dėstoma ir anglų k.)
15.
Video kūryba
ir medijos
(Dėstoma ir anglų k.)
16.
Tarptautinis verslas
(Dėstoma tik anglų k.)

SOCIALINIŲ MOKSLŲ KOLEGIJA
Alternatyvus mokslo modelis
SMK
SOCIALINIŲ MOKSLŲ KOLEGIJA
SAVITA
MODERNI
KŪRYBIŠKA
2600
1000
65%
Nuo

SMK
SOCIALINIŲ MOKSLŲ
KOLEGIJA

SMK
SOCIALINIŲ MOKSLŲ
KOLEGIJA

SM<
SOCIALINIŲ MOKSLŲ
KOLEGIJA

BROMBERG
CALLING 18
WWW.MOZG.PL
31.10.2017
MÓZG
BYDGOSZCZ
PARKOWA 2
START : 22:00
ENTRY : 20 PLN
MÓ
ZG
JERZY PRZEŹDZIECKI
DJ KEBS + FREEZE + MO
GRZANKO MUZYKANT
CHINO + PROJEKT UTOPIA
SOULITARY + ERDMANN

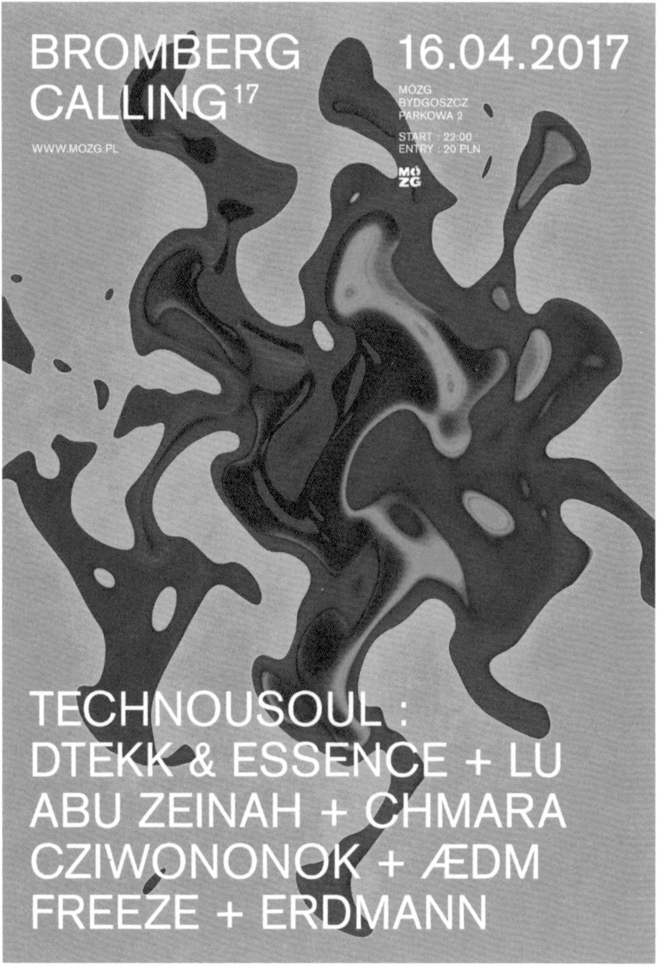
BROMBERG
CALLING17
WWW.MOZG.PL
16.04.2017
MÓZG
BYDGOSZCZ
PARKOWA 2
START : 22:00
ENTRY : 20 PLN
MÓ
ZG
TECHNOUSOUL :
DTEKK & ESSENCE + LU
ABU ZEINAH + CHMARA
CZIWONONOK + ÆDM
FREEZE + ERDMANN

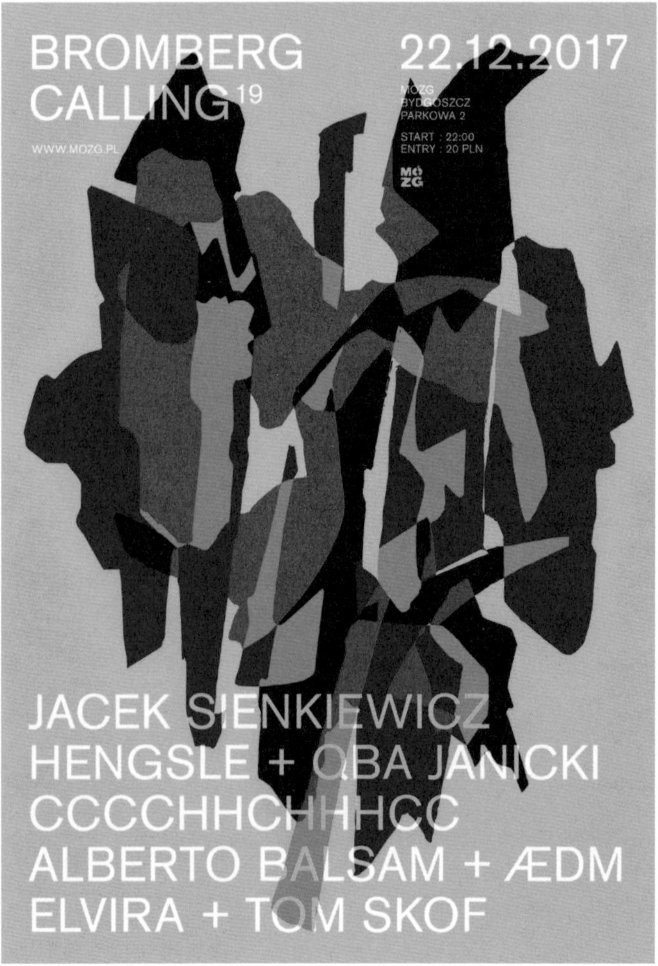
BROMBERG CALLING 19
WWW.MOZG.PL
22.12.2017
MÓZG
BYDGOSZCZ
PARKOWA 2
START : 22:00
ENTRY : 20 PLN
JACEK SIENKIEWICZ
HENGSLE + QBA JANICKI
CCCCHHCHHHCC
ALBERTO BALSAM + ÆDM
ELVIRA + TOM SKOF

BROMBERG
CALLING 22
WWW.MOZG.PL
21.04.2019
MÓZG
BYDGOSZCZ
PARKOWA 2
START : 22:00
ENTRY : 20/30 PLN
MÓ
ZG
DZUMA + HURAGAN
OSTROWSKI + DYKTANDO
COPY CORPO + GLOCK17
ERDMANN + FOQL + LESU

FRESH

FUCK

jam
PRESENT & CORRECT
INK
BUTTER
MARROWFAT
P&C

STOP
Present & Correct
Colour Wheel Notecards.
6 Notecards. 6 Envelopes. 6 Colours.
Red
Rouge
Rojo
Rot
Rosso

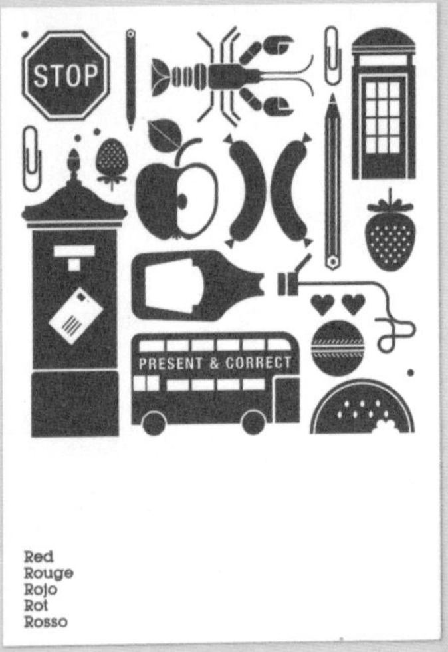
STOP
PRESENT & CORRECT
Red
Rouge
Rojo
Rot
Rosso

Orange
Orange
Naranja
Farbe
Arancione

MARROWFAT
Green
Vert
Verde
Grün
Verde

INK
Blue
Bleu
Azul
Blau
Azzurro

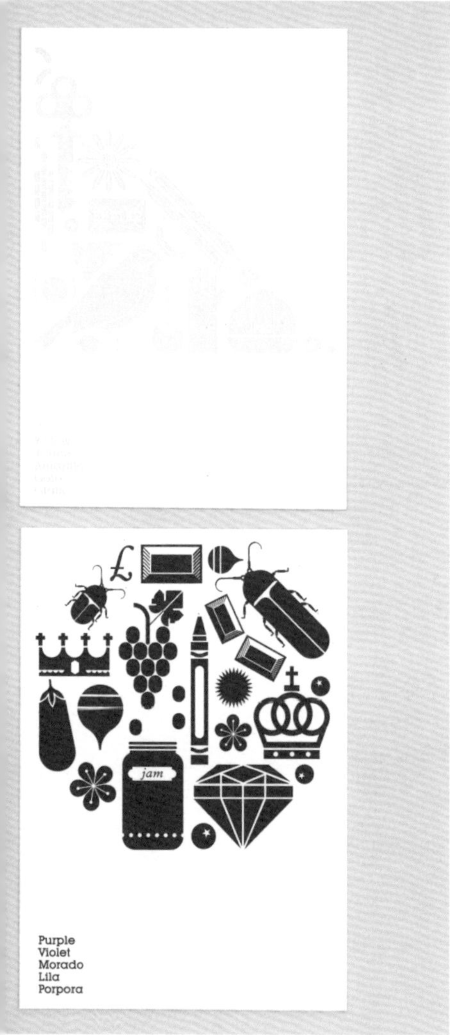
jam
Purple
Violet
Morado
Lila
Porpora

VOULEZ
– VOUS
CLICHER
CE SOIR
Studio Clicher
(à Mervilla)
Saturday 16th
8:00 p.m
La maison Clicher
ne ressemblera pas simplement
à une belle demeure de magazine.
La maison Clicher
va vibrer de tout son corps:
Creative
Libertaire
Internationale
Conceptuelle
Haut de gamme
Endomorphe
Respectueuse
Clicher

Studio Clicher
(à Mervilla)
La maison Clicher
ne ressemblera pas simplement
à une belle demeure de magazine.
La maison Clicher
va vibrer de tout son corps:
Creative

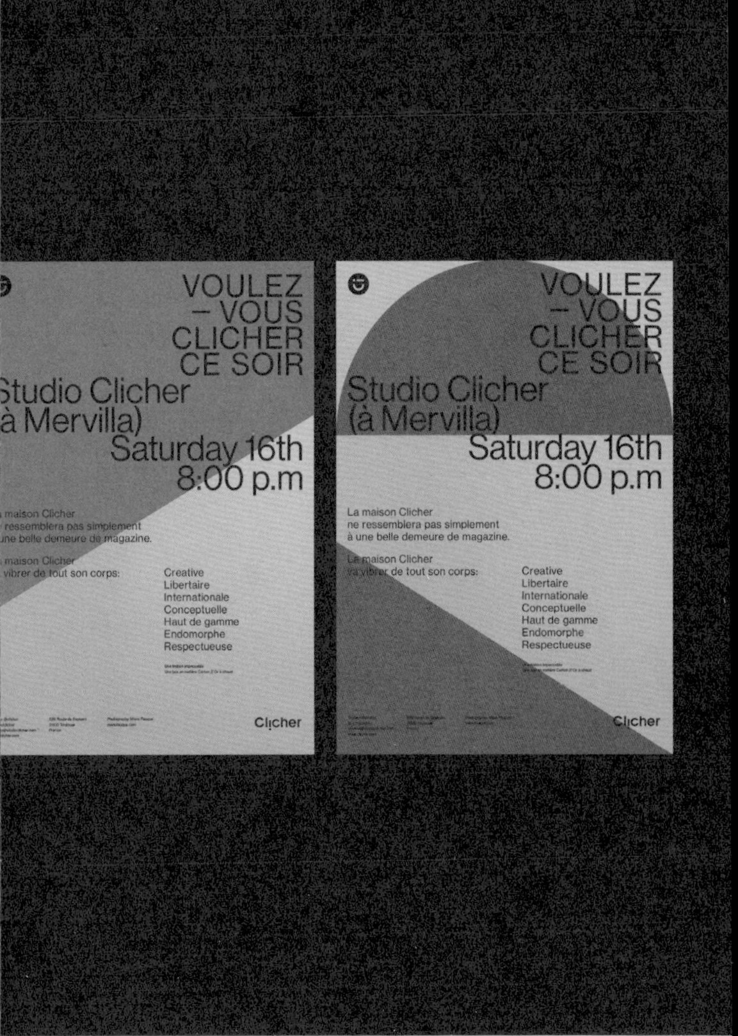
VOULEZ
– VOUS
CLICHER
CE SOIR
Studio Clicher
(à Mervilla)
Saturday 16th
8:00 p.m
La maison Clicher
ne ressemblera pas simplement
à une belle demeure de magazine.
La maison Clicher
va vibrer de tout son corps:
Creative
Libertaire
Internationale
Conceptuelle
Haut de gamme
Endomorphe
Respectueuse
Clicher

VOULEZ
– VOUS
CLICHER
CE SOIR
Studio Clicher
(à Mervilla)
Saturday 16th
8:00 p.m
La maison Clicher
ne ressemblera pas simplement
à une belle demeure de magazine.
La maison Clicher
va vibrer de tout son corps:
Creative
Libertaire
Internationale
Conceptuelle
Haut de gamme
Endomorphe
Respectueuse
Clicher

VOULEZ
– VOUS
CLICHER
CE SOIR
Studio Clicher
(à Mervilla)
Saturday 16th
8:00 p.m
La maison Clicher
ne ressemblera pas simplement
à une belle demeure de magazine.
La maison Clicher
va vibrer de tout son corps:
Creative
Libertaire
Internationale
Conceptuelle
Haut de gamme
Endomorphe
Respectueuse
Clicher

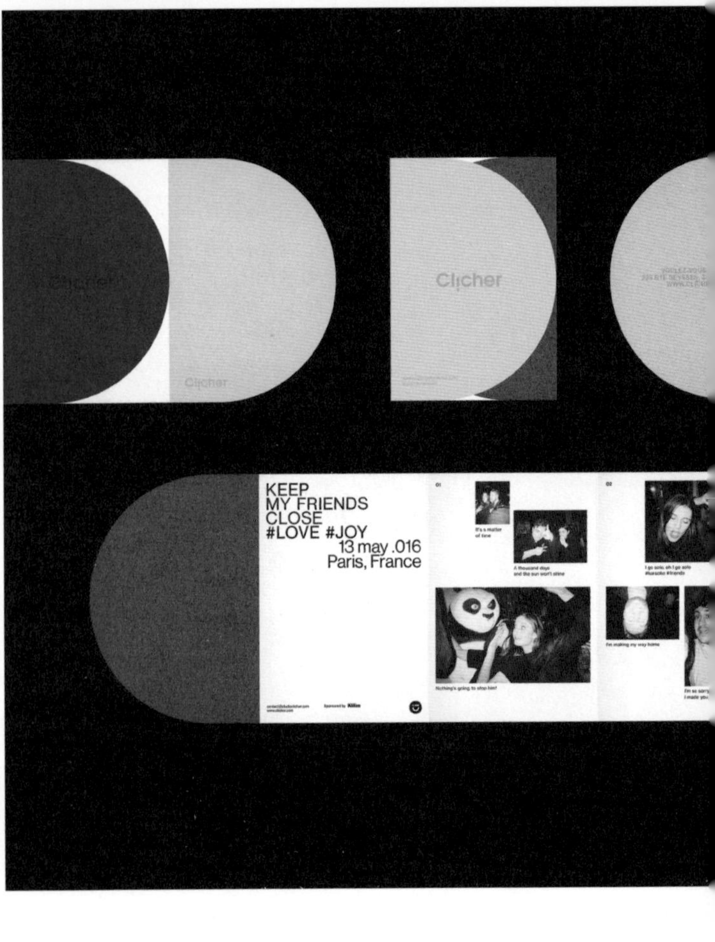
Clicher
Clicher
KEEP
MY FRIENDS
CLOSE
#LOVE #JOY
13 may .016
Paris, France
It's a matter
of time
A thousand days
and the sun won't shine
Nothing's going to stop him!
I'm making my way home

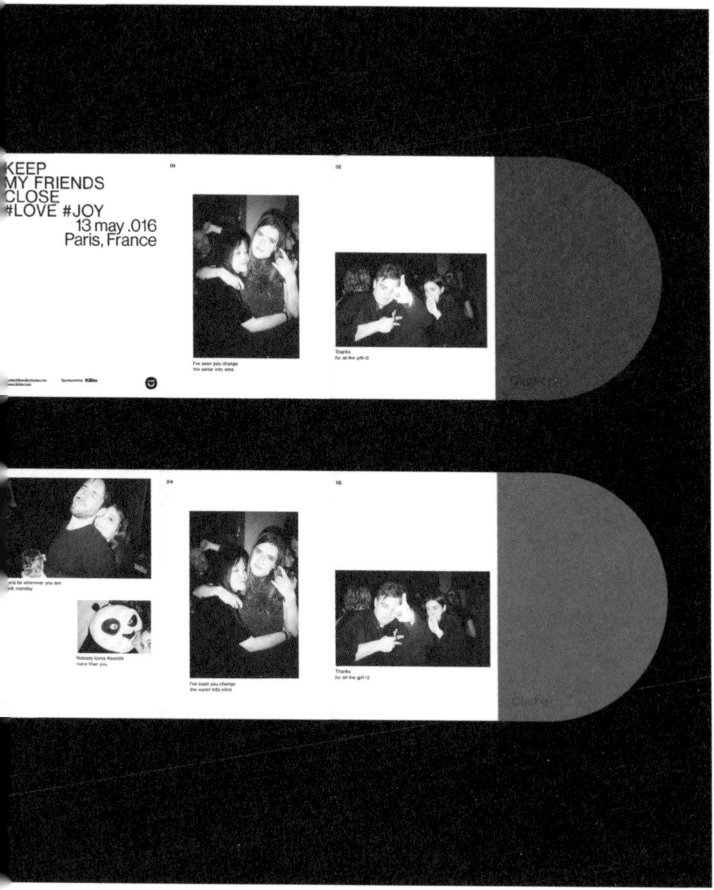
KEEP
MY FRIENDS
CLOSE
#LOVE #JOY
13 may .016
Paris, France
I've seen you change
the water into wine
Thanks
for all the gift<3
Nobody loves #panda
more than you
I've seen you change
the water into wine
Thanks
for all the gift<3

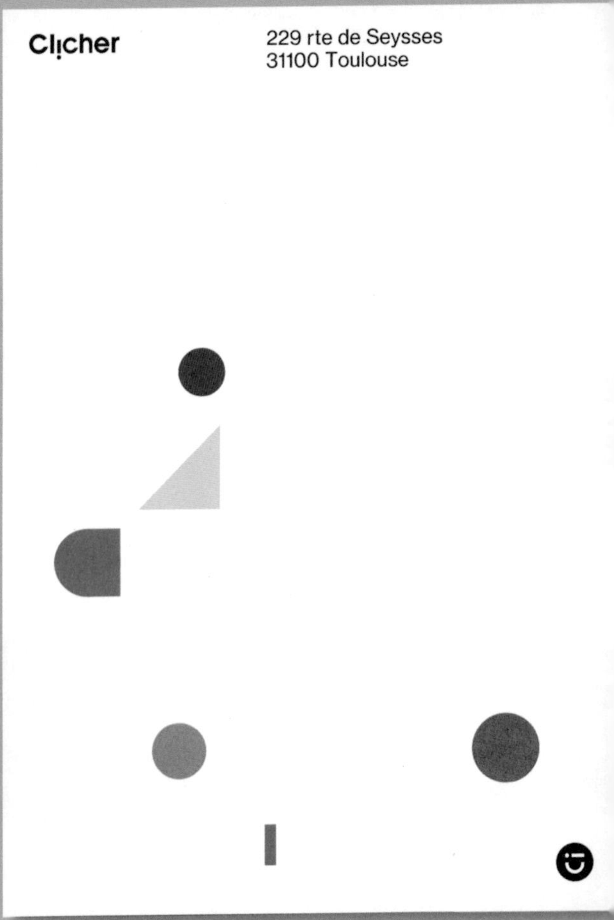
Clicher
229 rte de Seysses
31100 Toulouse

Clicher
229 rte de Seysses
31100 Toulouse

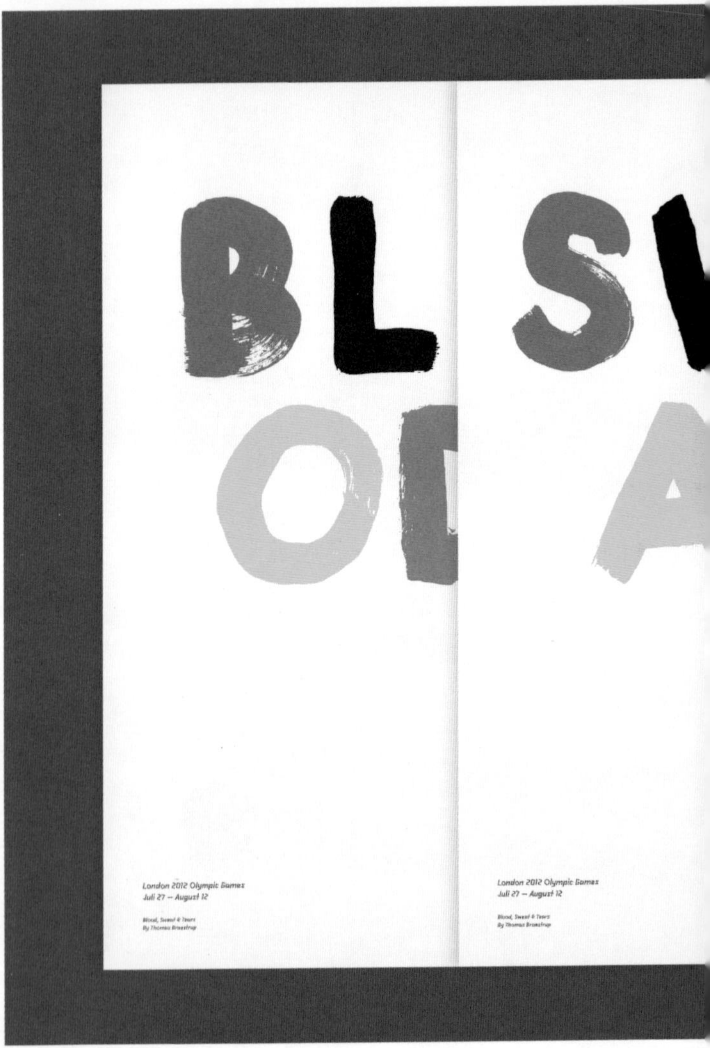
BL
OD
London 2012 Olympic Games
Juli 27 — August 12
London 2012 Olympic Games
Juli 27 — August 12

TEA
RS
London 2012 Olympic Games
Juli 27 – August 12

BLO SWE TEA
OD AT RS

HON MOR DRA
OR AL MA

POW GOA CLA
ER LS SS

JES OWE SPE
SE NS ED

PEA TEA SPO
CE MS RT

BLO
OD
EUROMAN

ENCRE
ACRYLIQUE

ENCRE
ACRYLIQUE
PROFESSIONNEL DE SÉRIGRAPHIE
INFOS

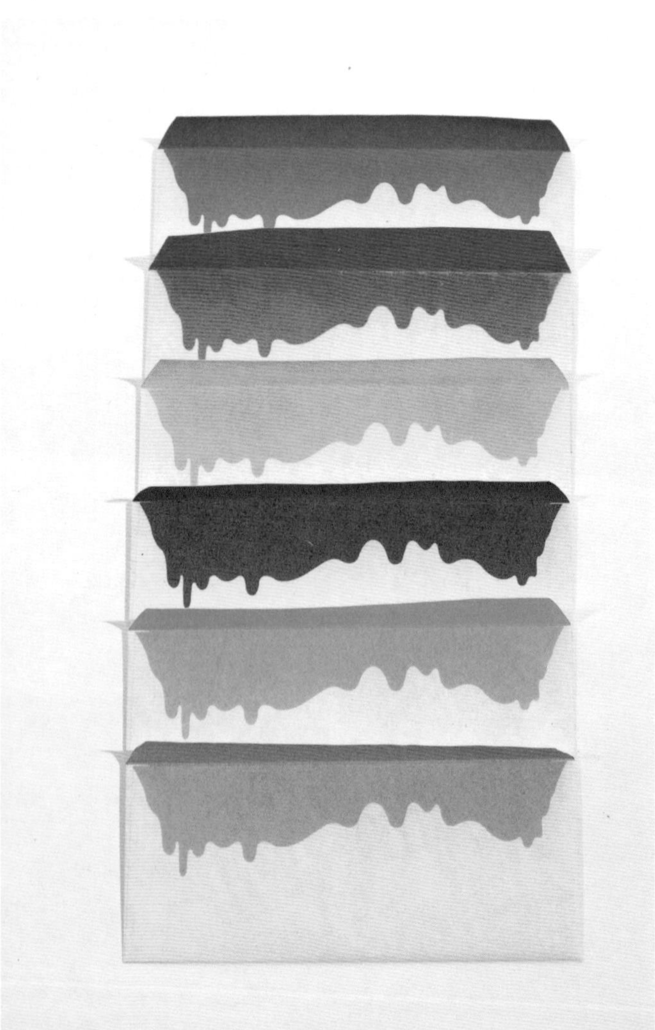

BANG
BANG
BANG

MAR
KL.19.30
DogA, Hausmannsgate 16
YourFriends
OSLO VOL.14
Music & Film
Million City
New Classic
complimentary drink
PechaKucha Night OSLO VOL.15
The right light
LUXO
25
NOV

Creator of movements
APR
KL. 19.30
Leirdal // Hugo Design
The right light
LUXO
MAR
complimentary drink
PechaKucha
VOL.19
// Fotball, fornuft og følelser
KL.19.30
DogA,
YourFriends
PechaKucha Night OSLO VOL.15
history of philosophy in 1-2-3
n + Marianne Boye // Design uten grenser
provisasjonsorkester
Hausmannsgate
All the world is a game
OSLO VOL.11

¿CÓMO QUEREMOS VIVIR?

La Ciudad de las Personas
UN LUGAR
MÁS SANO
La Ciudad de las Personas

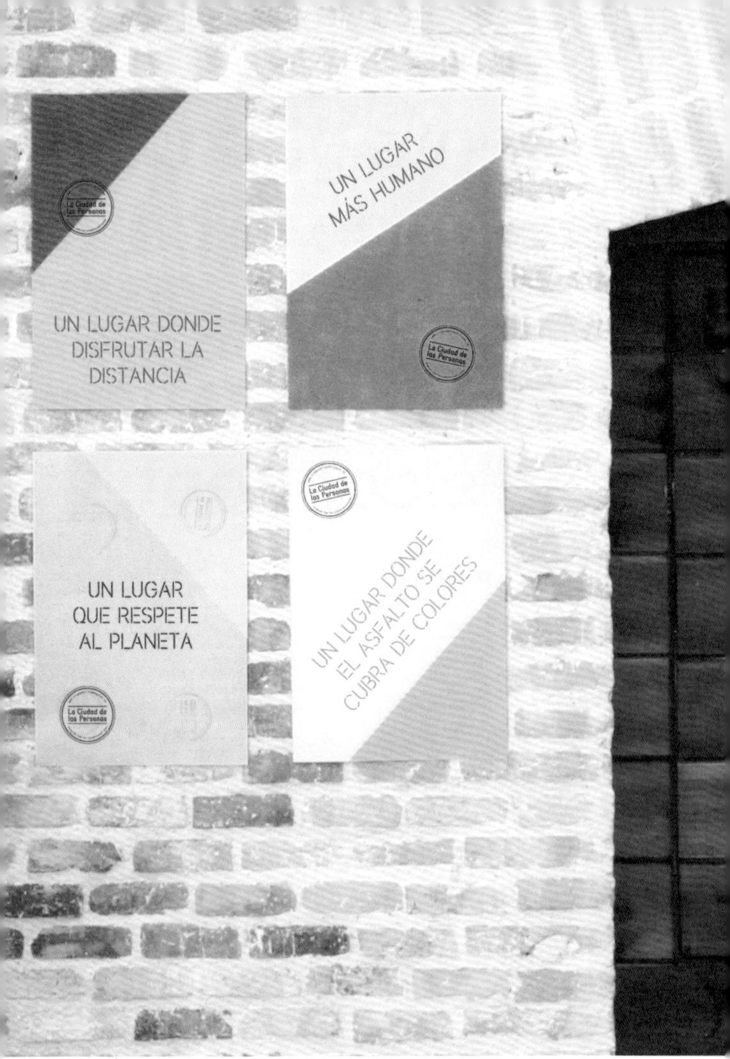
La Ciudad de las Personas
UN LUGAR DONDE DISFRUTAR LA DISTANCIA
UN LUGAR MÁS HUMANO
La Ciudad de las Personas
La Ciudad de las Personas
UN LUGAR QUE RESPETE AL PLANETA
La Ciudad de las Personas
UN LUGAR DONDE EL ASFALTO SE CUBRA DE COLORES

“The variety of gradients give us the chance to catch the eye and be coherent with the brand’s concept.”

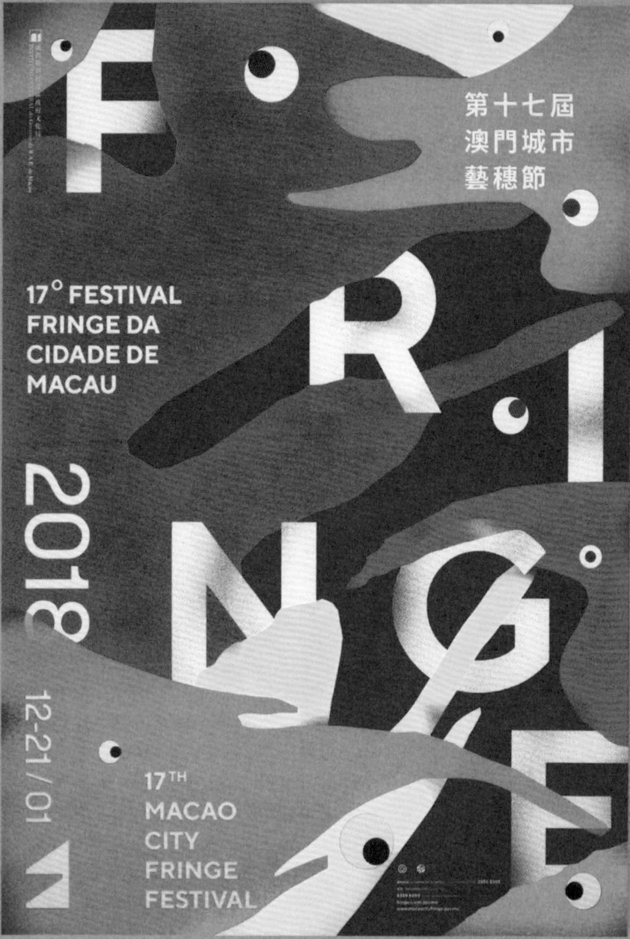
FRINGE
第十七屆
澳門城市
藝穗節
17° FESTIVAL
FRINGE DA
CIDADE DE
MACAU
2018
12-21/01
17TH
MACAO
CITY
FRINGE
FESTIVAL

第十七屆
澳門城市
藝穗節
FRINGE
2018
17°
FESTIVAL
FRINGE DA
CIDADE DE
MACAU
12-21/01
INSTITUTO CULTURAL
17TH
MACAO
CITY
FRINGE
FESTIVAL

MACAOCITYFRINGEFESTIVAL
場地
LOCAIS
VENUES

第十七屆
澳門城市藝穗節
17° FESTIVAL FRINGE DA CIDADE DE MACAU
17TH MACAO CITY FRINGE FESTIVAL
錦堂
JIN-TANG
12-14/01
2018
第十七屆
澳門城市藝穗節
2018

17TH MACAO
CITY FRINGE
FESTIVAL
16, 17/01
第十七屆
澳門城市藝穗節
17° FESTIVAL
FRINGE DA CIDADE
DE MACAU
17TH MACAO
CITY FRINGE
FESTIVAL
三段式動能
TRINAMICS
20, 21/01
2018

鄉愁的妮雅廬
NIYARO: ANSEIO PELA PÁTRIA
HOMELAND
12/1
13, 14/1
WORKSHOP SOBRE DANÇA, CANÇÕES ANTIGAS E ARTE PERFORMATIVA CONTEMPORÂNEA
WORKSHOP ON ANCIENT DANCE, SONGS AND CONTEMPORARY PERFORMANCE ART
TEATRO LANGASAN (TAIWAN)
O MEU PAI É MOTORISTA DE AUTOCARRO
MY OLD MAN IS A BUS DRIVER

愛情遺物拍賣會
LEILÃO DE HISTÓRIAS DE AMOR
THE AUCTION OF LOVE STORIES
14/1
15, 17/1
流浪兔
O COELHO VAGABUNDO
WANDERING RABBIT
節目表
CALENDÁRIO
CALENDAR
12
13
15
16
17
20
購票指南
AQUISIÇÃO DE BILHETES
BOOKING GUIDE

第十七屆
澳門城市
藝穗節
STIVAL
NGE
CIDADE
MACAU
17 TH
MACAO
CITY
FRINGE
FESTIVAL

第十七屆
澳門城市
藝穗節
2018
P.B.: 15000KGS
Sentados: 30
De Pé: 36

第十七屆
澳門城市
藝穗節
17°
FESTIVAL
FRINGE
DA CIDADE
DE MACAU
2018
12-21/01
文化局
INSTITUTO CULTURAL

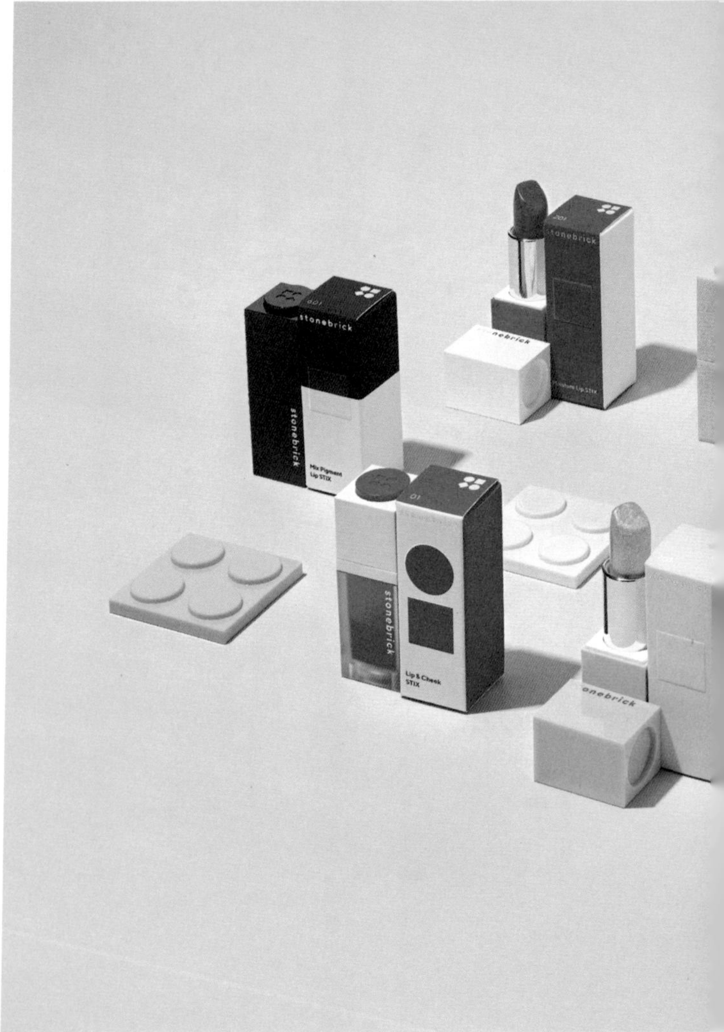
001
stonebrick
stonebrick
Mix Pigment
Lip STIX
201
stonebrick
01
stonebrick
Lip & Cheek
STIX

102
stonebrick
101
stonebrick
stonebrick
401
stonebrick
stonebrick
Glitter Pigment
Lip STIX

stonebrick
Moist BB Cushion
302
stonebrick
stonebrick
178
stonebrick
Mix Pigment
Lip STIX
stonebrick

01
Power Blush Box
stonebrick
401
stonebrick
Mix Pigment
Lip STIX
stonebrick

stonebrick
stonebrick
stonebrick
stonebrick

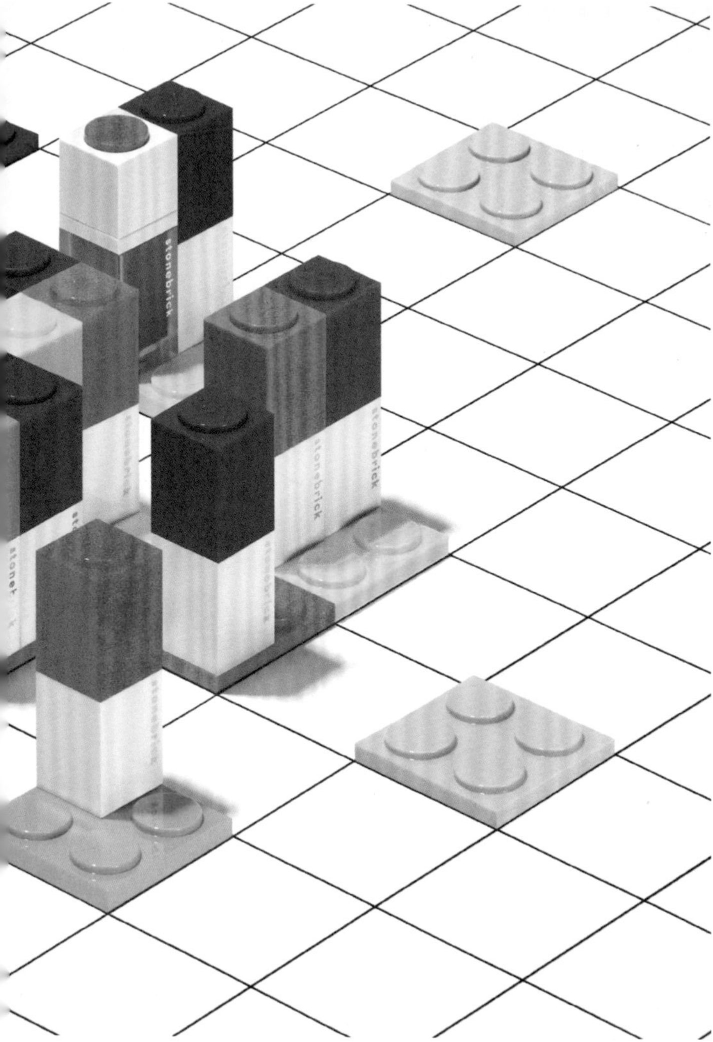
stonebrick
stonebrick
stonebrick
stonebrick

Nobel
Deutschsprachige
Literaturnobelpreisträger
German speaking
Winners of the Nobel
Prize in Literature
1902–2004
GOETHE-INSTITUT

Theodor Mommsen
Literaturnobelpreis 1902
Nobel Prize in Literature 1902

Hermann Hesse
Literaturnobelpreis 1946
Thomas Mann
Literaturnobelpreis 1929
Theodor Mommsen
Literaturnobelpreis 1902
Nobel Prize in Literature 1902
Nobel
Deutschsprachige
Literaturnobelpreisträger
German speaking
Winners of the Nobel
Prize in Literature
1902–2004
GOETHE-INSTITUT
Elfriede Jelinek
Günter Grass
Nobel Prize in Literature 1999
Heinrich Böll
Nelly Sachs

Carl Spitteler
Gerhart Hauptmann
Literaturnobelpreis 1912
Paul Heyse
Literaturnobelpreis 1910
Nobel Prize in Literature 1910
Rudolf Eucken
Literaturnobelpreis 1908

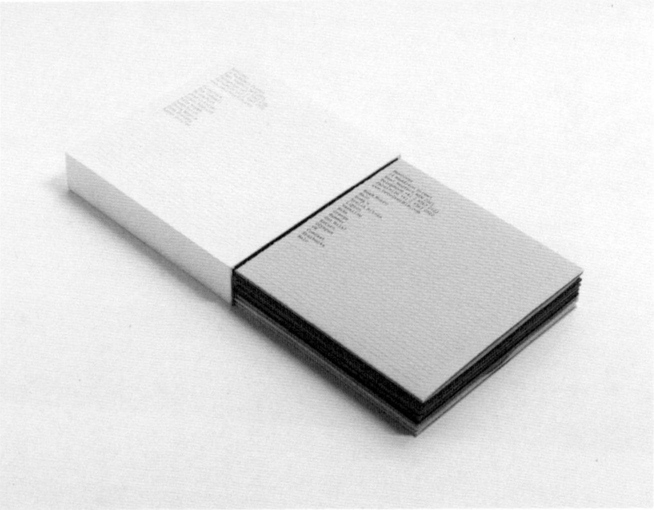

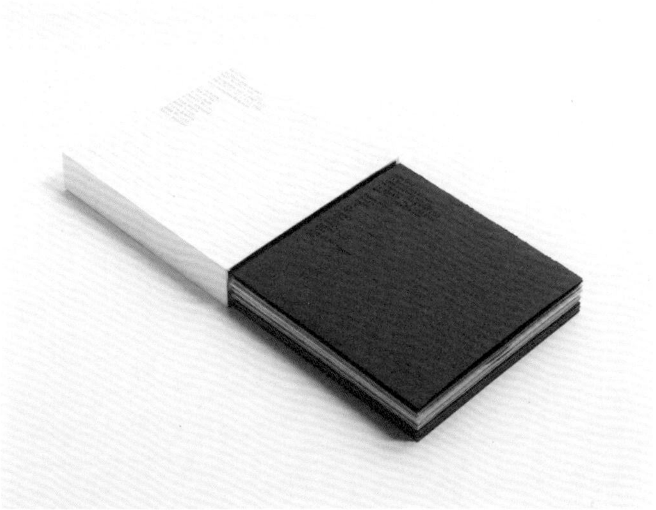

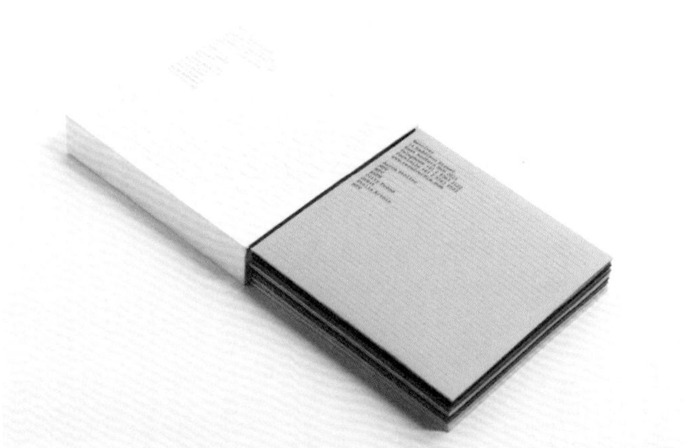

Revolver
14 Maddison Street
East Redfern NSW 2021
Telephone +61 2 9363 2122
Facsimile +61 2 9363 0522
www.revolverfilm.com

Directors
Tim Godsall
Bruce Hunt
Justin Kurzel
Simon McQuoid
Kris Moyes
Noam Murro
Steve Rogers
Glue Society
Aaron Stoller

1 - 500

BOURGEOIS

Phase One.

A visual collaboration between
D. Crooks and D Kim.

Note: This poster contains an element from
an unused commisioned project.

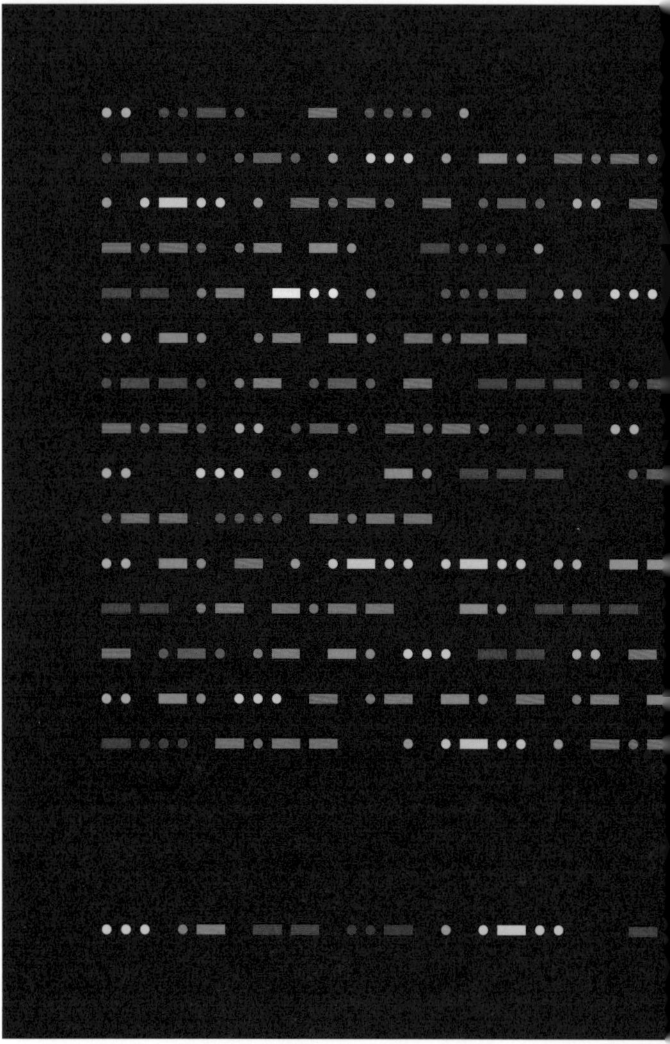

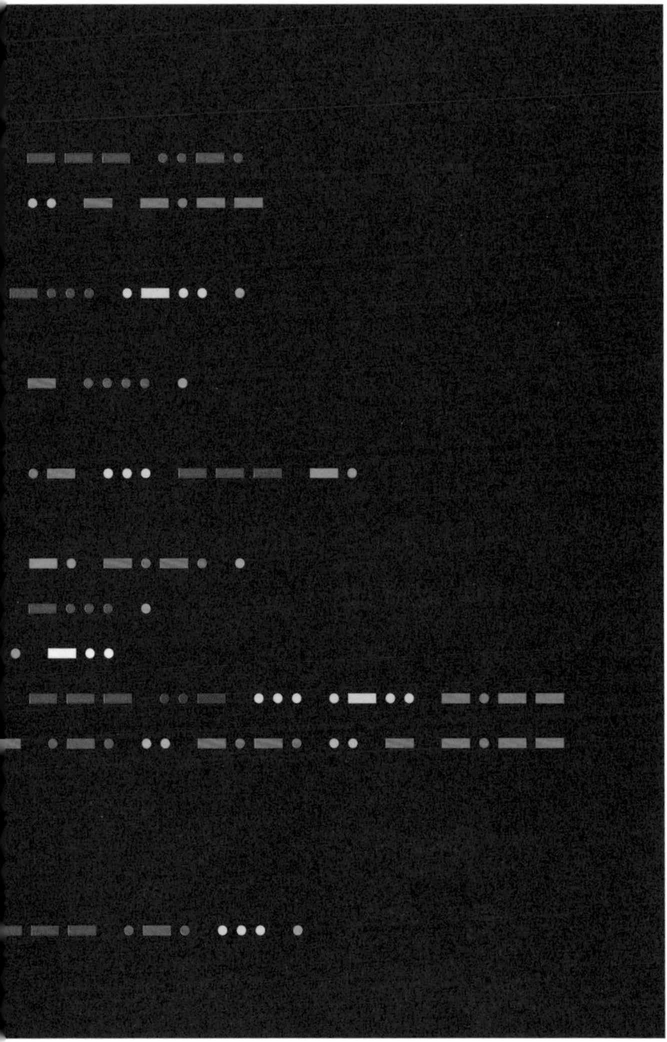

SONORAMA

SONORAMA

SONORAMA

SONORAMA

SONORAMA

SONORAMA

SONORAMA

SONORAMA

SON
OR
AM
A
09
BESANÇON
PAYSAGE
SONORE
INSTALLATIONS ET PARCOURS SONORES,
CONCERTS, FILMS MUSICAUX,
PERFORMANCES, SPECTACLES DE RUE...
8-11 OCTOBRE
WWW.SONORAMA-BESANÇON.COM

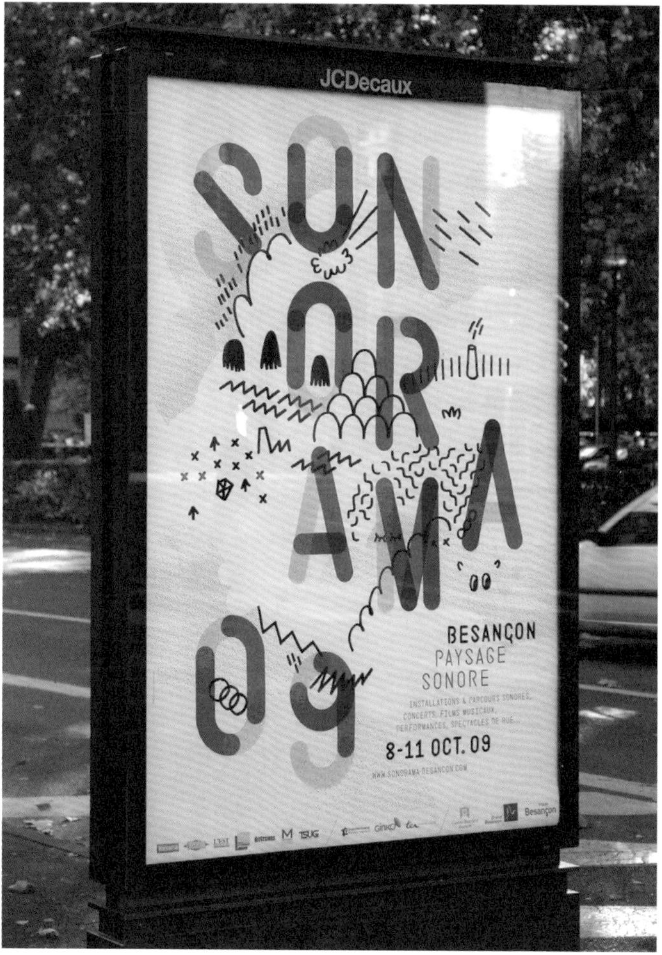
JCDecaux
SON
OR
AMA
09
BESANÇON
PAYSAGE
SONORE
INSTALLATIONS & PARCOURS SONORES,
CONCERTS, FILMS MUSICAUX,
PERFORMANCES, SPECTACLES DE RUE...
8-11 OCT. 09
WWW.SONORAMA-BESANCON.COM
Besançon

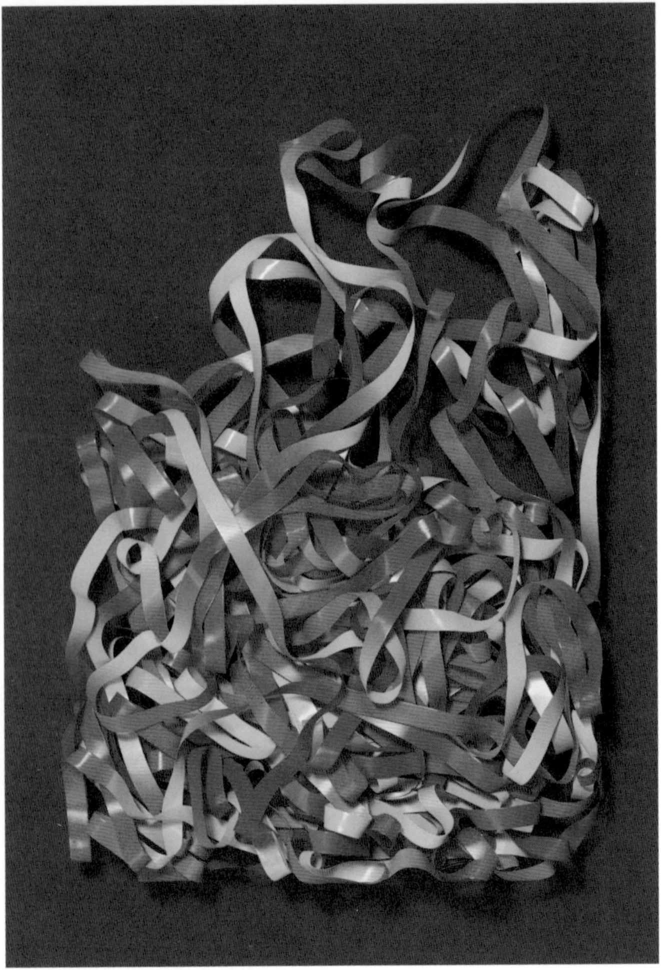

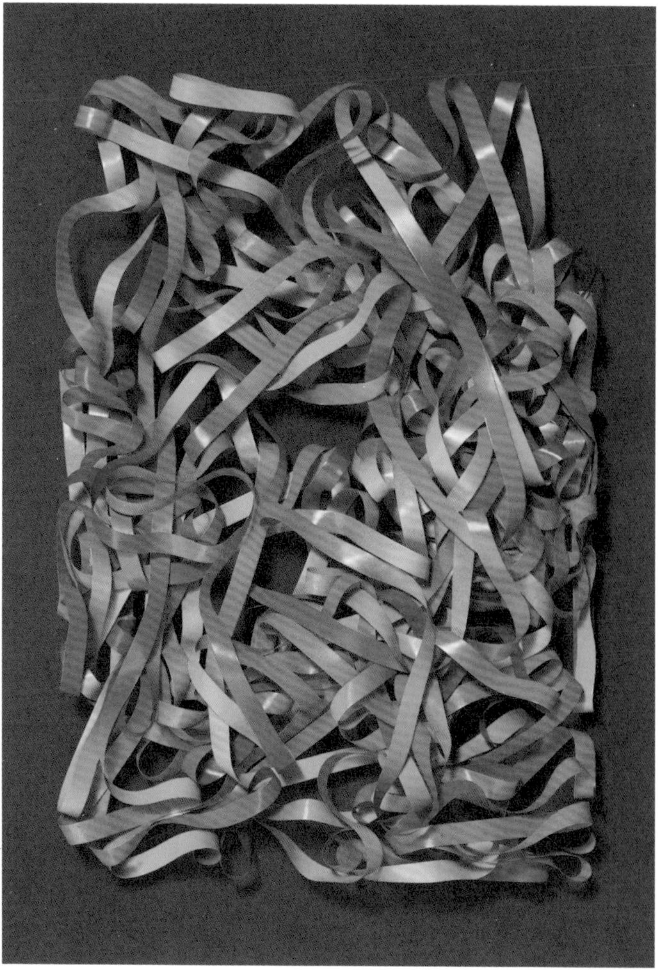

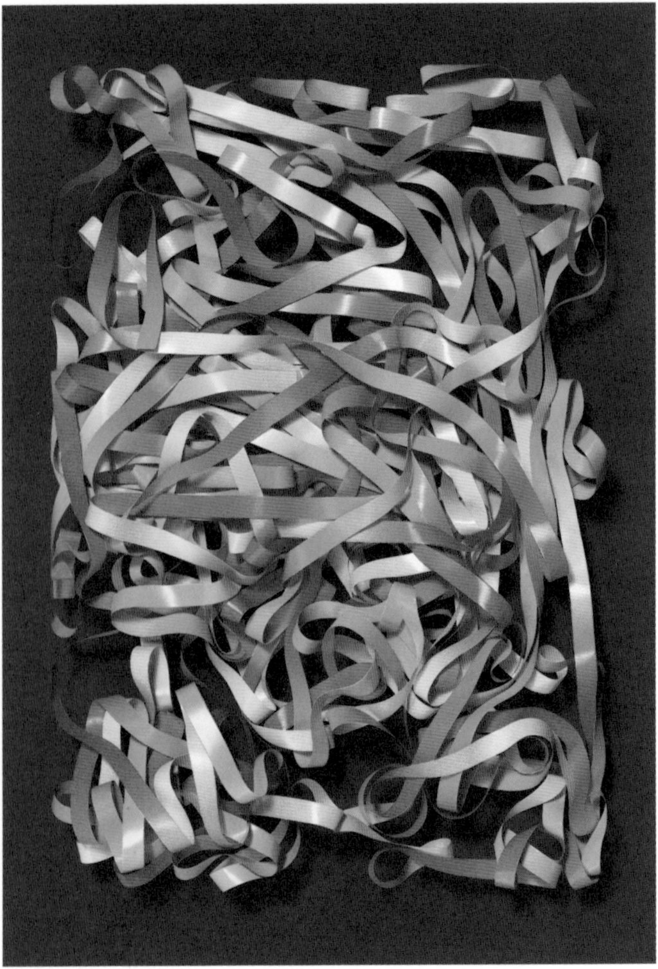

Hey

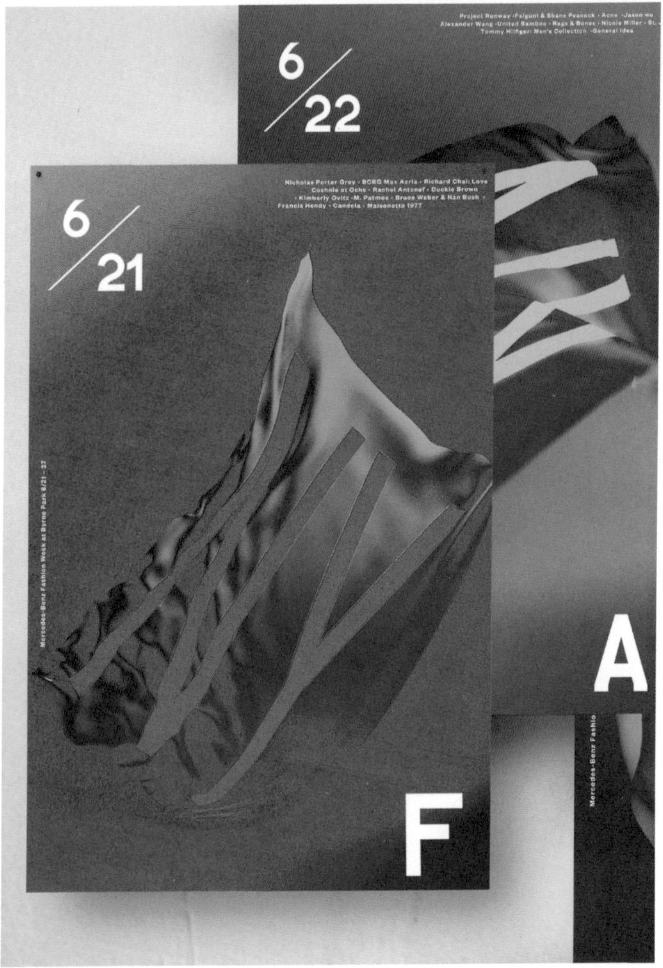
Project Runway · Falguni & Shane Peacock · Acne · Jason wu
Alexander Wang · United Bamboo · Rags & Bones · Nicole Miller · St.
Tommy Hilfiger: Men's Collection · General Idea
6/22
Nicholas Porter Grey · BCBG Max Azria · Richard Chai Love
Cushnie et Ochs · Rachel Antonof · Duckie Brown
· Kimberly Ovitz · M. Patmos · Bruce Weber & Nan Bush ·
Francis Hendy · Candela · Maisonette 1977
6/21
Mercedes-Benz Fashion Week at Byrne Park 6/21 – 27
F
A
Mercedes-Benz Fashio

6/23
Nicholas Porter Grey · BCBG Max Azria · Richard Chai: Love
Cushnie et Ochs · Rachel Antonof · Duckie Brown
· Kimberly Ovitz ·M. Patmos · Bruce Webe
Francis Hendy · Candela · Maisonette 1977
Mercedes-Benz Fashion Week at Byrne Park 6/21 – 27
S

6/24
Nicholas Porter Grey · BCBG Max Azria · Richard Chai: Love
Cushnie et Ochs · Rachel Antonof · Duckie Brown
· Kimberly Ovitz ·M. Patmos · Bruce Webe
Francis Hendy · Candela · Maisonette 1977
Mercedes-Benz Fashion Week at Byrne Park 6/21 – 27
H

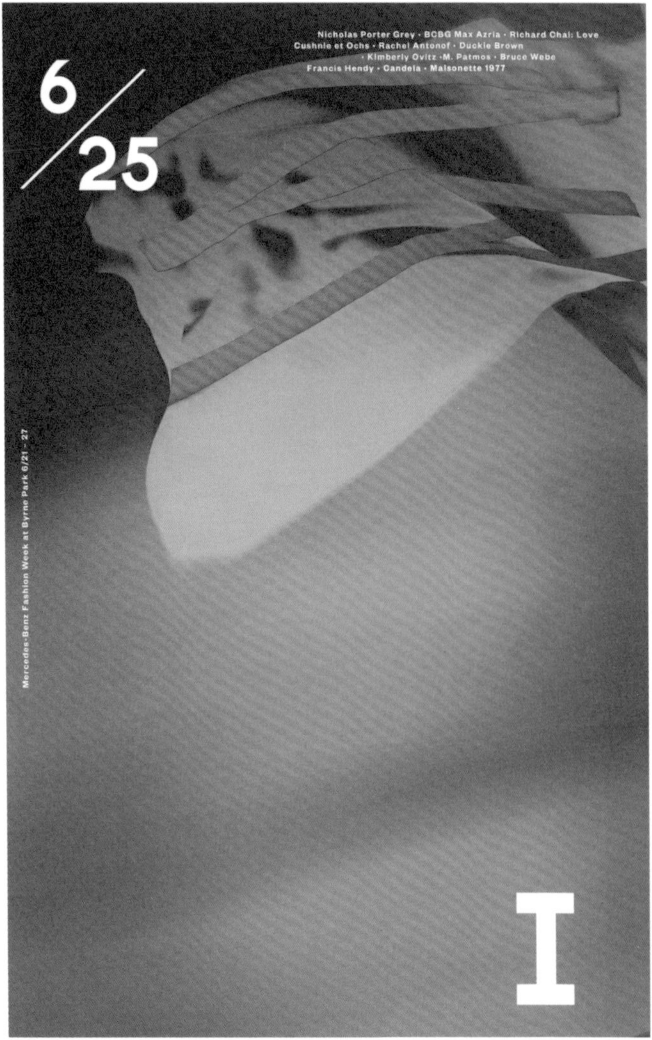
Nicholas Porter Grey · BCBG Max Azria · Richard Chai: Love
Cushnie et Ochs · Rachel Antonof · Duckie Brown
· Kimberly Ovitz ·M. Patmos · Bruce Webe
Francis Hendy · Candela · Maisonette 1977
6/25
Mercedes-Benz Fashion Week at Byrne Park 6/21 - 27
I

Nicholas Porter Grey · BCBG Max Azria · Richard Chai: Love
Cushnie et Ochs · Rachel Antonof · Duckie Brown
· Kimberly Ovitz ·M. Patmos · Bruce Webe
Francis Hendy · Candela · Maisonette 1977
6/26
Mercedes-Benz Fashion Week at Byrne Park 6/21 – 27
0

6/27
Nicholas Porter Grey · BCBG Max Azria · Richard Chai: Love
Cushnie et Ochs · Rachel Antonof · Duckie Brown
· Kimberly Ovitz ·M. Patmos · Bruce Webe
Francis Hendy · Candela · Maisonette 1977
Mercedes-Benz Fashion Week at Byrne Park 6/21 – 27
N

Pride Month
June 1–24
#PrideTO
pridetoronto.com
PATTISON

de
Festival
June 22–24
Pride
TD

June
22–24
2018
Pride
Pride
June
22–24
2018
Pride
Pride
Pride

June
22–24
2018
Pride
#prideTO
pridetoronto.com
Pride
TD

June
22–24
2018
June
22–24
Pride
Prid
#prideTO
pridetoronto.com
Pride
prideTO
idetoronto.com

2018
June
22–24
Pride
#prideTO
pridetoronto.com
Pride
TD
2018
June
22–24
Pride
#prideTO
pridetoronto.com

Pride
#prideTO
pridetoronto.com
Pride
TORONTO
TD
Pride
TORONTO
TD
Festival
Guide
June
22—24
2018
Festival
Guide

Pride
Pride
#prideTO
pridetoronto.com
prideTO
pridetoronto.com
June
22—24
2018
Festival
Guide
June
22—24
2018
Pride

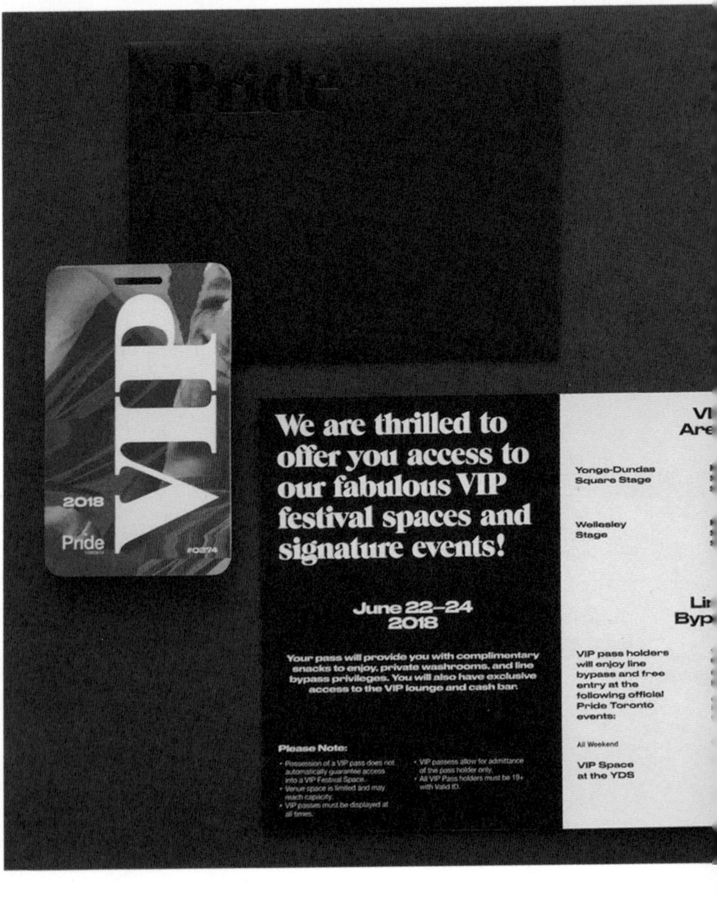
VIP
2018
Pride
#0274
We are thrilled to offer you access to our fabulous VIP festival spaces and signature events!
June 22–24 2018
Your pass will provide you with complimentary snacks to enjoy, private washrooms, and line bypass privileges. You will also have exclusive access to the VIP lounge and cash bar.
Please Note:
• Possession of a VIP pass does not automatically guarantee access into a VIP Festival Space.
• Venue space is limited and may reach capacity.
• VIP passes must be displayed at all times.
• VIP passes allow for admittance of the pass holder only.
• All VIP Pass holders must be 19+ with Valid ID.
Yonge-Dundas Square Stage
Wellesley Stage
VIP pass holders will enjoy line bypass and free entry at the following official Pride Toronto events:
All Weekend
VIP Space at the YDS

5:30–11pm
2–11pm
2–11pm
5pm–2am
2pm–2am
2pm–11pm

June
22—24
2018
Festival
Guide
Pride
#prideTO
pridetoronto.com

June
22–24
2018
Pride
#prideTO
pridetoronto.com
The numbers involved are
significant, and could result
in billions of pounds being
lost to the Treasury if a
number of people had
decided they wanted to
"Investors will be able to
build an investment
portfolio which should allow
them to continue to grow
their capital, while also
taking an income – although
this of course depends

Accent Fresco
Gesso
270gsm
Accent Fresco
270gsm
Mohawk Options
PC100 iTone
148gsm
Mohawk Options
PC100 iTone
118/148/176/216/298/352gsm
Colorplan
Factory Yellow
350gsm
Colorplan
135/175/270/350gsm
Mohawk Navajo
Brilliant White Smooth
148gsm
Mohawk Navajo
118/148/270/352gsm
Paper from GF Smith

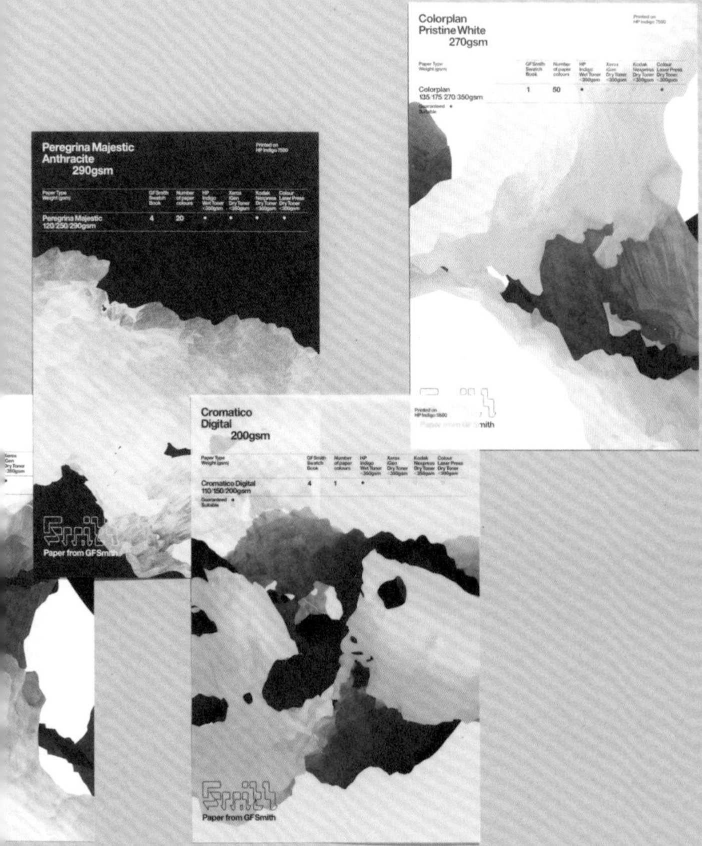
Colorplan
Pristine White
270gsm
Colorplan
135/175/270/350gsm
Peregrina Majestic
Anthracite
290gsm
Peregrina Majestic
120/250/290gsm
Paper from GF Smith
Cromatico
Digital
200gsm
Cromatico Digital
110/150/200gsm
Paper from GF Smith

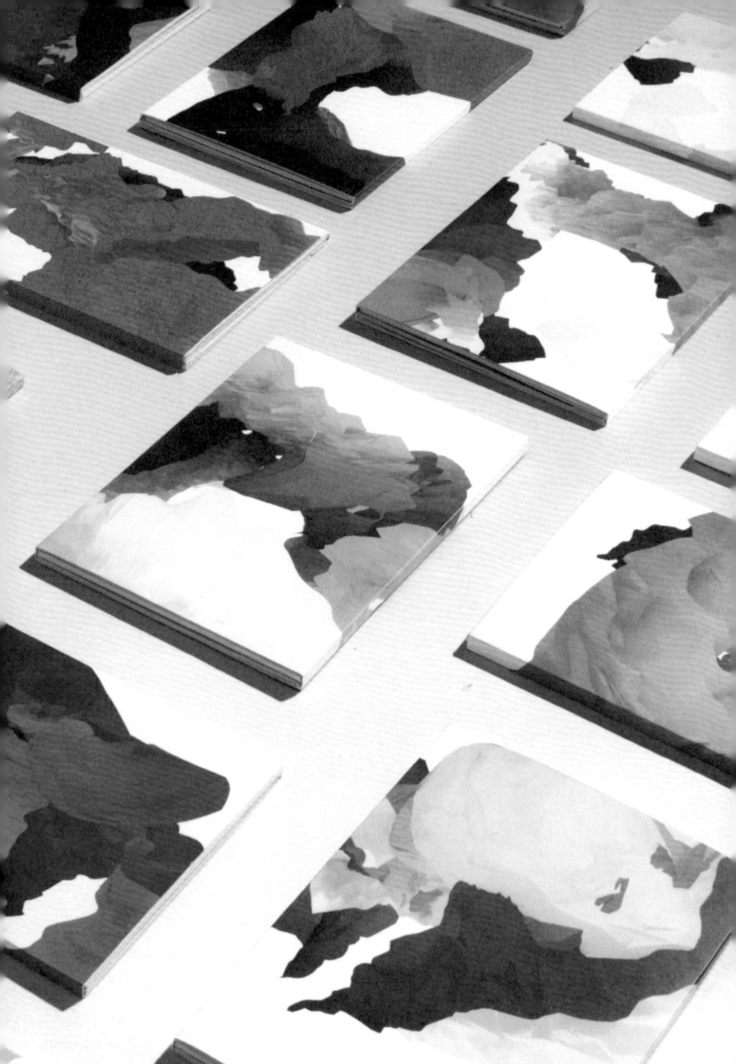

G
W
S
P
T
Y
I
U
R
A

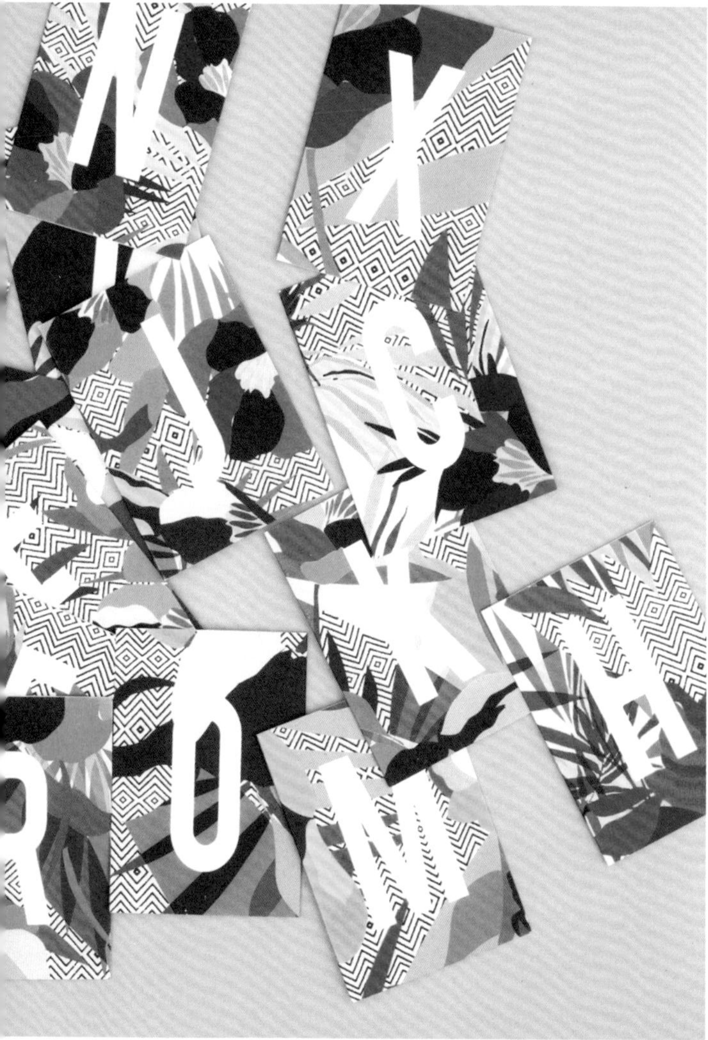

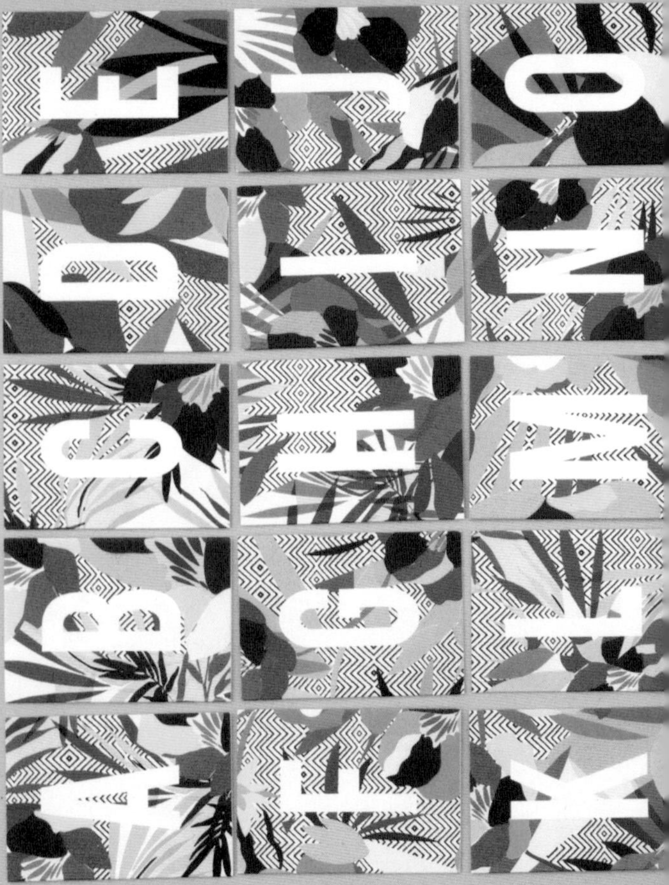
A
B
C
D
E
F
G
H
I
J
K
L
M
N
O

P
Q
R
S
T
U
V
W
X
Y
Z

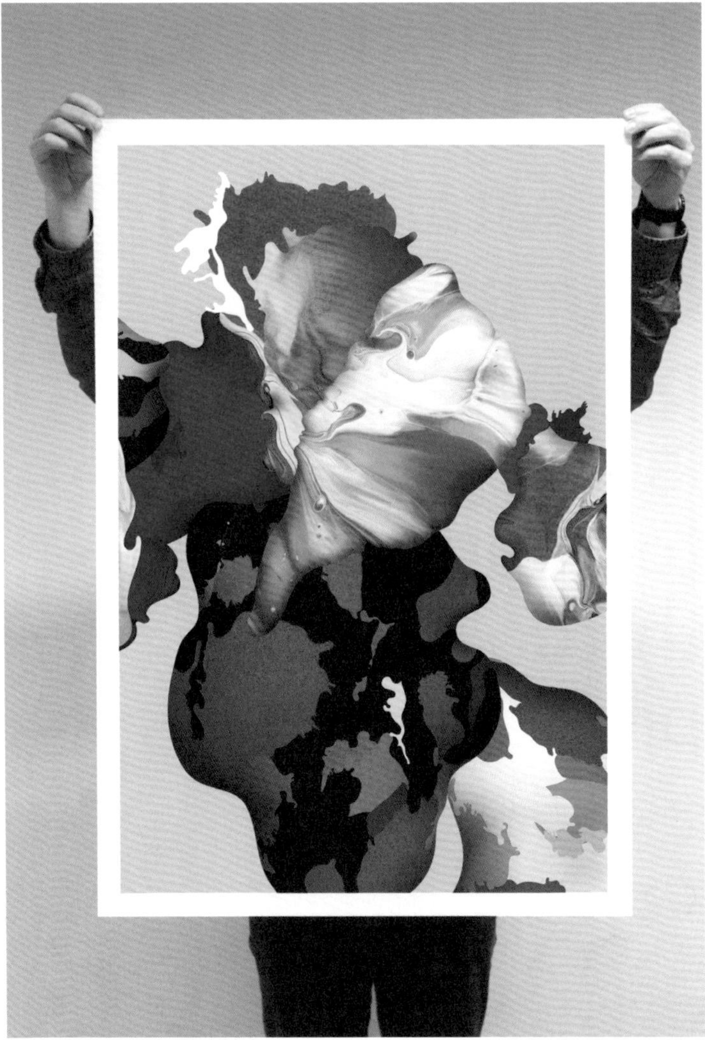

“If relevant, colour is a key ingredient to revitalise and dramatise. In this project, colour is a key element to interpret the colourful products.”

ST KILDA
FILM
FESTIVAL
2012
AUSTRALIA'S
TOP 100
SHORT FILMS
22-27 MAY
THE ASTOR THEATRE
PALAIS THEATRE
STKILDAFILMFESTIVAL.COM.AU
PROUDLY PRODUCED
& PRESENTED BY
GOVERNMENT PARTNERS
Screen
Australia
FILM VICTORIA
AUSTRALIA
MAJOR SPONSOR
RENAULT
THE ST KILDA FILM FESTIVAL ACKNOWLEDGES THE FINANCIAL ASSISTANCE OF SCREEN AUSTRALIA AND FILM VICTORIA.

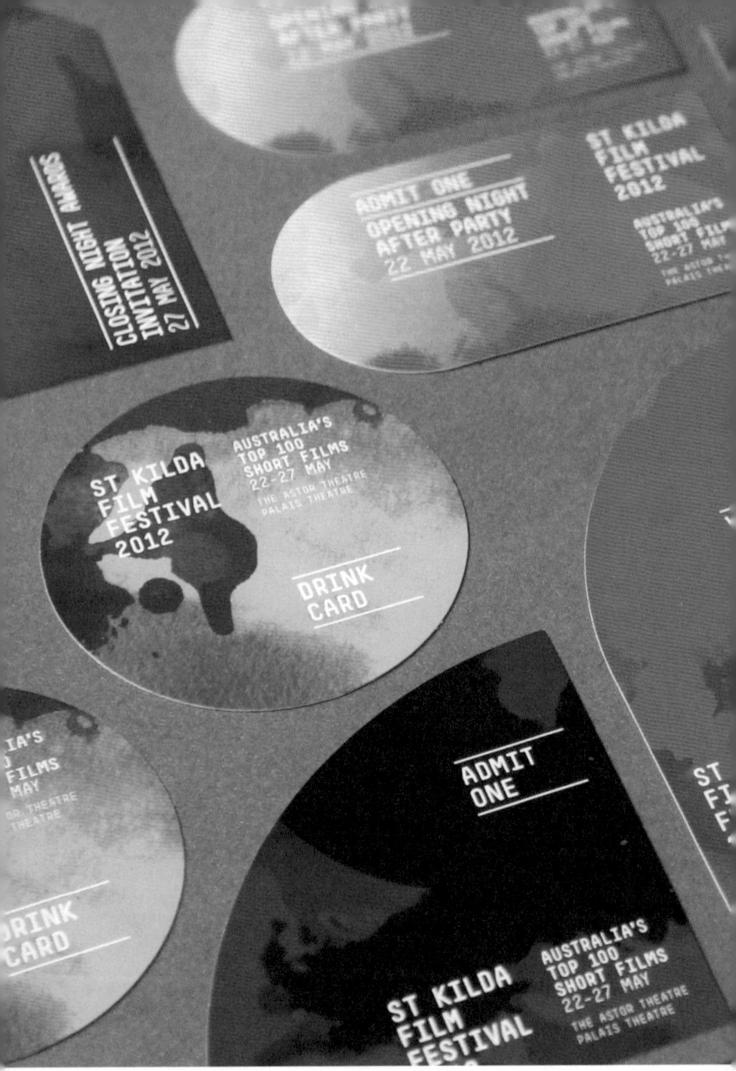
CLOSING NIGHT AWARDS
INVITATION
27 MAY 2012
ADMIT ONE
OPENING NIGHT
AFTER PARTY
22 MAY 2012
ST KILDA
FILM
FESTIVAL
2012
ST KILDA
FILM
FESTIVAL
2012
AUSTRALIA'S
TOP 100
SHORT FILMS
22-27 MAY
THE ASTOR THEATRE
PALAIS THEATRE
DRINK
CARD
ADMIT
ONE
ST KILDA
FILM
FESTIVAL
AUSTRALIA'S
TOP 100
SHORT FILMS
22-27 MAY
THE ASTOR THEATRE
PALAIS THEATRE

FILMMAKER
DEVELOPMENT
FORUM PROGRAM
SATURDAY 26 MAY
Forum Hall across the road from The Astor
CAMERA TALK WITH
CINEMATOGRAPHER
JOHN BRAWLEY
Presented by LEMAC
12.30PM-2PM
DISTRIBUTING
AND MARKETING
SHORT FILMS
Presented by Open Channel and Shaun Miller Lawyers
2.15PM-3.15PM
FOCUS ON EDITING
Presented by Australian Screen Editors Guild
3.30PM-4.30PM
ACT. WRITE.
DIRECT.
A CONVERSATION
WITH THOSE
WHO DO IT ALL.
(See over page for details)
INDUSTRY OPEN DAY
FEATURED EXHIBITORS
Australian Screen Editors Guild
Digital Pictures, LEMAC
Music & Effects, National Film & Sound Archive
Open Channel, Profile Creative
Screen Hub, Screen Producers
Association of Australia (SPAA)
Screen Rights, Swinburne University
St Kilda Film Festival International
VCA School of Film & Television
PROUDLY PRODUCED & PRESENTED BY
GOVERNMENT PARTNERS
Screen Australia
FILM
THE ST KILDA FILM FESTIVAL ACKNOWLEDGES THE FINANCIAL ASSISTANCE OF
DRINKS
SING NIGHT
ARDS
NVITATION
27 MAY 2012
STKILDAFILMFESTIVAL.COM.AU
ST KILDA
FILM
FESTIVAL
2012
AUSTRALIA'S
TOP 100
SHORT FILMS
22-27 MAY
THE ASTOR THEATRE
PALAIS THEATRE

STKILDAFILMFESTIVAL.COM.AU

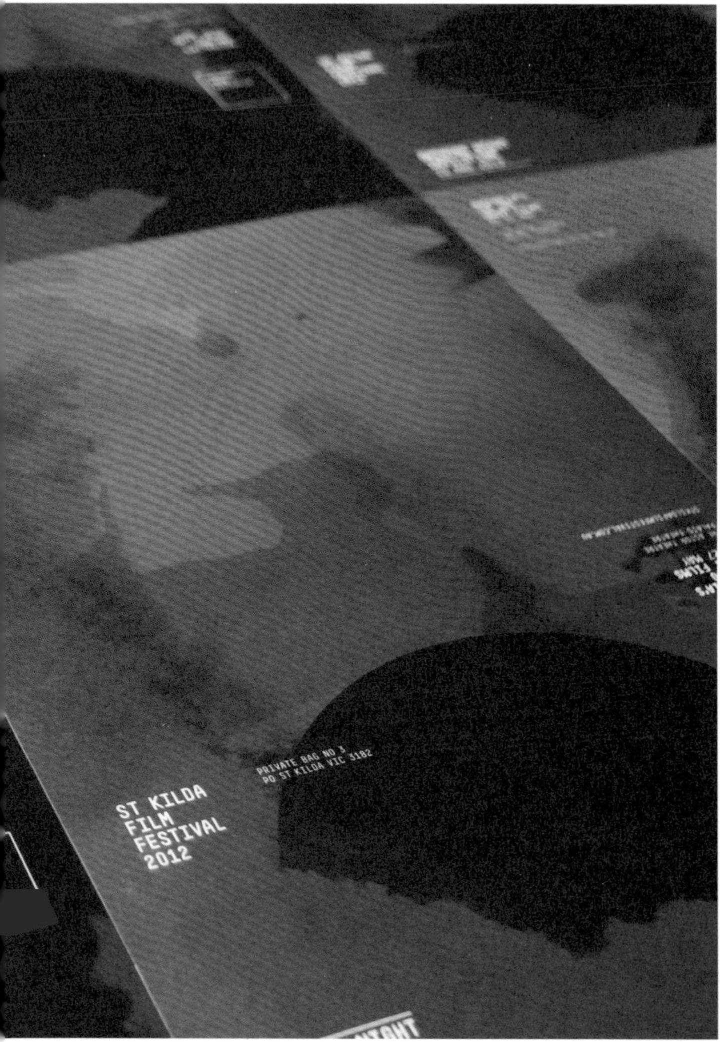
PRIVATE BAG NO 3
PO ST KILDA VIC 3182
ST KILDA
FILM
FESTIVAL
2012

Cro
Pep

cker
!

Crocker
Pep!

Crocker
Pep!

Help mee
aan een oplossing
voor Alzheimer
alzheimer
nederland
alzheimer
nederland

Leven met dementie
Als thuis wonen niet meer gaat
Is het dementie?
Word donateur
Bank 2502
alzheimer nederland

ik weet
dat
ik het
niet
meer
weet
alzheimer nederland

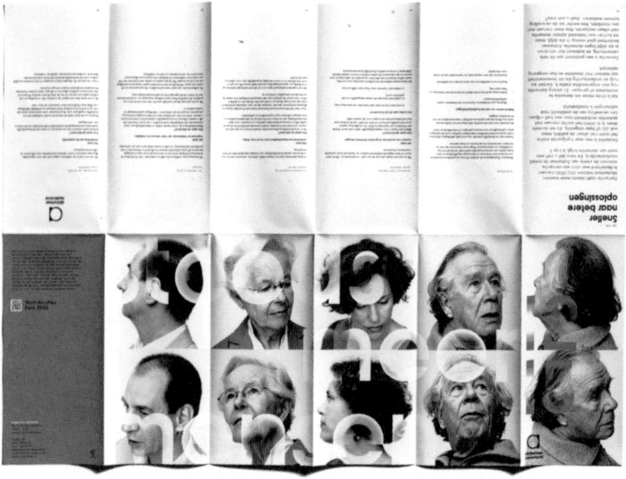
Sneller naar betere oplossingen

alzheimer
nederland
alzheimer
nederland
alzheimer
nederland
alzheimer
nederland

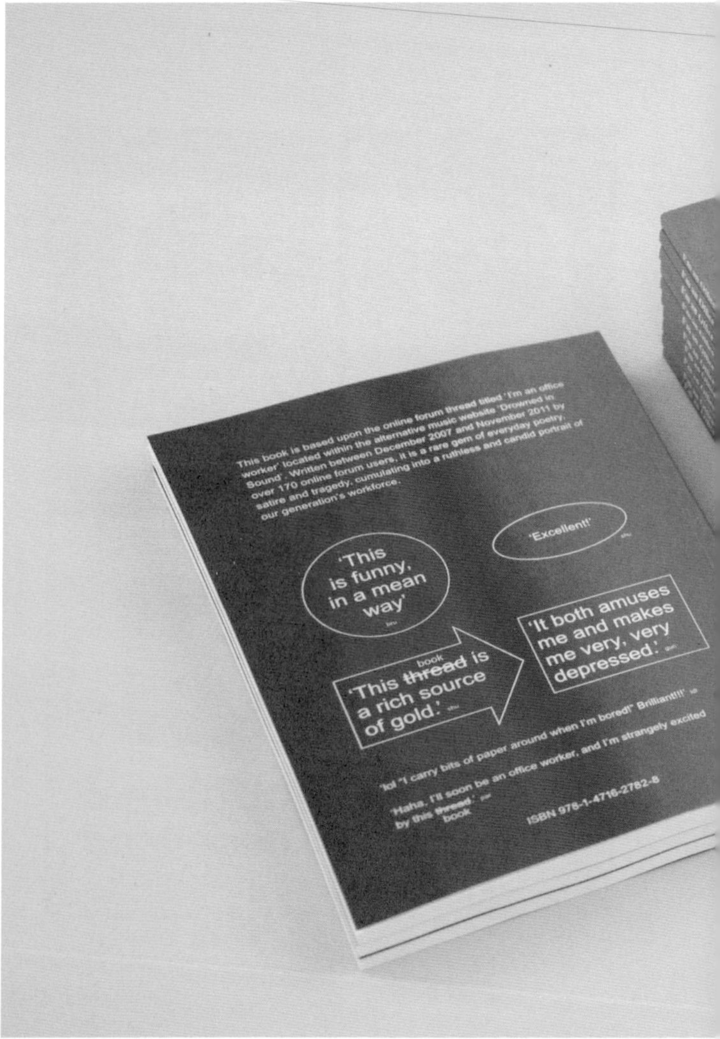
This book is based upon the online forum thread titled 'I'm an office worker' located within the alternative music website 'Drowned in Sound'. Written between December 2007 and November 2011 by over 170 online forum users, it is a rare gem of everyday poetry, satire and tragedy, cumulating into a ruthless and candid portrait of our generation's workforce.
'Excellent!'
'This is funny, in a mean way'
'This ~~thread~~ book is a rich source of gold.'
'It both amuses me and makes me very, very depressed.'
'lol "I carry bits of paper around when I'm bored!" Brilliant!!!'
'Haha, I'll soon be an office worker, and I'm strangely excited by this ~~thread~~ book.'
ISBN 978-1-4716-2782-8

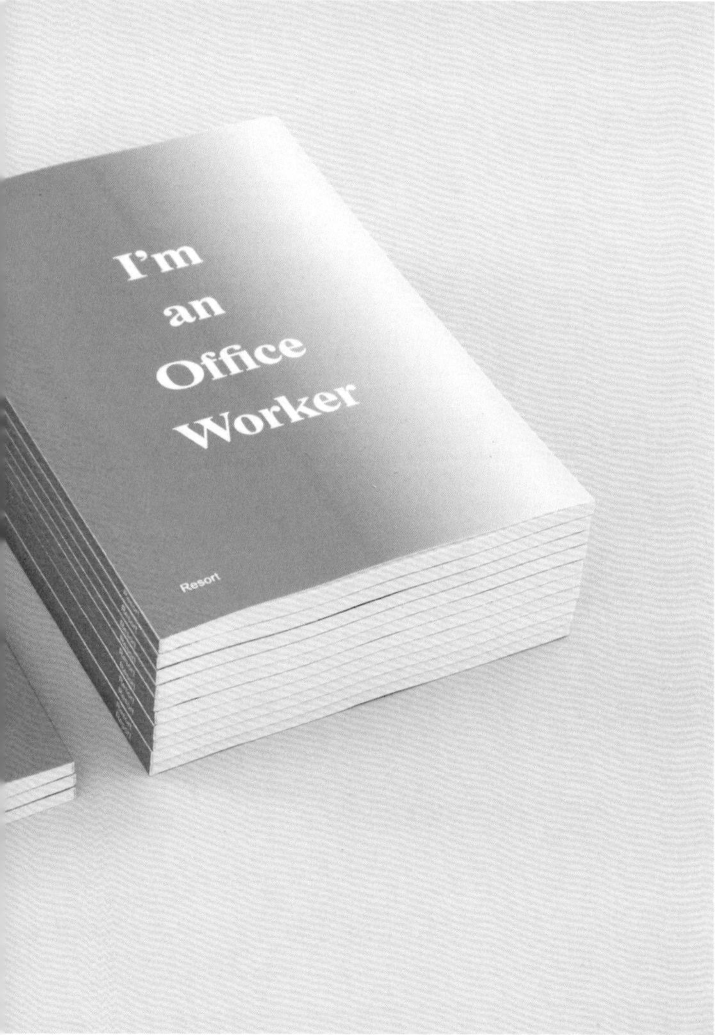
I'm
an
Office
Worker
Resort

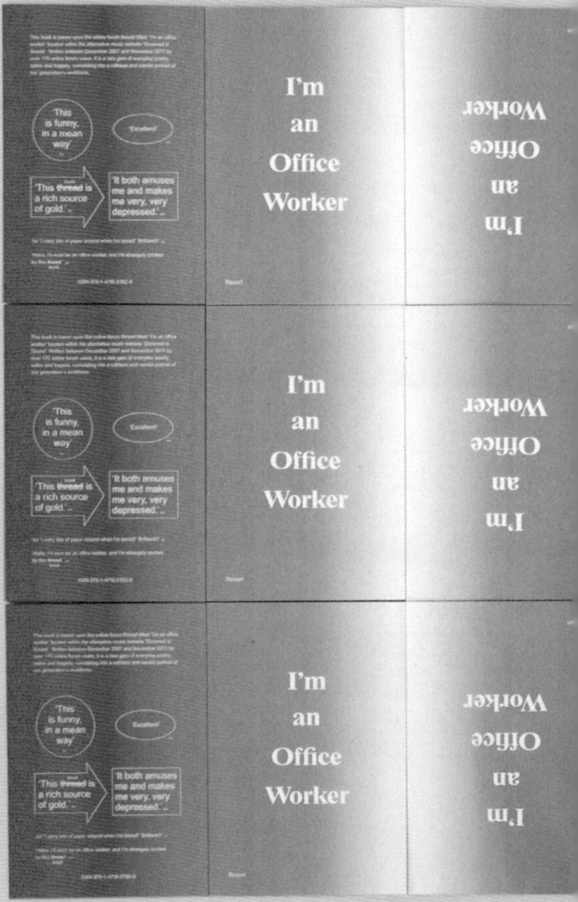
I'm
an
Office
Worker
'This
is funny,
in a mean
way'
'This thread is a rich source of gold.'
'It both amuses me and makes me very, very depressed.'

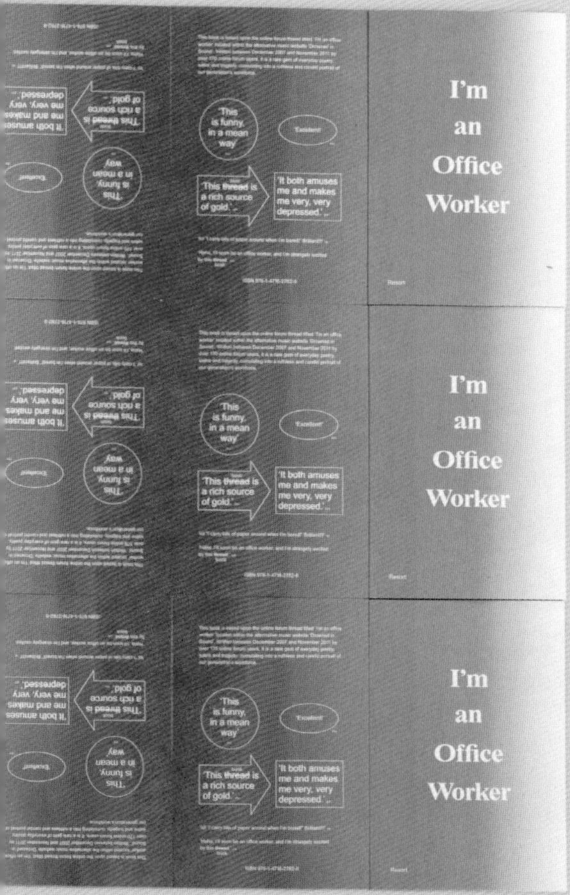
I'm an Office Worker
'This is funny, in a mean way'
'This thread is a rich source of gold.'
'It both amuses me and makes me very, very depressed.'

INGREDIENTES:
RICO TAMARINDO, FRUTAS DESHIDRATADAS
& CRUJIENTES HOSTIAS.
CANTIDAD:
14
ELABORADO POR:
BERMELLON.MX

INGREDIENTES:
RICO TAMARINDO, FRUTAS DESHIDRATADAS & CRUJIENTES HOSTIAS.
CANTIDAD:
14
ELABORADO POR:
BERMELLÓN

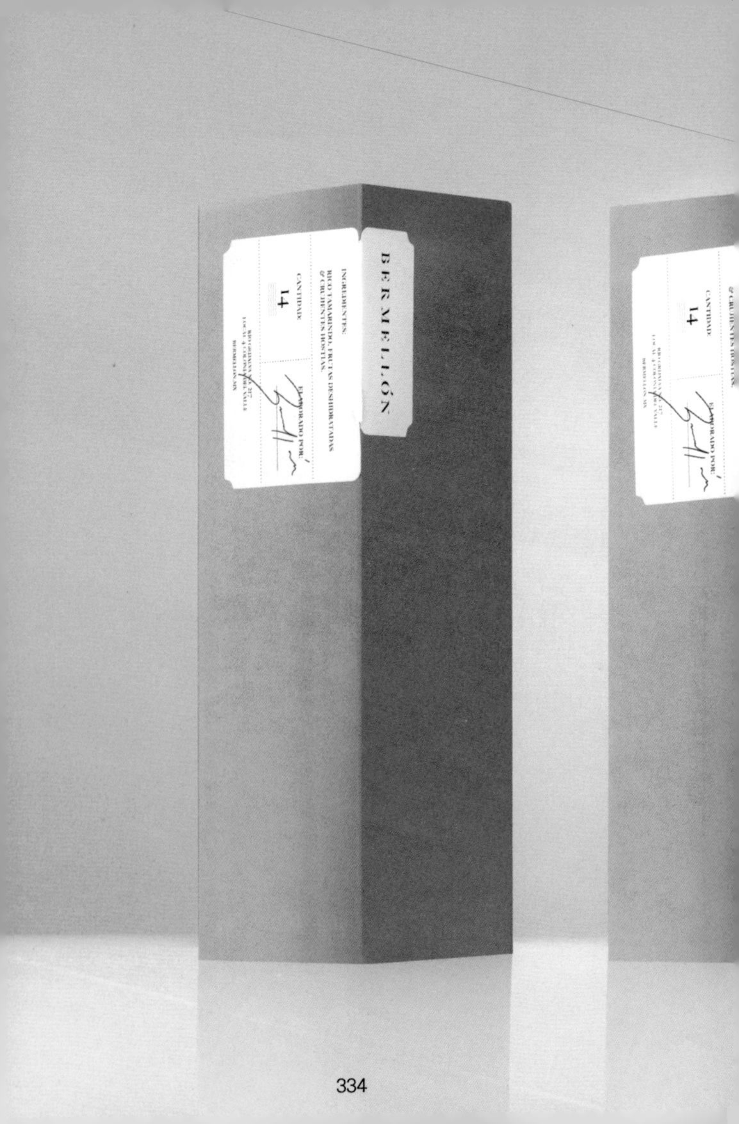
BERMELLÓN
INGREDIENTES:
RICO TAMARINDO, FRUTAS DESHIDRATADAS
& CRUJIENTES HOSTIAS.
CANTIDAD:
14
ELABORADO POR:

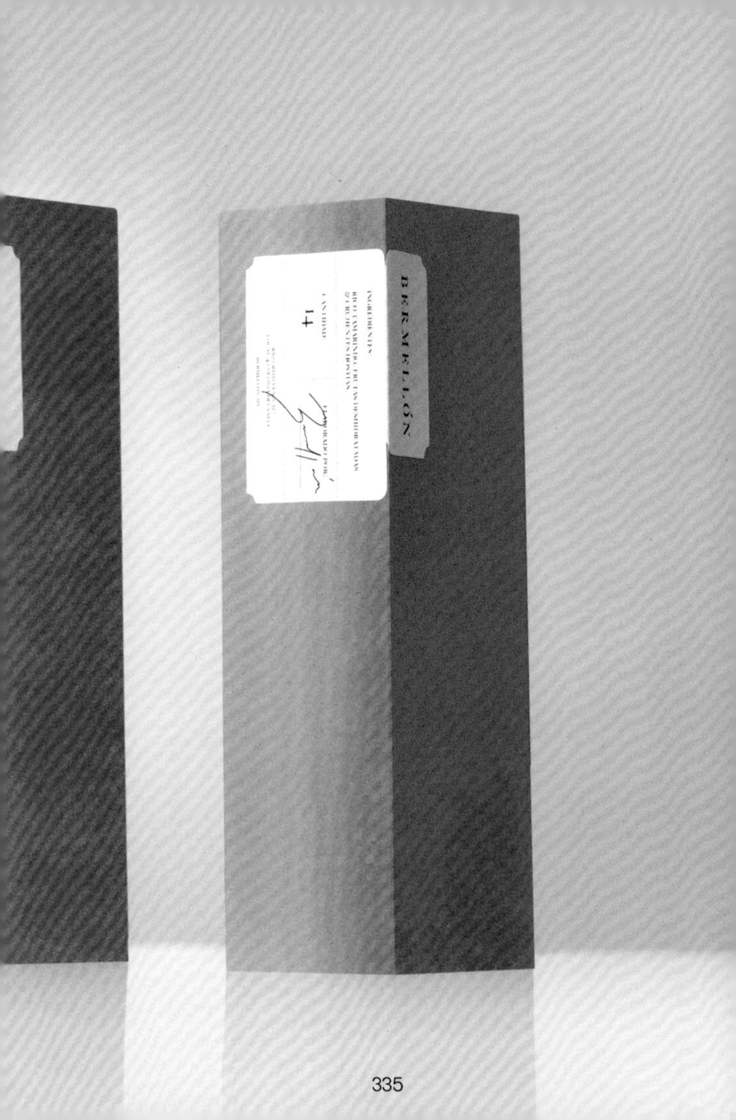
BERMELLÓN
INGREDIENTES
CANTIDAD
14
ELABORADO POR:

235 ML
BERMELLÓN
CRUDITÉS
SELECCIÓN DE BOTANAS PREPARADAS CON RICOS INGREDIENTES DE ORIGEN NATURAL Y NUESTRO TOQUE PICOSITO.
CONTENIDO:
CRUDITÉS, PAPAS, FRUTOS SECOS O CACAHUATES.
INGREDIENTES:
RICO TAMARINDO, FRUTAS DESHIDRATADAS & CRUJIENTES HOSTIAS.
CANTIDAD:
14

LIGERA
BERMELLÓN

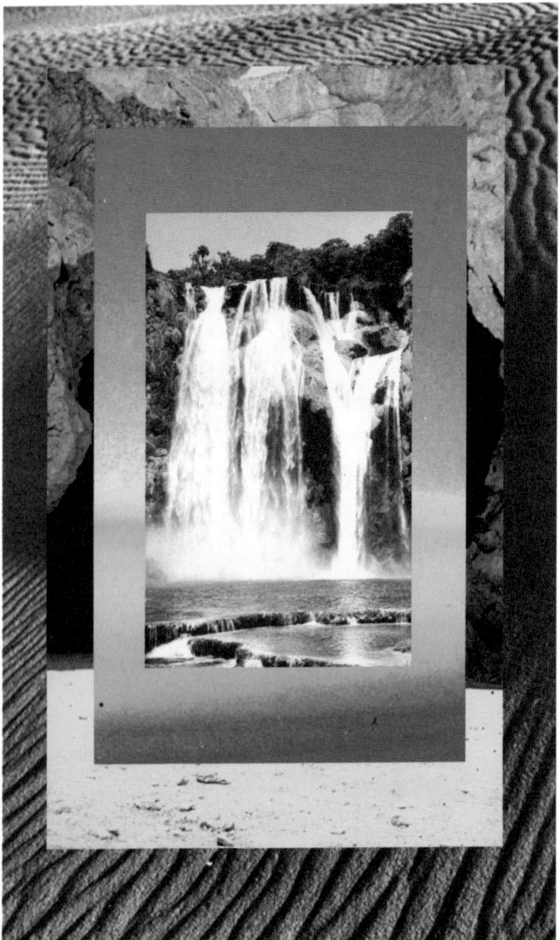

CHIMERA ~ CAVERN

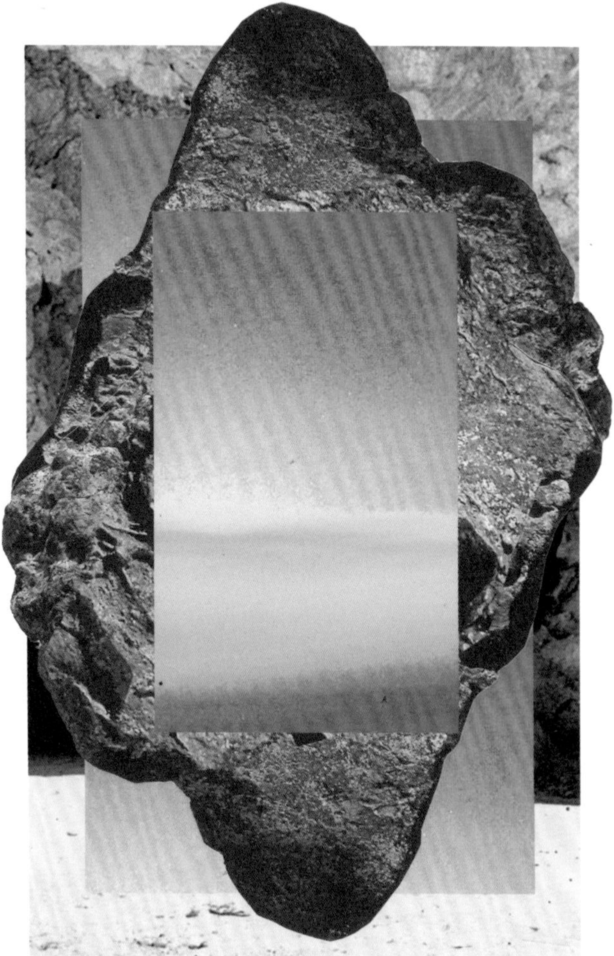

CHIMERA ~ CAVERN

CAN XALANT 2009/2010
CX
09
10
CX
09
10
CX
09
10

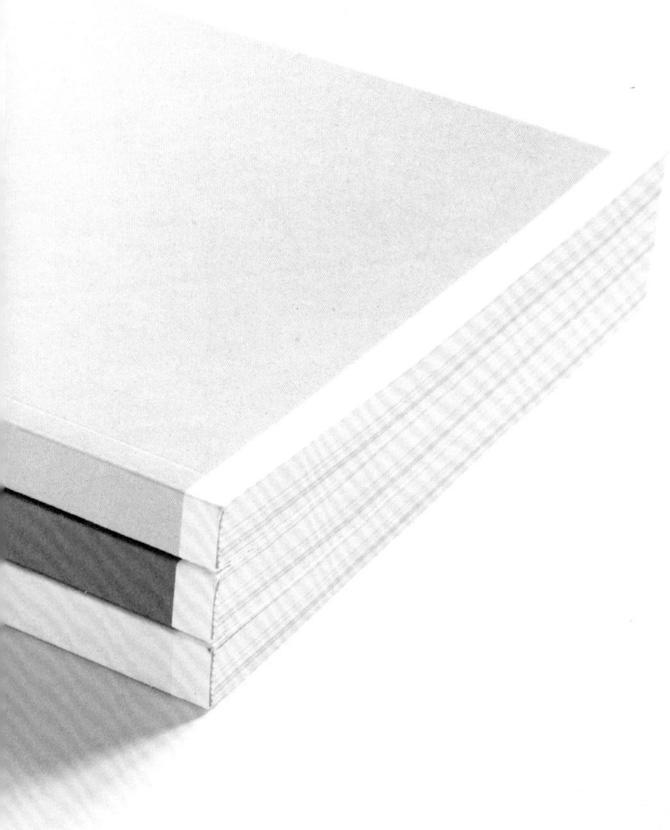

CAN XALANT 2009/2010

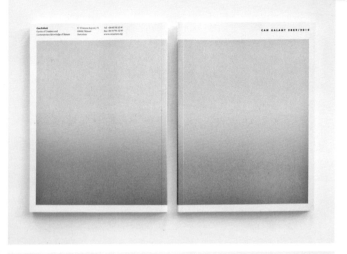
CAN XALANT 2009/2010

CAN XALANT 2009/2010

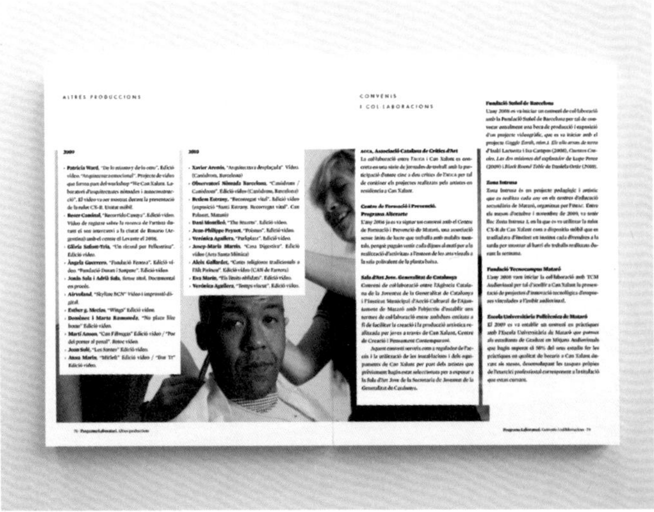
ALTRES PRODUCCIONS
CONVENIS
I COL·LABORACIONS

FEBRUARY
UNNAMED
FOLDER
2019
JUNE
MAY
UNNAMED FOLDER 2019
BALANCER
PRODUCTION
MON
WED
THU
SUN

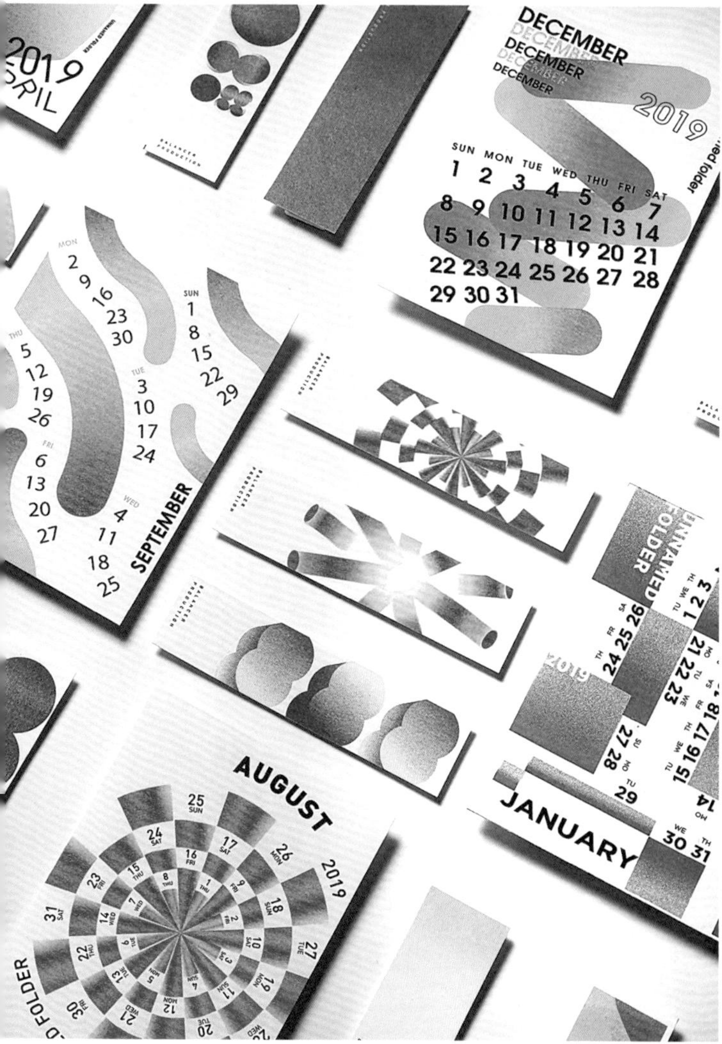
DECEMBER
2019
SUN MON TUE WED THU FRI SAT
1 2 3 4 5 6 7
8 9 10 11 12 13 14
15 16 17 18 19 20 21
22 23 24 25 26 27 28
29 30 31
2019
APRIL
SEPTEMBER
AUGUST
2019
JANUARY
UNNAMED FOLDER

平衡
制作
UNNAMED
FOLDER
2019
CALENDAR

MON
UNNAMED
FOLDER
SUN

DECEMBER
DECEMBER
DECEMBER
2019
SUN MON TUE WED THU FRI SAT
1 2 3 4 5 6 7
8 9 10 11 12 13 14
15 16 17 18 19 20 21
22 23 24 25 26 27 28
29 30 31
unnamed folder
FEBRUARY
UNNAMED
FOLDER
2019
UNNAMED FOLDER
UNNAMED FOLDER
AUGUST
25 SUN
24 SAT

JULY
2019
UNNAMED FOLDER
MARCH
JANUARY
MAY
UNNAMED FOLDER 2019

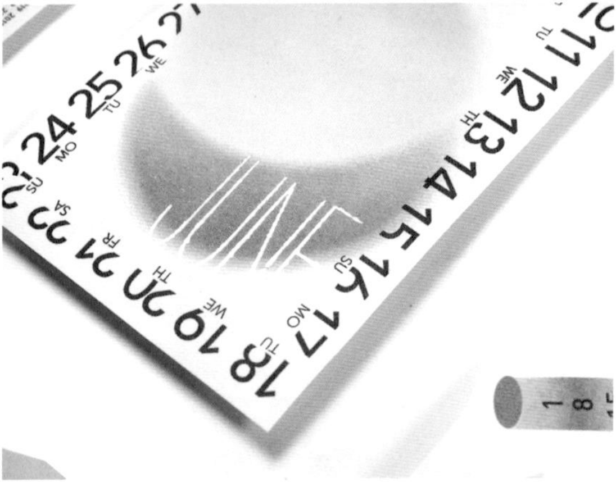
JUNE

EMBER
folder

BALANCER PRODUCTION

BALANCER PRODUCTION
BALANCER PRODUCTION
BALANCER PRODUCTION
BALANCER PRODUCTION
BALANCER PRODUCTION
BALANCER PRODUCTION

DEAR
DEAR
DEAR
DEAR
NEIGHBOUR

217
201
235
285

TOILETS
↘
TOILETS
DISABLED
TOILET
FEM
TOI
MA
TOI
TOI
↙

PRIVATE
TOILETS
CLOAK-
ROOM

brion

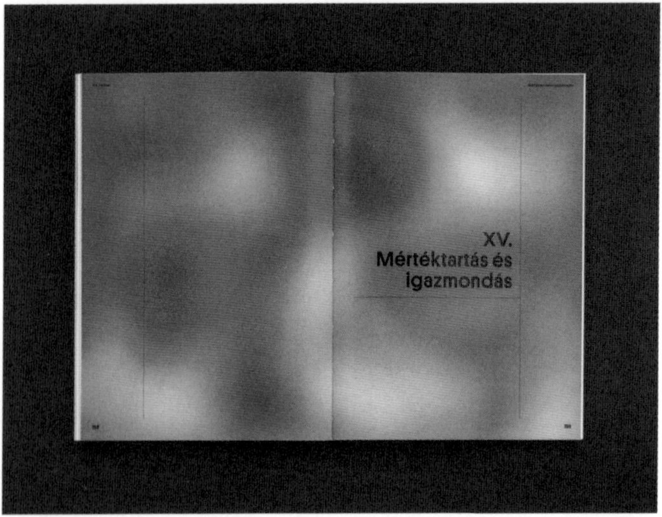
XV.
Mértéktartás és
igazmondás

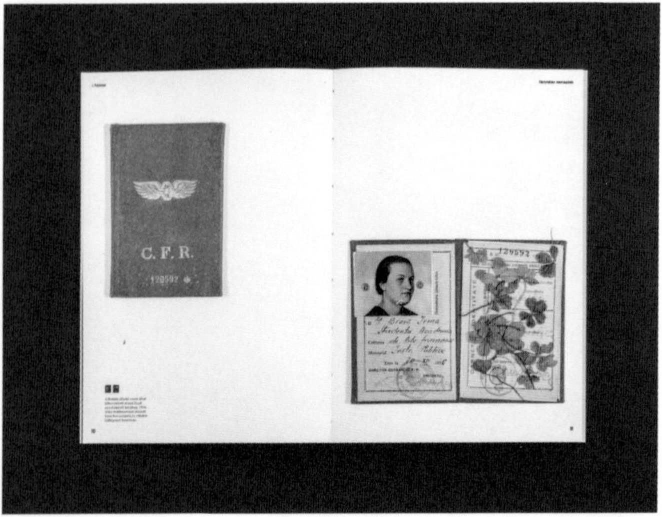
C. F. R.
129592
129592

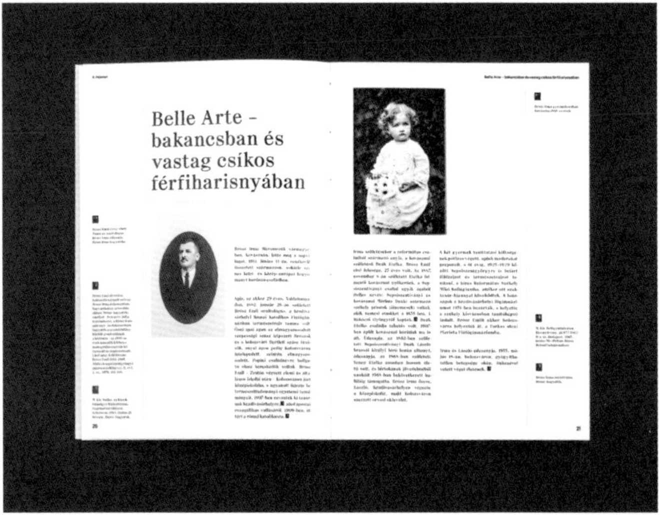
Belle Arte –
bakancsban és
vastag csíkos
férfiharisnyában

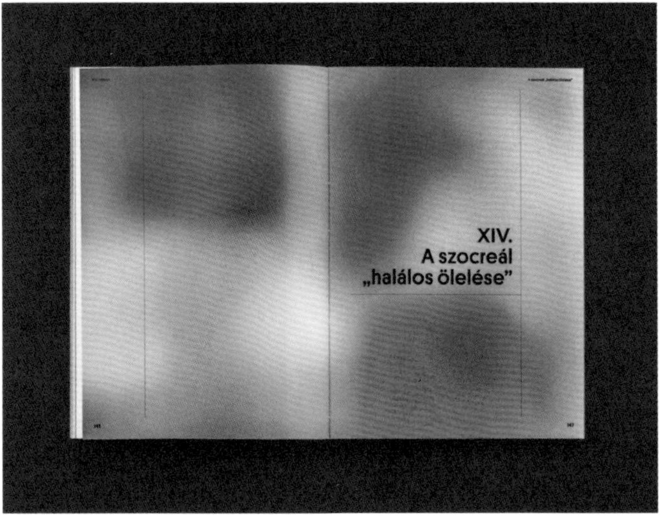
XIV.
A szocreál
„halálos ölelése”

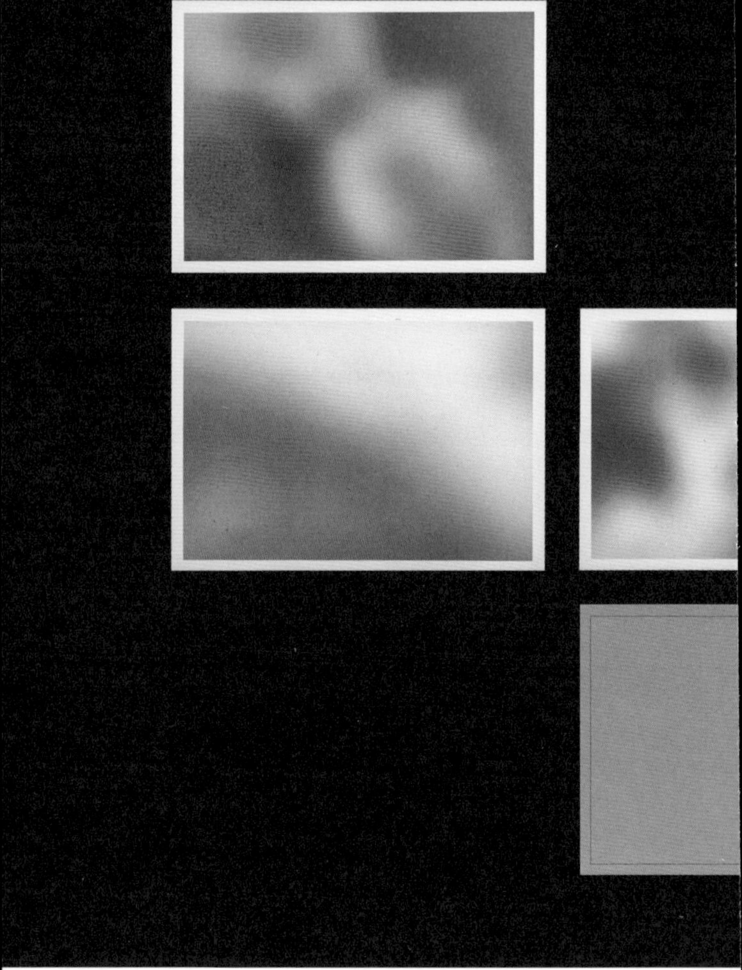

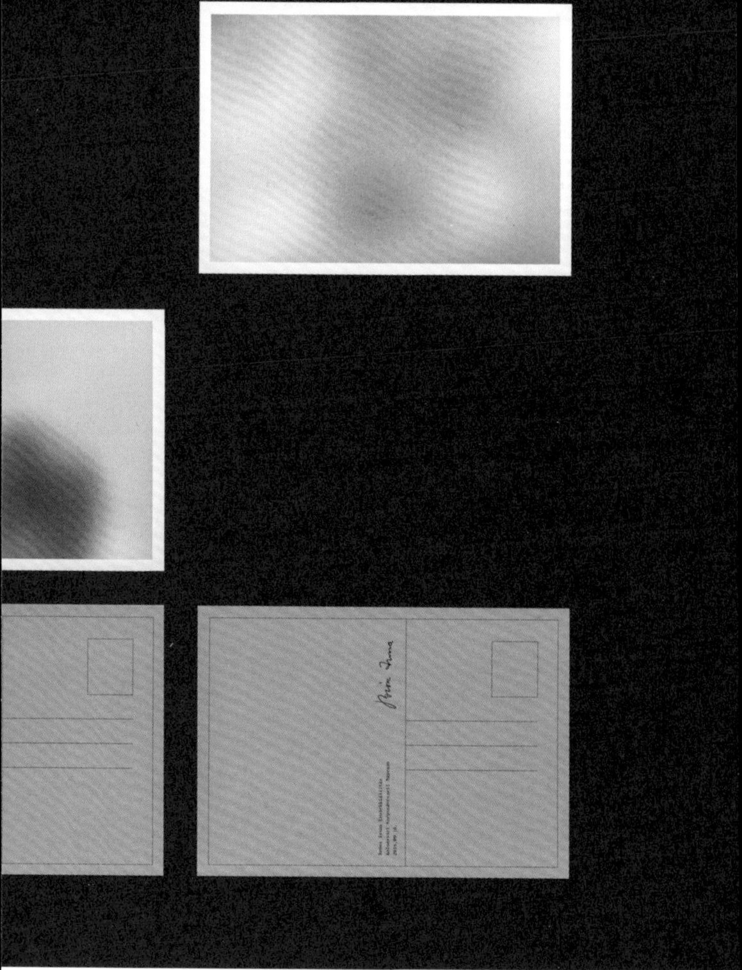

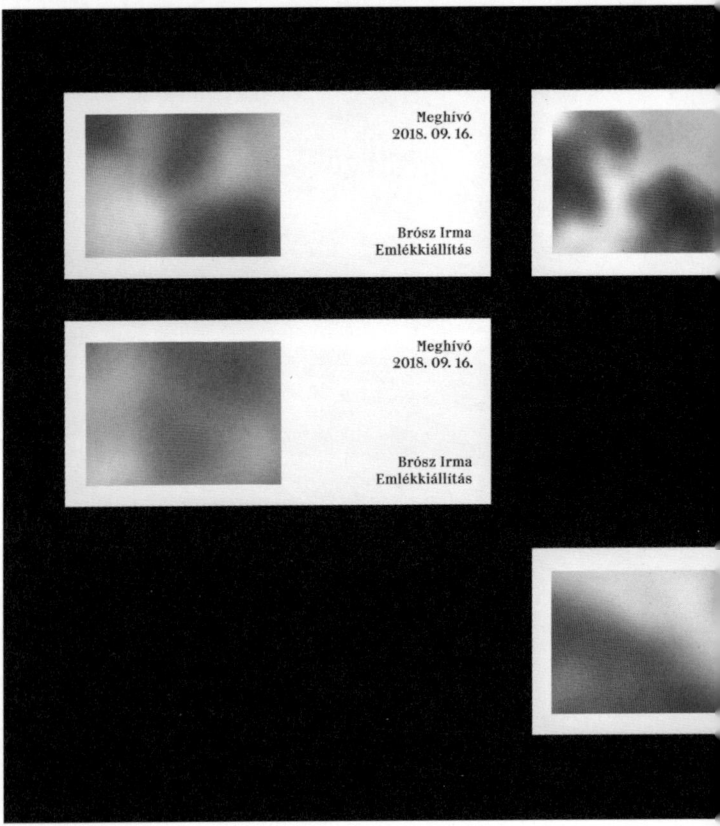
Meghívó
2018. 09. 16.
Brósz Irma
Emlékkiállítás
Meghívó
2018. 09. 16.
Brósz Irma
Emlékkiállítás

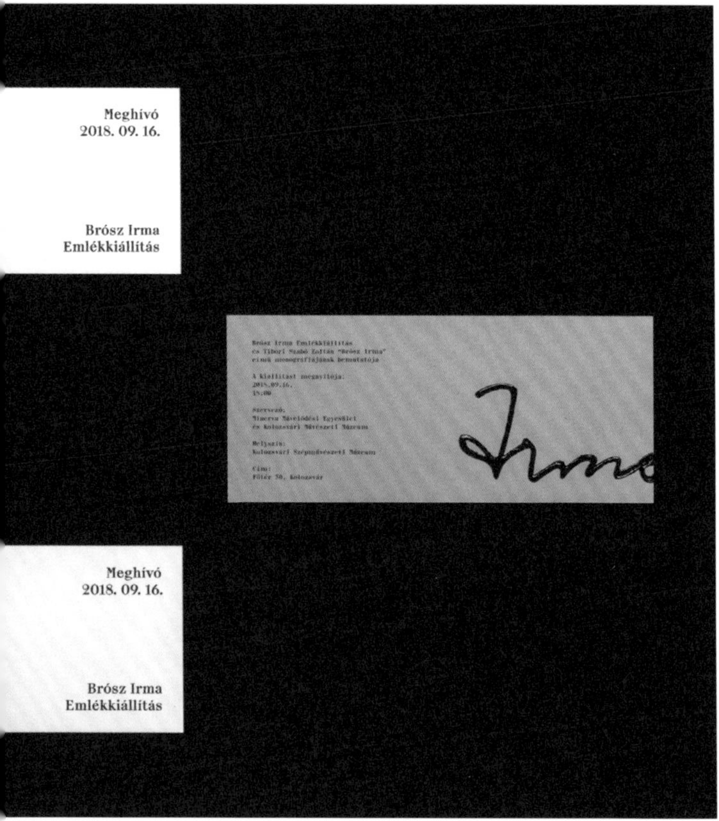
Meghívó
2018. 09. 16.
Brósz Irma
Emlékkiállítás
Meghívó
2018. 09. 16.
Brósz Irma
Emlékkiállítás

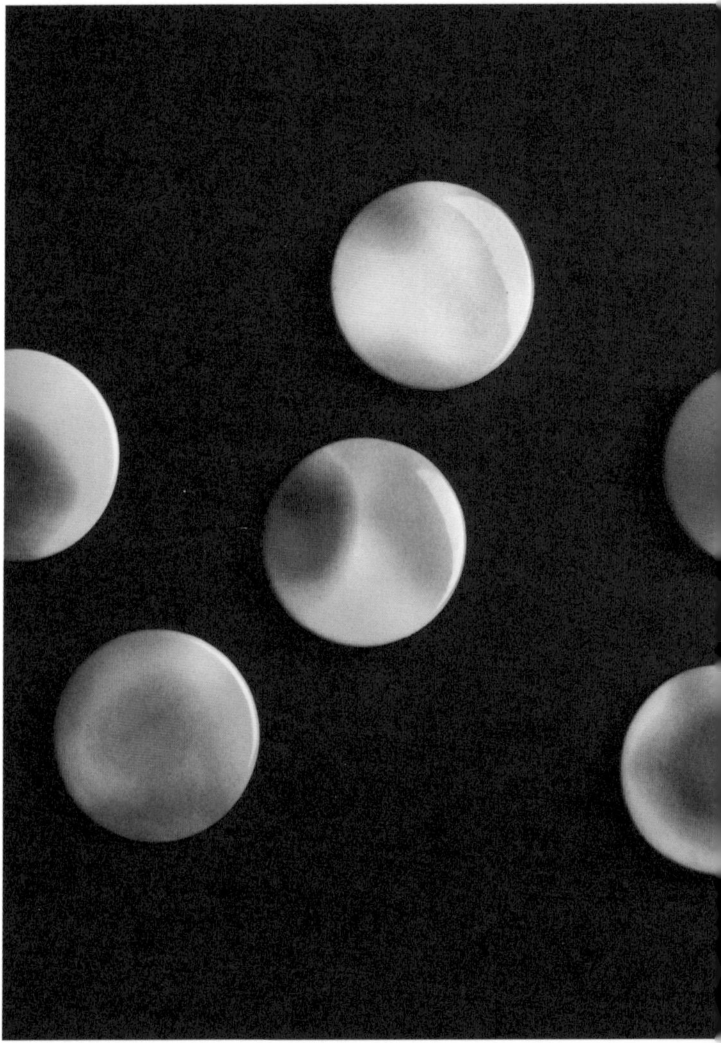

TROMMER
SKOLE
STYRKE
UTDANNING
HÅP
FREMTID
HELSE
#SOLIDARITET
VALG
ARBEID
Undervisningshefte for
UNGDOMSSKOLEN
Internasjonal uke
10.–21. oktober
OD-dagen
27. oktober
OD 2011
Ikke se
så svart
på det
Arbeidskort
OD 2011
Ikke se så svart på det

OD 2011
Ikke se
så svart
på det
Ressurshefte for
Internasjonal uke
OD-dagen
OD 2011
Ikke se
så svart
på det
Årets
prosjekt
OD 2011
Ikke se
så svart
på det
OD 2011
Ikke se
så svart
på det

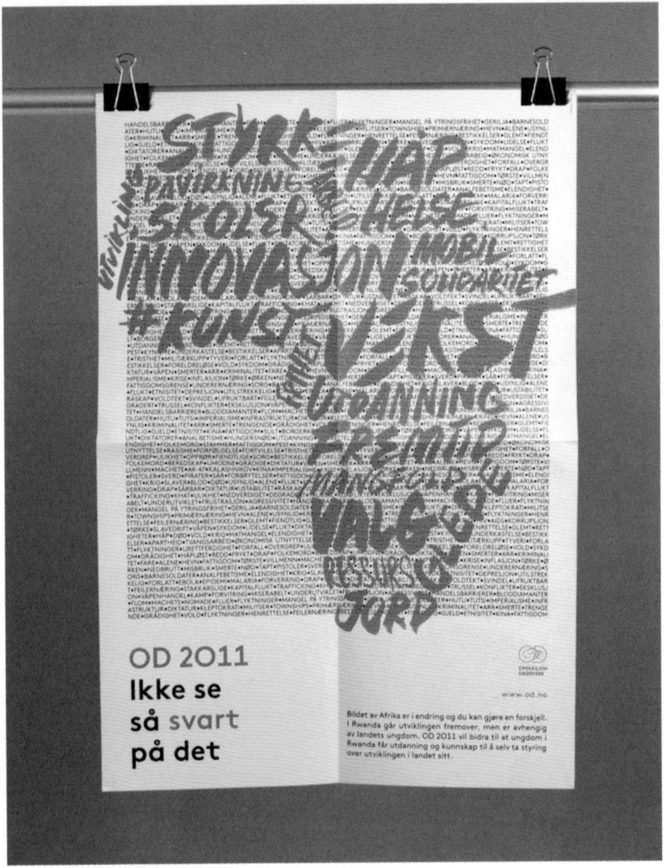
HÅP
HELSE
SKOLER
INNOVASJON
MOBIL
SOLIDARITET
#KUNST
VEKST
UTDANNING
FREMTID
VALG
JORD
OD 2011
Ikke se
så svart
på det
www.od.no
Bildet av Afrika er i endring og du kan gjøre en forskjell. I Rwanda går utviklingen fremover, men er avhengig av landets ungdom. OD 2011 vil bidra til at ungdom i Rwanda får utdanning og kunnskap til å selv ta styring over utviklingen i landet sitt.

Undervisnings-
opplegg

Arbeidskort
Del 1 — Til arbeidsgiver
2011

wtp
PROFESSIONAL
GUMBOOTS
REAR KICK-OFF RIBS
BIO PROTECT
FULLY LINED
STEEL TOES
STORAGE
COMFORTGEL INSOLE

wrp
PAINTBRUSH
PAINTBRUSH
wrp
PAINTROLLER
BOILERSUIT

wtp
wtp
wtp
wtp

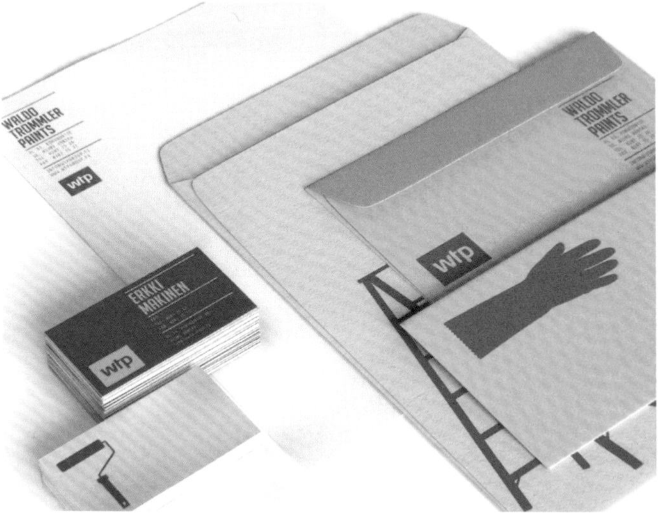
WALDO
TROMMLER
PAINTS
wtp
ERKKI
MAKINEN
wtp
WALDO
TROMMLER
PAINTS
wtp

wtp
KAUKO
LEFTTINEN
wtp

PROFESSIONAL
GUMBOOTS
RETAIN SUPPLENESS AT
TEMPERATURES UP TO -30C
REAR KICK-OFF RIBS

FULLY LINED
EU VOC 2004/42/
EC-LIMIT VALUE
STEEL TOES
APPROX. 1.5 KG/L
STORAGE
PROTECT
FROM FROST
HYPOALLERGENIC
COMFORT GEL INSOLE
PAINT
PAINTROLLER

wtp
SOLID COLOR WATERPROOFING
WOOD SATIN
WOOD

wtp
ADIATO
wtp
LOOR
ALL
wtp
THRO
LING

TAKE YOUR PLEASURES SERIOUSLY.
NOT WHAT YOU SEE
PAINTS
ULJAS LONNBOHM
KAUKO LEFTTINEN
wtp
ERKKI MAKINEN
ALKYD PAINT
ARVO SNELLMANN
WALDO TROMMLER PAINTS
IF YOU CAN PAINT ONE THING, YOU CAN PAINT

HANNU
POLVIANDER
TOIVO
JARVINEN
ULJAS
LONNBOHM
wtp
WALDO
TROMMLER
PAINTS
CREATIVITY
IS THE DRUG
I CANNOT
LIVE
WITHOUT
FLOOR
LACQUER

“Colour is pure emotion and emotion is what moves people.”

THE BUILDING
BLOCKS OF YOUR
NEXT BIG IDEA
THE
PLUS
SERIES
PANTONE®
PANTONE®
PANTONE®
PANTONE®
PANTONE®
pantone.com/plus
Introducing, The Plus Series, the next generation fo the Pantone Matching System.
The Plus Series supercharges it with a host of new colors, features, and digital tools.

ink films
Bays 34–36 Pegholme Mill
Wharfebank Business Centre
Ilkley Road, Otley, LS21 3JP
ink films
Bay's 34–36 Pegholme Mill
Wharfebank Business Centre
Ilkley Road, Otley, LS21 3JP

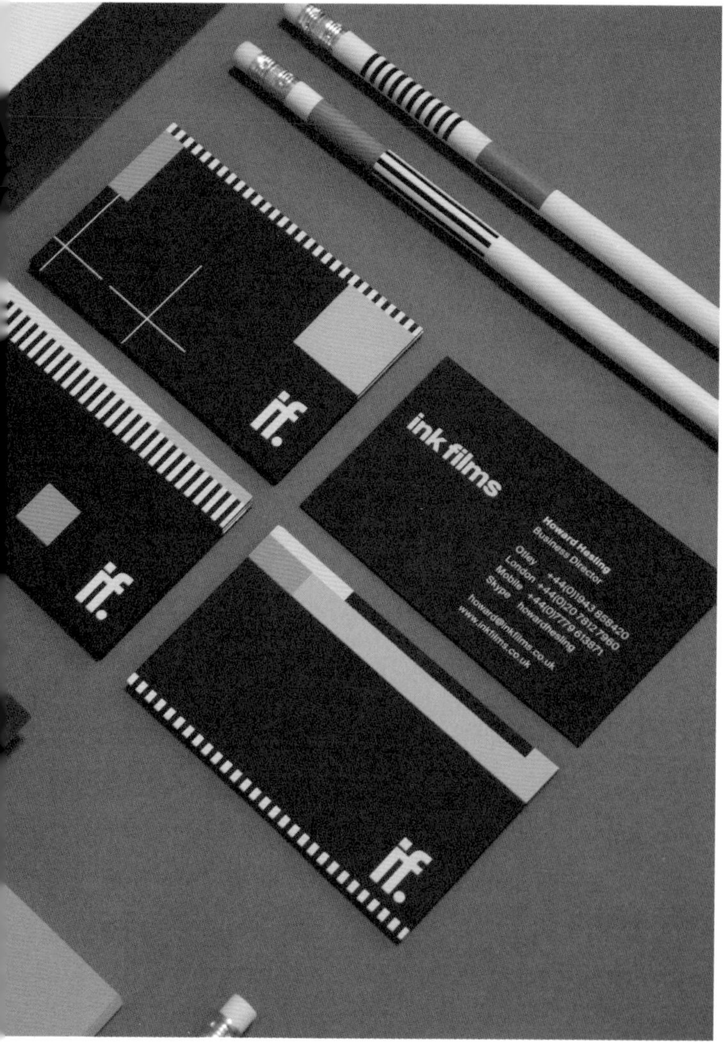
ink films
Howard Hesling
Business Director
Otley +44(0)1943 858420
London +44(0)20 7812 7980
Mobile +44(0)7779 613871
Skype howardhesling
howard@inkfilms.co.uk
www.inkfilms.co.uk

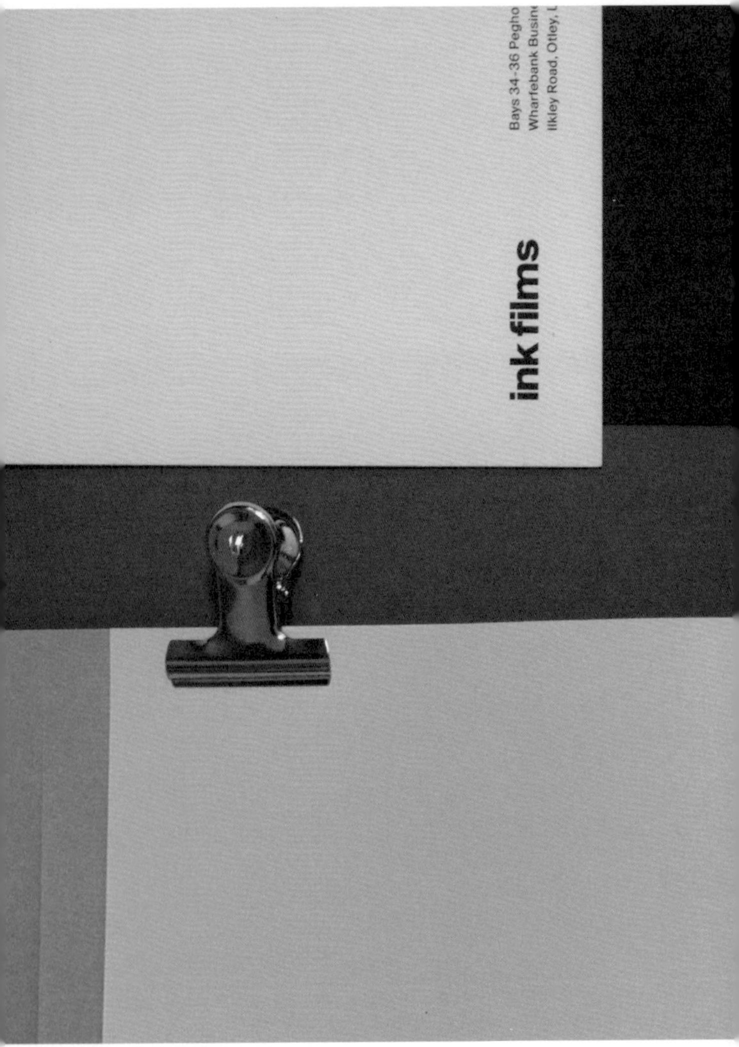
ink films
Bays 34-36 Pegho
Wharfebank Busin
Ilkley Road, Otley,

if.
if.
ink films

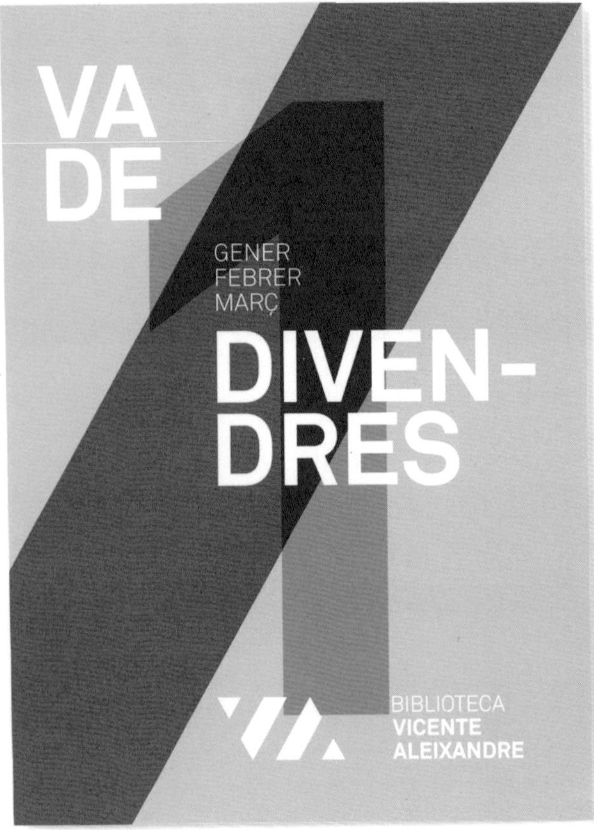
VA
DE
GENER
FEBRER
MARÇ
DIVEN-
DRES
BIBLIOTECA
VICENTE
ALEIXANDRE

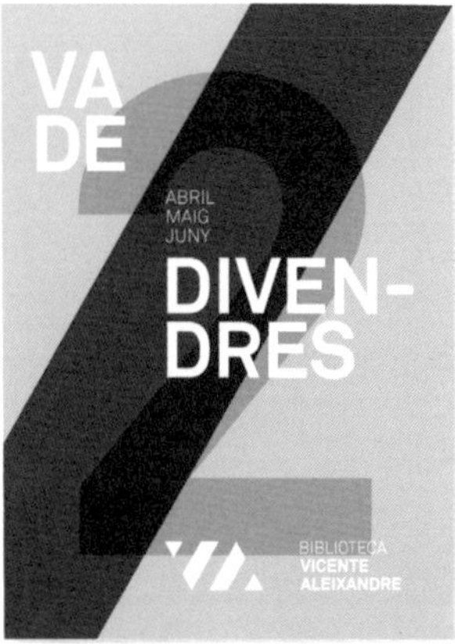
VA
DE
ABRIL
MAIG
JUNY
DIVEN-
DRES
BIBLIOTECA
VICENTE
ALEIXANDRE

VA
DE
JULIOL
AGOST
SETEMBRE
DIVEN-
DRES
BIBLIOTECA
VICENTE
ALEIXANDRE

VA
DE
OCTUBRE
NOVEMBRE
DESEMBRE
DIVEN-
DRES
BIBLIOTECA
VICENTE
ALEIXANDRE

UN ESPAI
PER ALS
PETITS LECTORS
(DE 0 A 3 ANYS)
LA
BEBE-
TECA
BIBLIOTECA
VICENTE
ALEIXANDRE

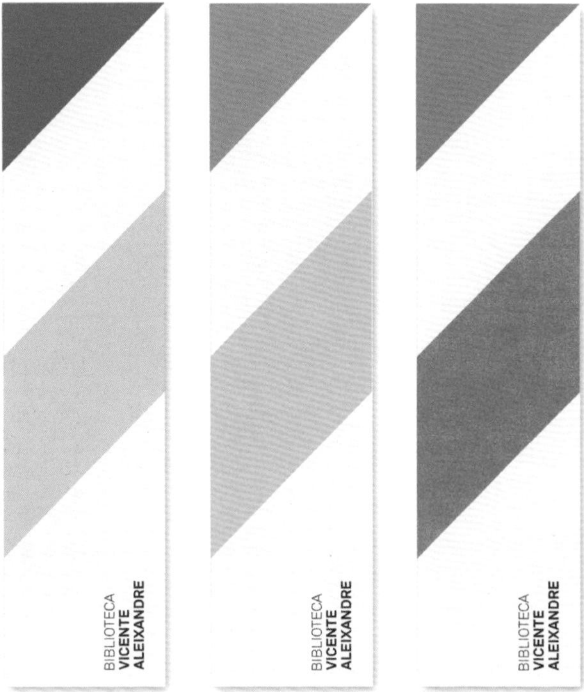
BIBLIOTECA
VICENTE
ALEIXANDRE
BIBLIOTECA
VICENTE
ALEIXANDRE
BIBLIOTECA
VICENTE
ALEIXANDRE

On The Way – Three Young Artists' Exhibit
Young Artists' Communicate Exhibition
Rock and a Soft Place 2009/06/28 - 2009/07/28
Qingying Time – Dong Wensheng's Video Work
Fang Wei: Gemini, Free Gate & Time Machin
Artists' Video Work Screening
Invitational Exhibition by Greentow
2011/05/05 Sonelle De Klerk: Displa
Space at LISTE Basel 2012/03/03
2012/07/10 Candida Höfer
Invitational Exhibition
Group Exhibition
of Designers in Hangzho
2013/06/30 Make I
Drips Project by
2013/10/31
Exhibition
by Che

Zhou Yilun: R3PM3
Coordinates – Group Exhibit
Candida Höf
Elian: Demibeast
ON AIR NO/2
Whole Year Video Screen Project
Chen Dor
2017/04/01 - 2017/06/04
Walter Robinson: WALTER ROBINSON
Eyes Moving Pencil
2018/06/23 - 2018/08/

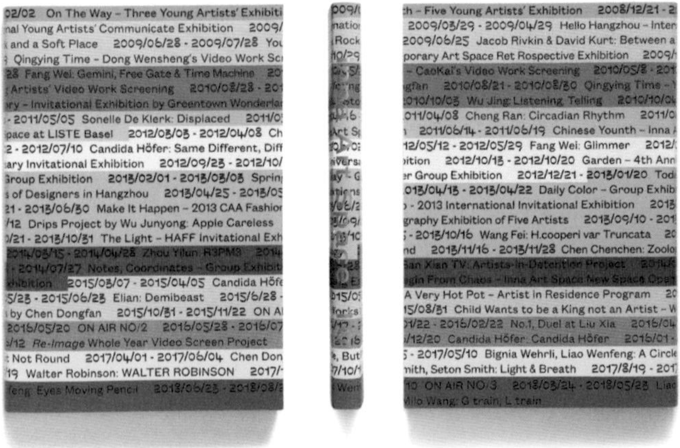
02/02 On The Way – Three Young Artists' Exhibiti
nal Young Artists' Communicate Exhibition 2009/
and a Soft Place 2009/06/28 - 2009/07/28 You
Qingying Time – Dong Wensheng's Video Work Sc
28 Fang Wei: Gemini, Free Gate & Time Machine
Artists' Video Work Screening 2010/03/28 - 20
ry – Invitational Exhibition by Greentown Wonderla
- 2011/05/05 Sonelle De Klerk: Displaced 2011/0
pace at LISTE Basel 2012/03/03 - 2012/04/08 Ch
2 - 2012/07/10 Candida Höfer: Same Different, Diff
ary Invitational Exhibition 2012/09/23 - 2012/10/
Group Exhibition 2013/02/01 - 2013/03/03 Sprin
s of Designers in Hangzhou 2013/04/25 - 2013/05
21 - 2013/06/30 Make It Happen – 2013 CAA Fashio
/12 Drips Project by Wu Junyong: Apple Careless
/21 - 2013/10/31 The Light – HAFF Invitational Exh
2014/03/15 - 2014/04/28 Zhou Yilun: R3PM3
- 2014/07/27 Notes, Coordinates – Group Exhibit
xhibition 2015/03/07 - 2015/04/05 Candida Höfe
5/23 - 2015/06/23 Elian: Demibeast 2015/6/28 -
by Chen Dongfan 2015/10/31 - 2015/11/22 ON A
2016/05/20 ON AIR NO/2 2016/05/28 - 2016/07
/12 Re-Image Whole Year Video Screen Project
Not Round 2017/04/01 - 2017/06/04 Chen Don
19 Walter Robinson: WALTER ROBINSON 2017/
feng: Eyes Moving Pencil 2018/06/23 - 2018/08/
h – Five Young Artists' Exhibition 2008/12/21 -
2009/03/29 - 2009/04/29 Hello Hangzhou – Inter
2009/06/25 Jacob Rivkin & David Kurt: Between a
porary Art Space Ret Rospective Exhibition 2009/
– CaoKai's Video Work Screening 2010/05/8 - 20
gfan 2010/08/21 - 2010/08/30 Qingying Time –
2010/10/03 Wu Jing: Listening, Telling 2010/10/0
011/04/08 Cheng Ran: Circadian Rhythm 2011/0
2011/06/14 - 2011/06/19 Chinese Younth – Inna
12/05/12 - 2012/05/29 Fang Wei: Glimmer 2012/
bition 2012/10/13 - 2012/10/20 Garden – 4th Ann
er Group Exhibition 2012/12/21 - 2013/01/20 Tod
013/04/13 - 2013/04/22 Daily Color – Group Exhib
- 2013 International Invitational Exhibition 2013
graphy Exhibition of Five Artists 2013/09/10 - 201
- 2013/10/16 Wang Fei: H.cooperi var Truncata 20
nd 2013/11/16 - 2013/11/28 Chen Chenchen: Zoolo
an Xian TV: Artists-in-Detention Project 2014/
gin From Chaos – Inna Art Space New Space Ope
A Very Hot Pot – Artist in Residence Program 20
15/08/31 Child Wants to be a King not an Artist – W
1/22 - 2016/02/22 No.1, Duel at Liu Xia 2016/04
/12/20 Candida Höfer: Candida Höfer 2016/01 -
- 2017/05/10 Bignia Wehrli, Liao Wenfeng: A Circle
mith, Seton Smith: Light & Breath 2017/8/19 - 201
10 ON AIR NO/3 2018/03/24 - 2018/05/28 Lia
Milo Wang: G train, L train

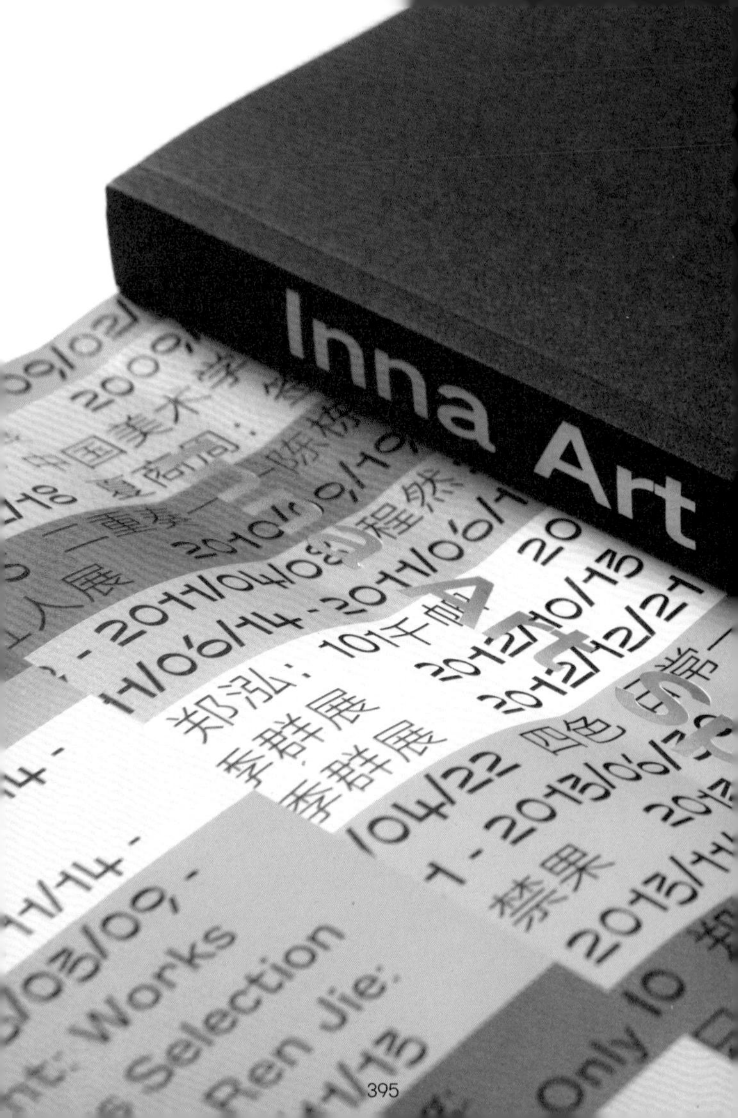
Inna Art

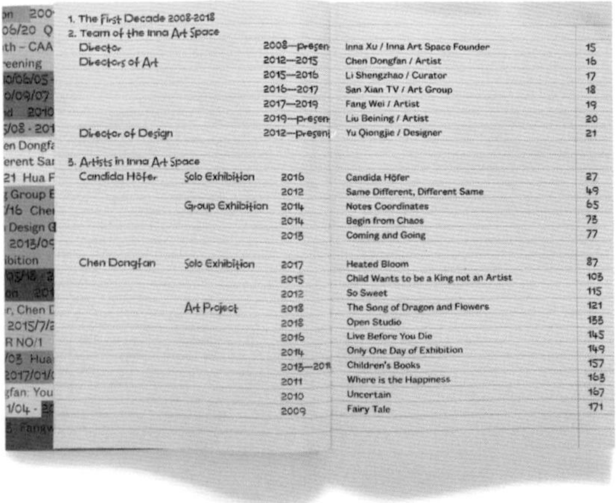

1. The First Decade 2008-2018
2. Team of the Inna Art Space

Director		2008—presen	Inna Xu / Inna Art Space Founder	15
Directors of Art		2012—2015	Chen Dongfan / Artist	16
		2015—2016	Li Shengzhao / Curator	17
		2016—2017	San Xian TV / Art Group	18
		2017—2019	Fang Wei / Artist	19
		2019—presen	Liu Beining / Artist	20
Director of Design		2012—present	Yu Qiongjie / Designer	21

3. Artists in Inna Art Space

Candida Höfer	Solo Exhibition	2016	Candida Höfer	27
		2012	Same Different, Different Same	49
	Group Exhibition	2014	Notes Coordinates	65
		2014	Begin from Chaos	73
		2013	Coming and Going	77
Chen Dongfan	Solo Exhibition	2017	Heated Bloom	87
		2015	Child Wants to be a King not an Artist	103
		2012	So Sweet	115
	Art Project	2018	The Song of Dragon and Flowers	121
		2018	Open Studio	133
		2016	Live Before You Die	145
		2014	Only One Day of Exhibition	149
		2013—2011	Children's Books	157
		2011	Where is the Happiness	163
		2010	Uncertain	167
		2009	Fairy Tale	171

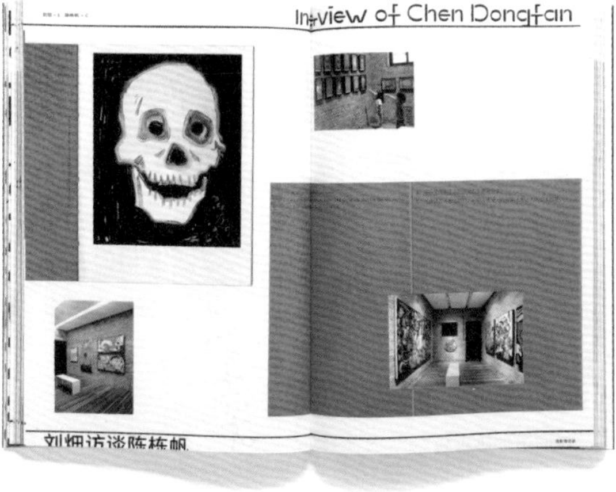
Interview of Chen Dongfan

Notes
Coordinates
笔记 坐标
2014 group exhibition
艺术家
Candida Höfer
2014 年 6 月 28 日 —— 7 月 27 日

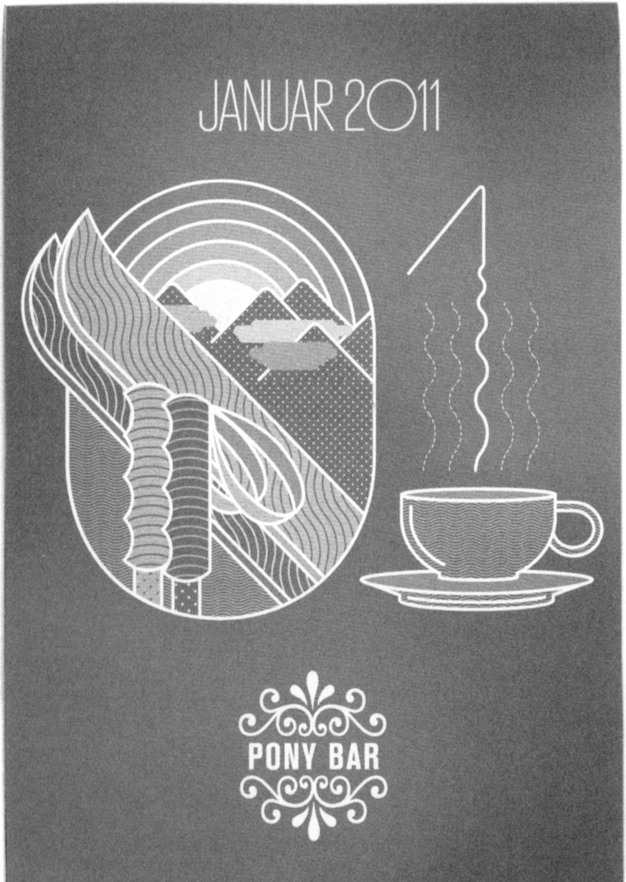
JANUAR 2011
PONY BAR

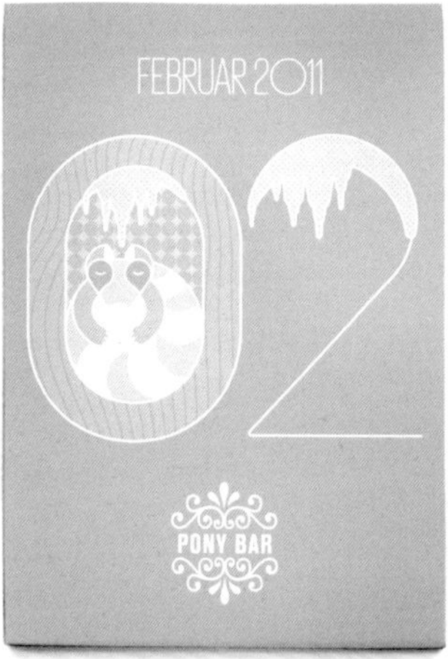
FEBRUAR 2011
PONY BAR
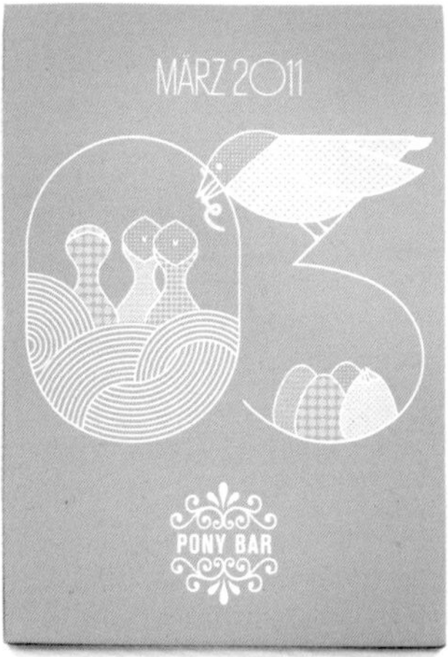
MÄRZ 2011
PONY BAR

APRIL 2011
PONY BAR
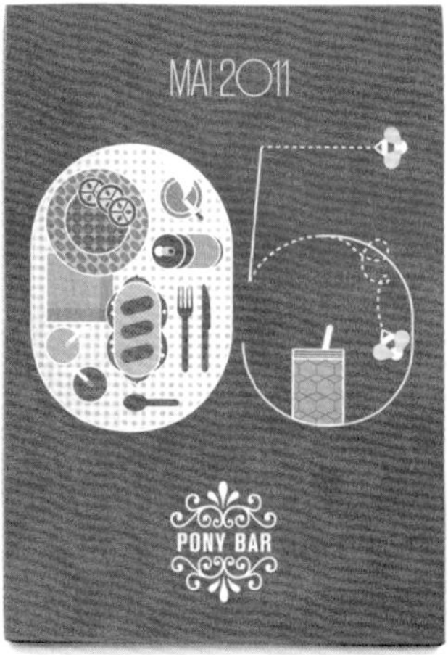
MAI 2011
PONY BAR

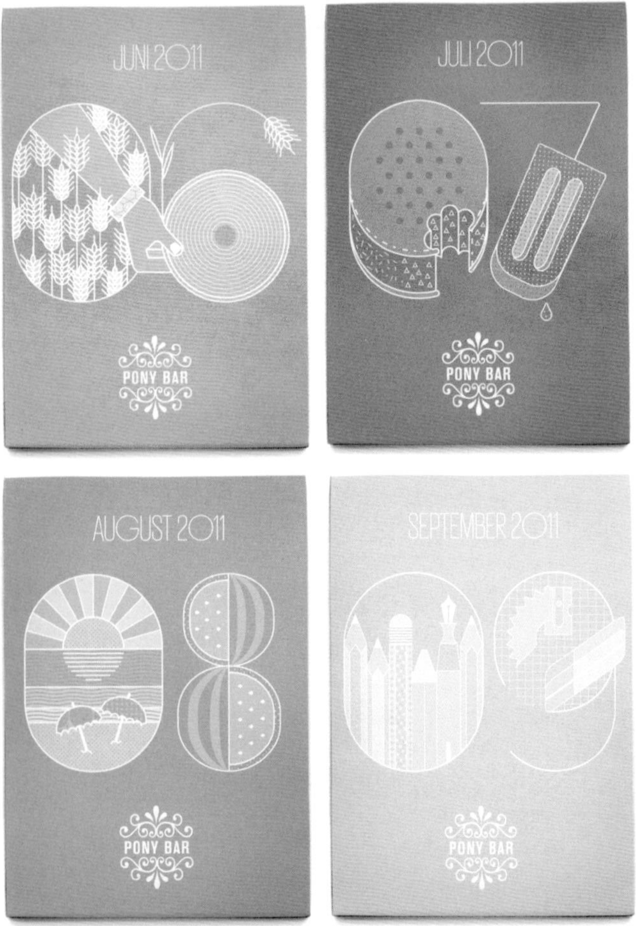
JUNI 2011
PONY BAR
JULI 2011
PONY BAR
AUGUST 2011
PONY BAR
SEPTEMBER 2011
PONY BAR

OKTOBER 2010
PONY BAR

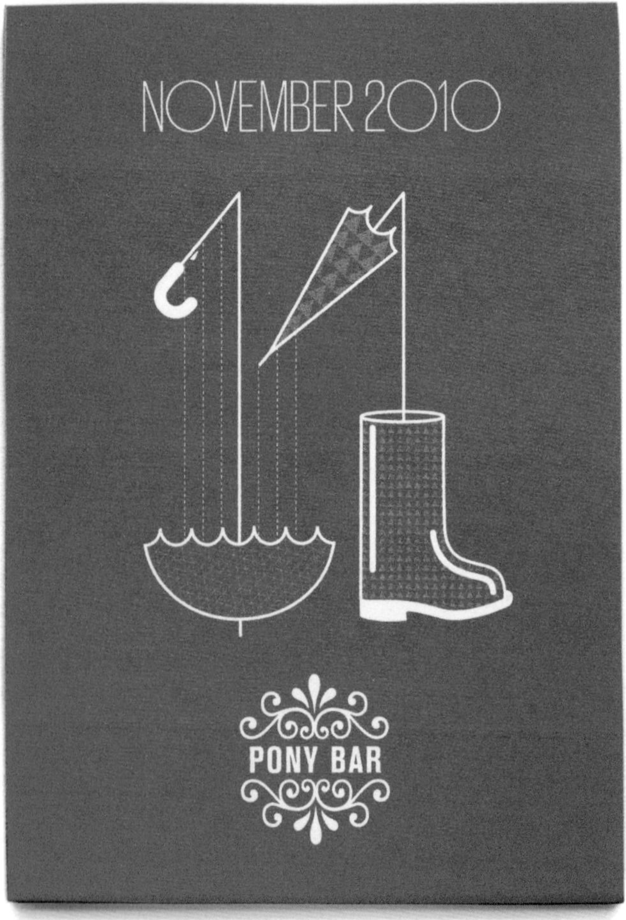
NOVEMBER 2010
PONY BAR

DEZEMBER 2010
PONY BAR

THE BEARDSHOP
LOVELY THINGS & LIMITED DESIGNS
VERY TEMPORARY 1
SAT
17.DEC
19:00
TEILFELD 8
WWW.THEBEARDSHOP.DE
D M

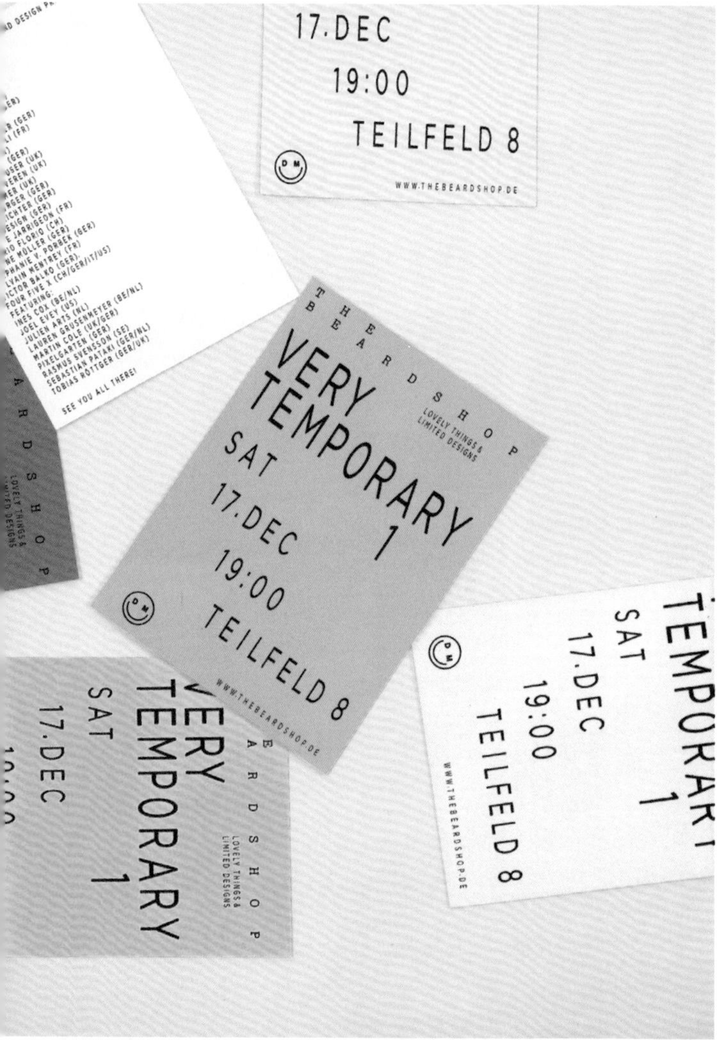
17.DEC
19:00
TEILFELD 8
WWW.THEBEARDSHOP.DE
FEATURING:
INES COX (BE/NL)
JOEL EVEY (US)
JULIEN ARTS (NL)
LAUREN GRUSENMEYER (BE/NL)
MARTIN COLE (UK/GER)
PIXELGARTEN (GER)
RASMUS SVENSSON (SE)
SEBASTIAN PATAKI (GER/NL)
TOBIAS RÖTTGER (GER/UK)
SEE YOU ALL THERE!
THE BEARDSHOP
VERY TEMPORARY
LOVELY THINGS & LIMITED DESIGNS
SAT
17.DEC
1
19:00
TEILFELD 8
WWW.THEBEARDSHOP.DE
SAT
17.DEC
19:00
TEILFELD 8
WWW.THEBEARDSHOP.DE
VERY TEMPORARY
SAT
17.DEC
1
LOVELY THINGS & LIMITED DESIGNS

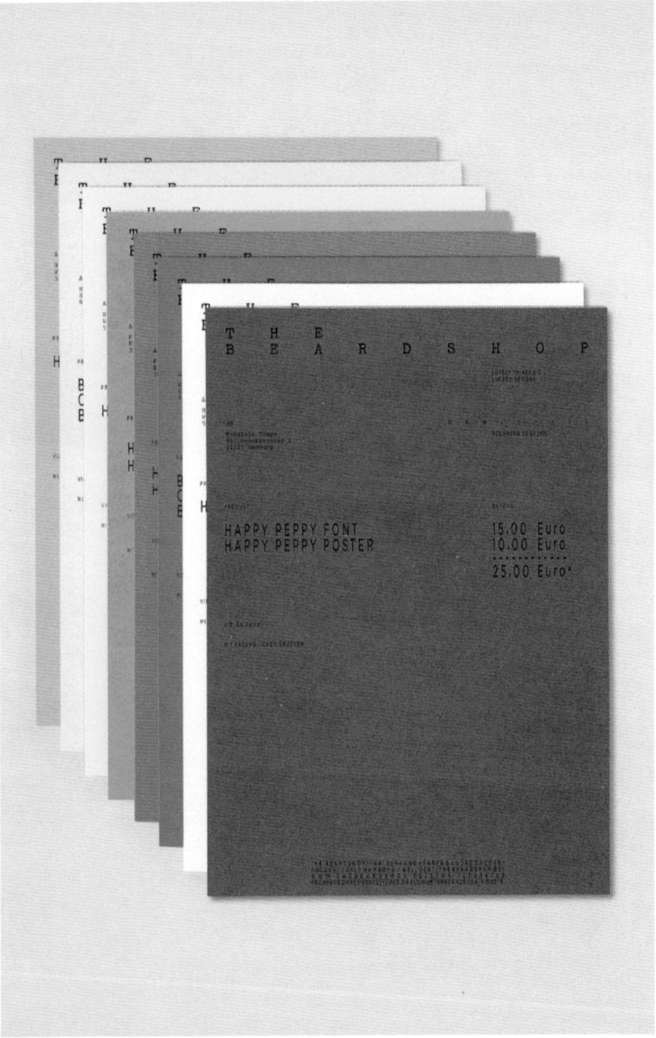
T H E
B E A R D S H O P
HAPPY PEPPY FONT
HAPPY PEPPY POSTER
15,00 Euro
10,00 Euro
25,00 Euro*

T
B

V
T

S

T H E
B E A R D S H O P
LOVELY THINGS &
LIMITED DESIGNS
VERY
TEMPORARY
1
SAT
17.DEC
19:00
TEILFELD8
A SELECTION OF
LIMITED ART AND
DESIGN PRINTS.
D M
WWW.THEBEARDSHOP.DE

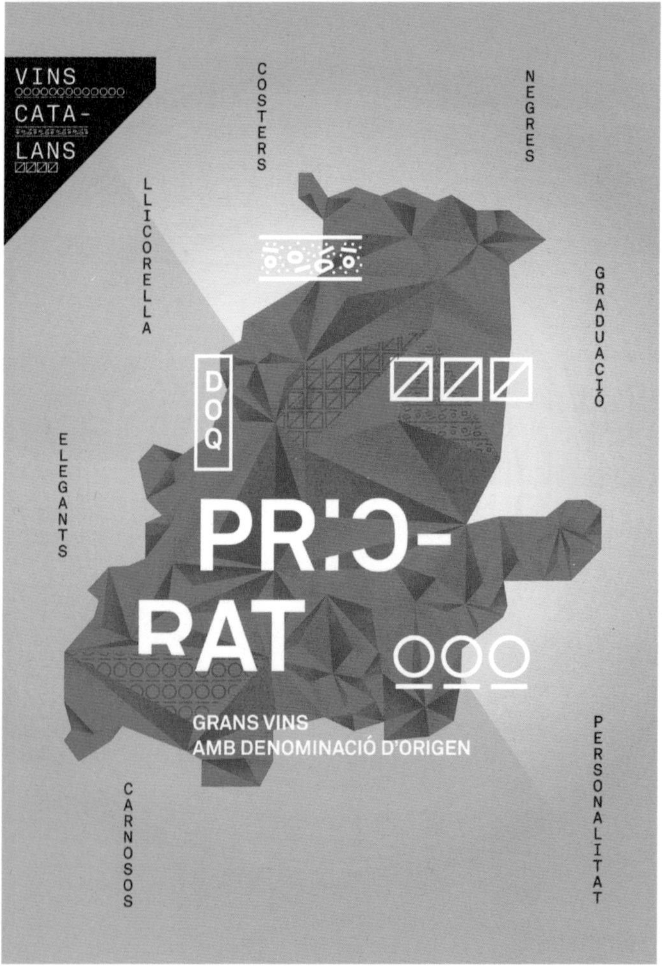
VINS
CATA-
LANS
COSTERS
NEGRES
LLICORELLA
GRADUACIÓ
DOQ
ELEGANTS
PRIO-
RAT
GRANS VINS
AMB DENOMINACIÓ D'ORIGEN
CARNOSOS
PERSONALITAT

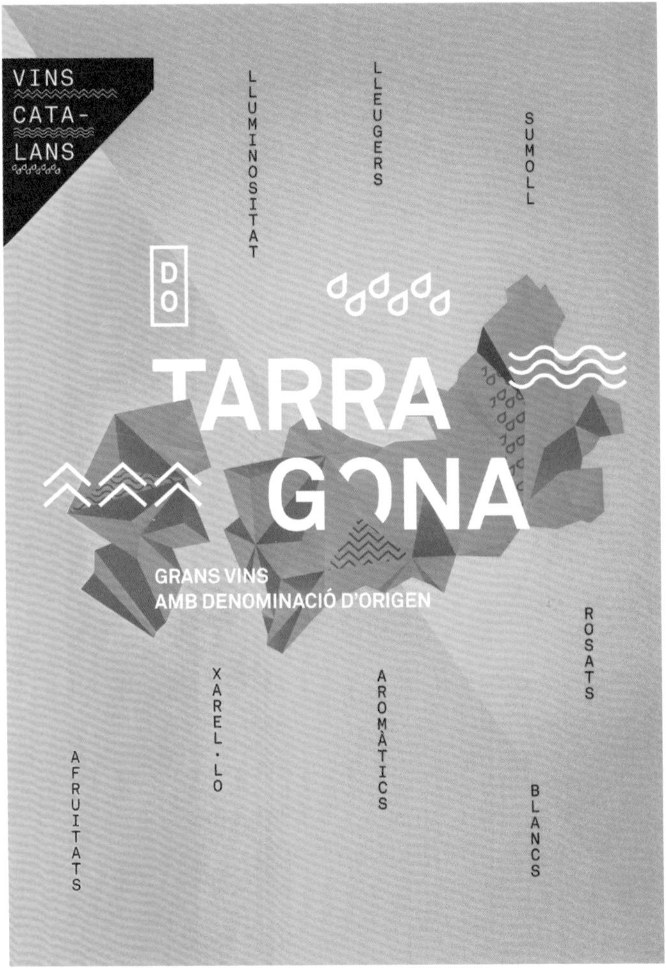
VINS
CATA-
LANS
LLUMINOSITAT
LLEUGERS
SUMOLL
DO
TARRA
GONA
GRANS VINS
AMB DENOMINACIÓ D'ORIGEN
ROSATS
XAREL·LO
AROMÀTICS
AFRUITATS
BLANCS

VINS
CATA-
LANS
DO
CA-
VA
GRANS VINS
AMB DENOMINACIÓ D'ORIGEN
DEGOLLAMENT
PENEDÈS
XAREL·LO
PARELLADA
SOLS VARIATS
SUCRE

VINS
CATA-
LANS
35 VARIETATS
MONASTRELL
MALVASIA
SOL
DO
CATA-
LUNYA
GRANS VINS
AMB DENOMINACIÓ D'ORIGEN
ESPATLLERA
MODERNS

VINS
CATA-
LANS
ROBUSTOS
MACABEU
AMPLIS
DO
TERRA
ALTA
BLANCS
GRANS VINS
AMB DENOMINACIÓ D'ORIGEN
CORPULENTS
TERRASSES
MEDITERRANI
POTENTS

VINS
CATA-
LANS
TRADICIÓ
FRANCOLÍ
TREPAT
DO
CON-
CA DE
BAR-
BERÀ
CHARDONNAY
FRESCOR
GRANS VINS
AMB DENOMINACIÓ D'ORIGEN
TANINS

VINS CATA- LANS
DO
MO- NT- SANT
GRANS VINS
AMB DENOMINACIÓ D'ORIGEN
BLANCS
LLEUGERS
PISSARRA
CARNOSOS
AROMÀTICS
SYRAH

VINS CATA- LANS
DO
COS- TERS DEL SEGRE
GRANS VINS
AMB DENOMINACIÓ D'ORIGEN
ESTRUCTURA
MUNTANYES
INNOVACIÓ
ESTRUCTURATS
SOL
POTENTS
CONTINENTAL

DO
PLA DE BAGES
GRANS VINS
AMB DENOMINACIÓ D'ORIGEN
FRESCOR
ARGILA
ESPATLLERES
FARIGOLA
PICAPOLL
MEDITERRANI
GEWÜRZTRAMINER

VINS CATA- LANS
DO
EM- PORDÀ
GRANS VINS
AMB DENOMINACIÓ D'ORIGEN
GARNATXA
FRUITATS
TRAMUNTANA
CORPULENT
CARINYENA
TANINS
LLEDONER

Rítmia
Rítmia
Musicoteràpia i educació social

Rítmia
Celia Castillo López
Rítmia
Música activa!
Dinàmiques amb ritme!
Centre Cívic Ateneu Fort Pienc
Octubre 2012

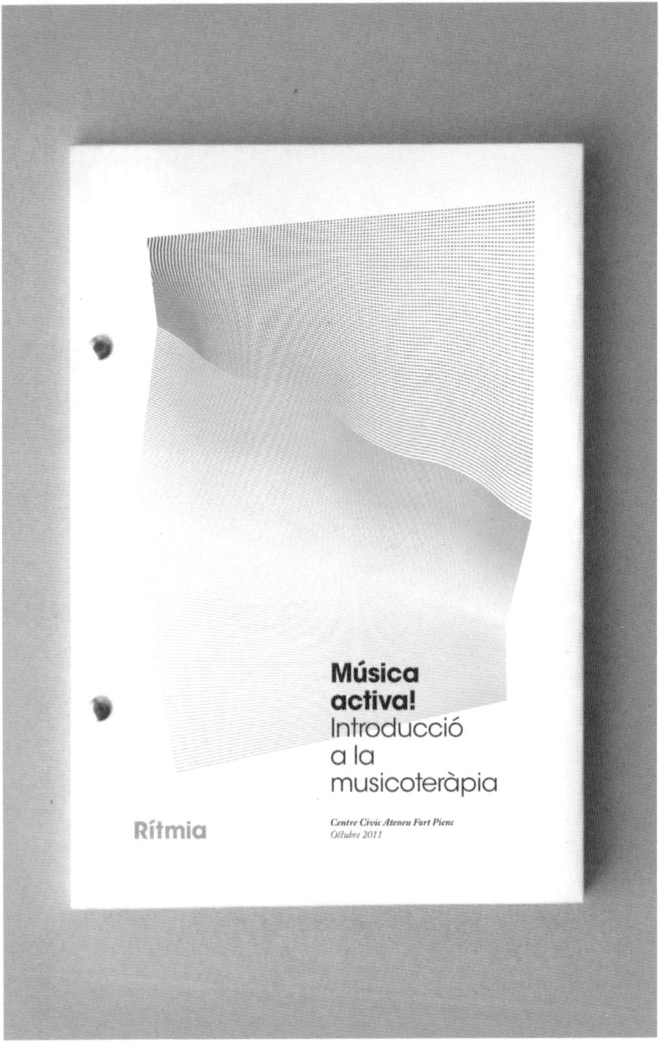
Música
activa!
Introducció
a la
musicoteràpia
Rítmia
Centre Cívic Ateneu Fort Pienc
Octubre 2011

Rítmia
Celia Castillo López
Musicoterapeuta i educadora social
+34 607 706 830
celia@ritmia.cat
www.ritmia.cat

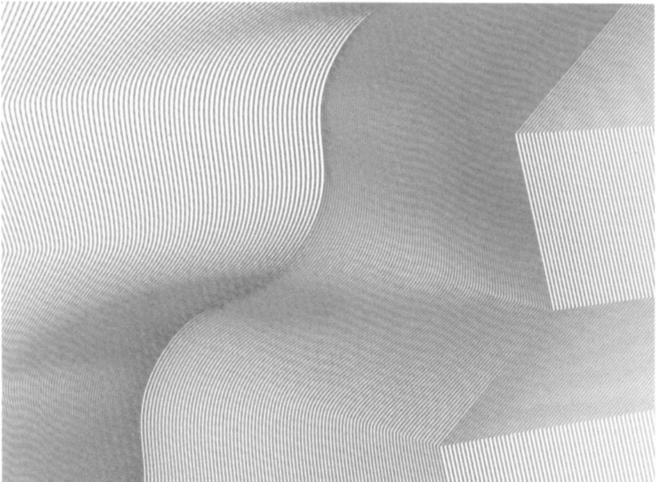

Rítmia
Musicoteràpia i educació social
Amb la musicoteràpia
aprendràs coses noves
de tu mateix, aprendràs
a relaxar-te, a relacionar-te,
a compartir experiències
i passaràs una estona
agradable.
En definitiva,
una nova forma

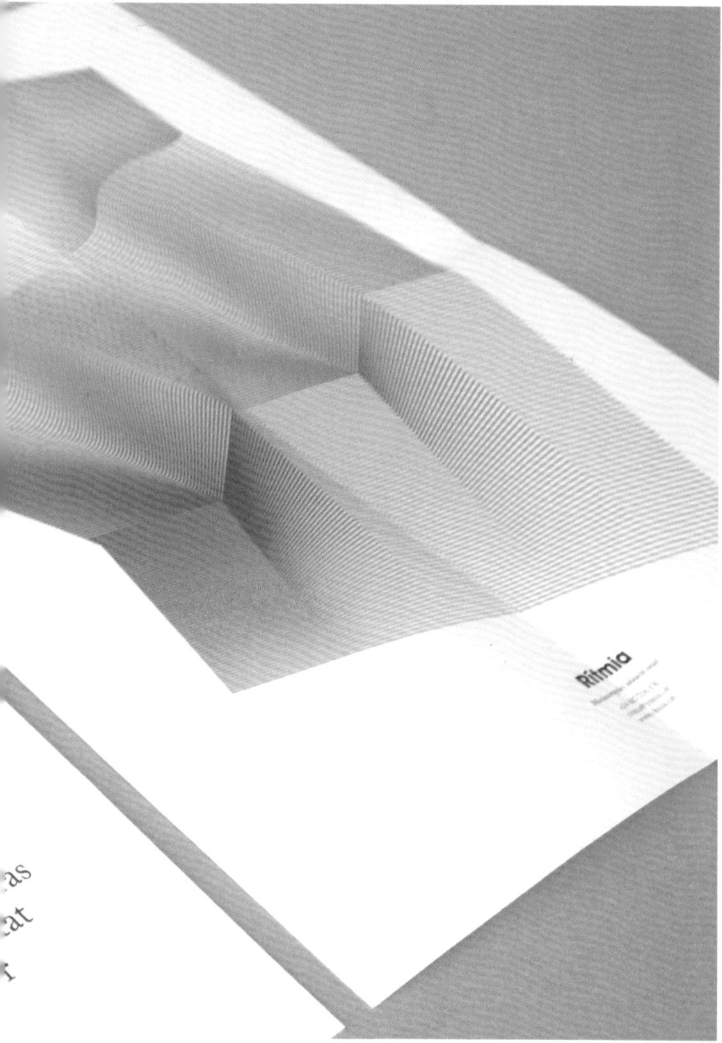
Ritmia

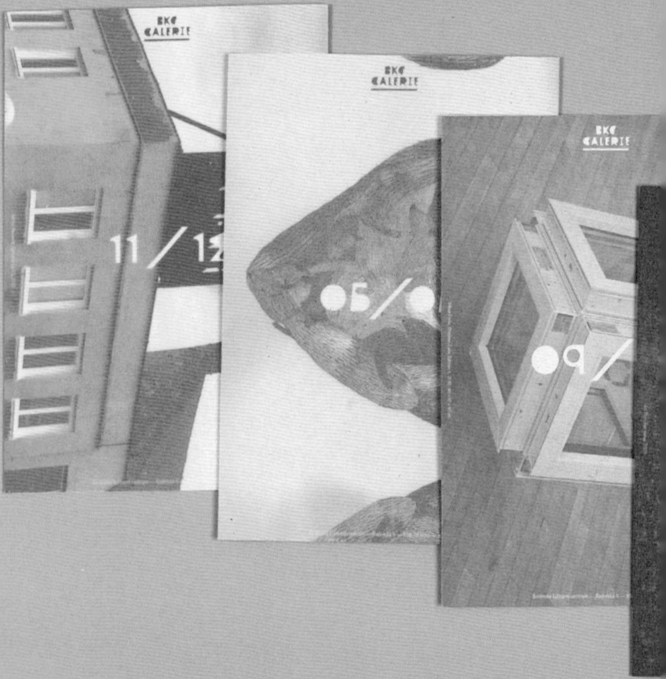
BKC GALERIE
11 / 12
BKC GALERIE
BKC GALERIE

BKC
GALERIE
07/
03/
BKC
GALERIE
01/02

EVERMORE LONDON
FLORE
EVERMORE LONDON
LIGHT
EVERMORE LONDON

EVERMORE LONDON
GROVE
EVERMORE LONDON
NORTH
EVERMORE LONDON
EVERMORE LONDON
TIDES

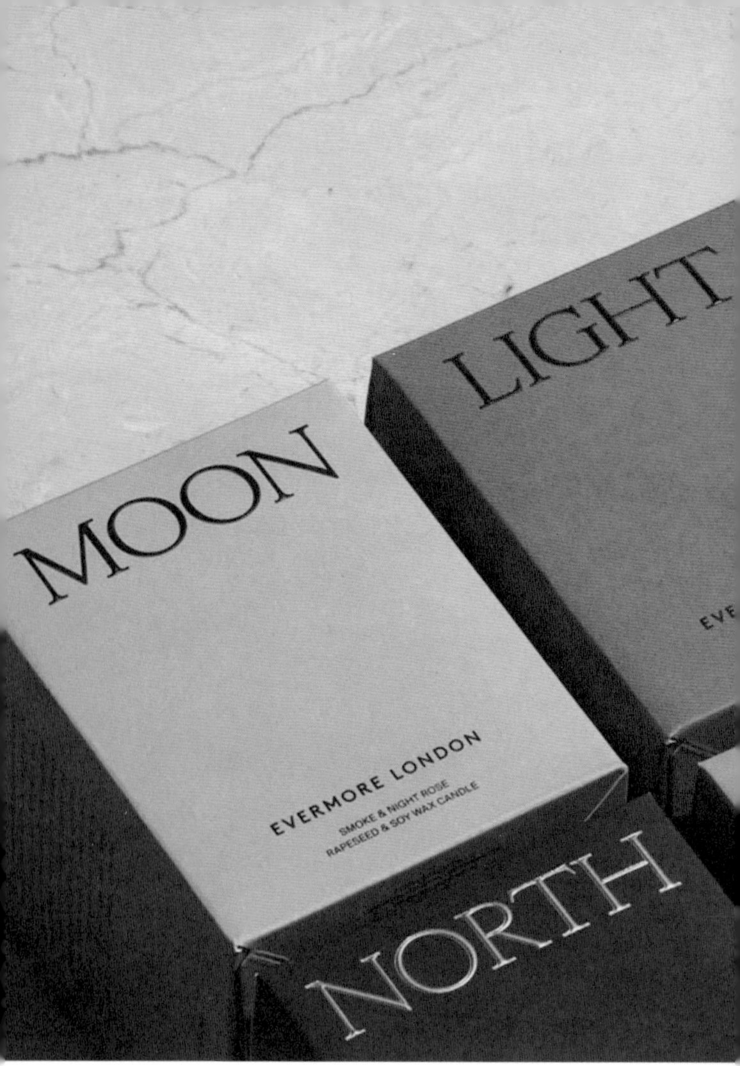
LIGHT
EVE
MOON
EVERMORE LONDON
SMOKE & NIGHT ROSE
RAPESEED & SOY WAX CANDLE
NORTH

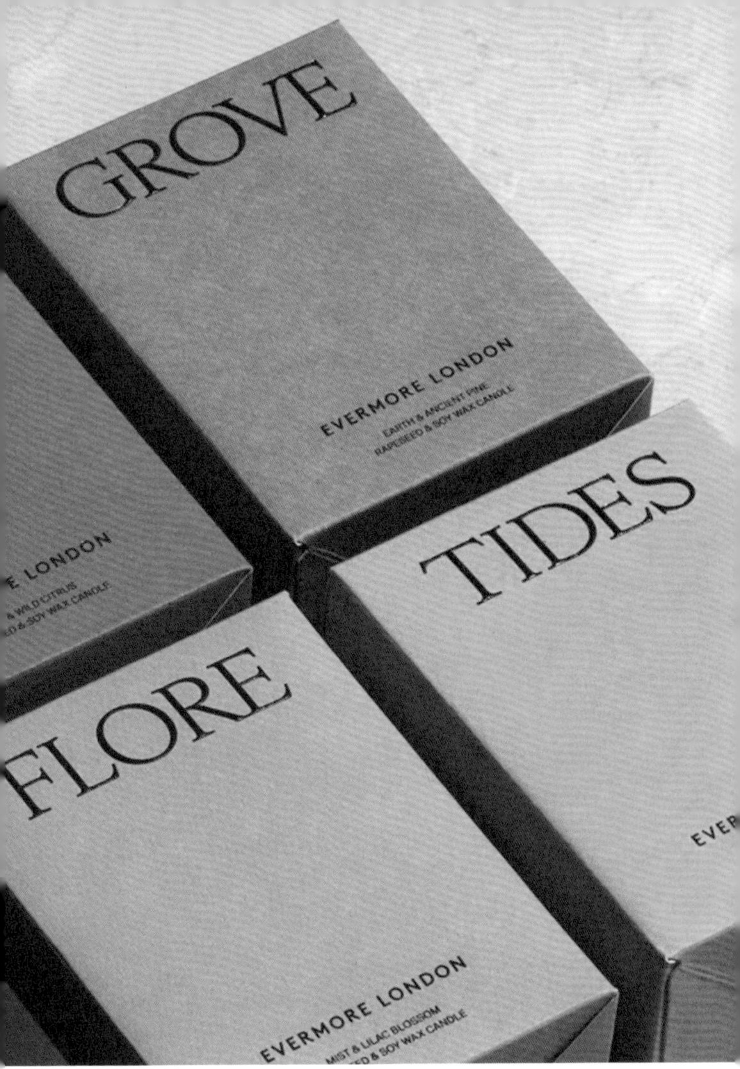
GROVE
EVERMORE LONDON
EARTH & ANCIENT PINE
RAPESEED & SOY WAX CANDLE
TIDES
FLORE
EVERMORE LONDON
MIST & LILAC BLOSSOM

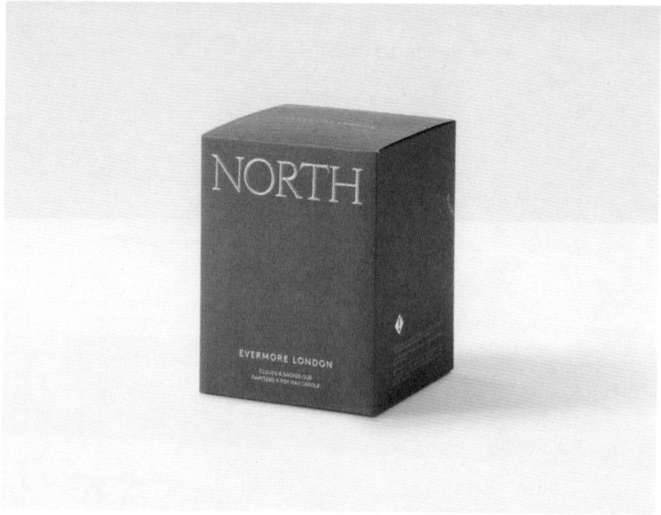
NORTH
EVERMORE LONDON

LIGHT
EVERMORE LONDON
SUN & WILD CITRUS
RAPESEED & SOY WAX CANDLE
LIGHT
EVERMORE LONDON

LIGHT
EVERMORE LONDON

NORTH
EVERMORE LONDON

TIDES
EVERMORE LONDON

FLORE
EVERMORE LONDON

GROVE
EVERMORE LONDON

CED
TGC110
KIYOMI
TANGENTGC
TGC108
CEDAR
organic
TANGENTGC
SUGAR
CEDAR

TGC109
CLOVER
GAR
TGC110
KIYOMI
TANGENTGC
organic
DAR
TGC109
CLOVER
SUGAR

CEDAR
TGC103
SUGAR
TANGENTGC
CLOVER
organic
TGC109
deos
KIYOMI
TGC110
SUGAR
TANGENTGC
organic
CLOVER
TGC109

CEDAR
TANGENTGC
TGC109
CLOVER
organic
TGC110
TANGENTGC
CLOVER
TGC109
organic
TANGENTGC
TGC110

100 EMOTIONS
09——10 16——17 DEC 2017
UNIT 6A SHIU FAT INDUSTRIAL BUILDING,
139-141 WAI YIP STREET, KLN, HK
BE INUNDATED WITH
A MULTITUDE OF FEELINGS
ERROR / EFFECT /
FUNDAMENTAL-STUDIO.COM

ERROR / EFFECT /
100 GRAPHICS
100 EMOTIONS
BE INUNDATED WITH
A MULTITUDE OF FEELINGS
09——10 16——17 DEC 2017
UNIT 6A SHIU FAT INDUSTRIAL BUILDING,
139-141 WAI YIP STREET, KLN, HK
FUNDAMENTAL-STUDIO.COM

ERROR / EFFECT /

ERROR / EFFECT /

ERROR / EFFECT /

EFFECT

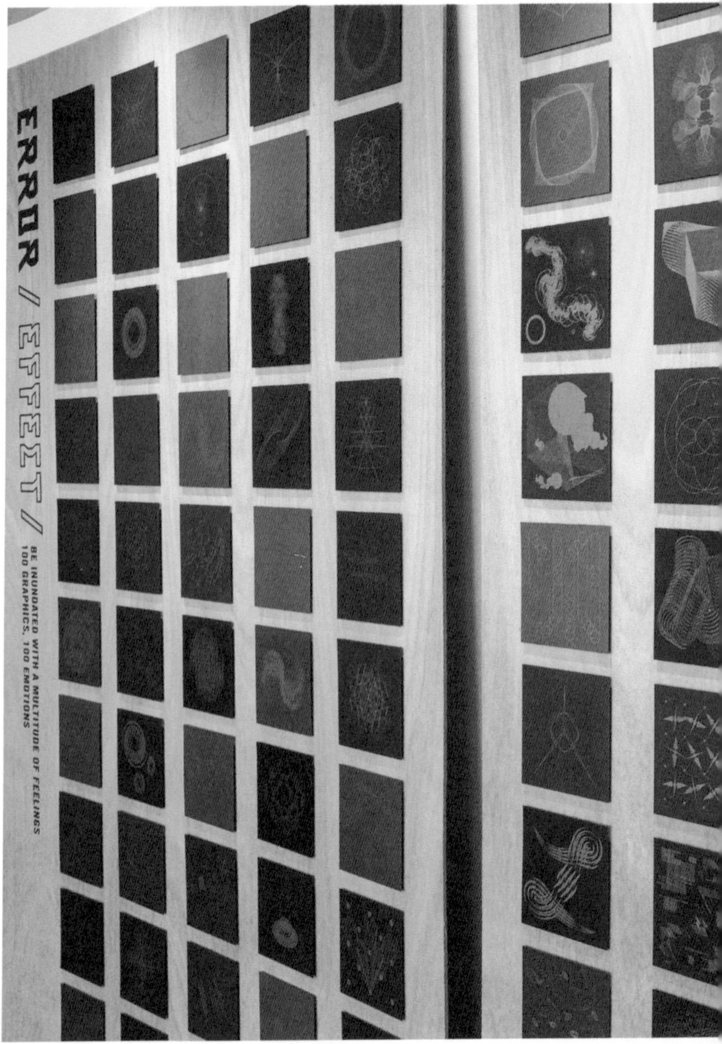
ERROR / EFFECT /
BE INUNDATED WITH A MULTITUDE OF FEELINGS
100 GRAPHICS, 100 EMOTIONS

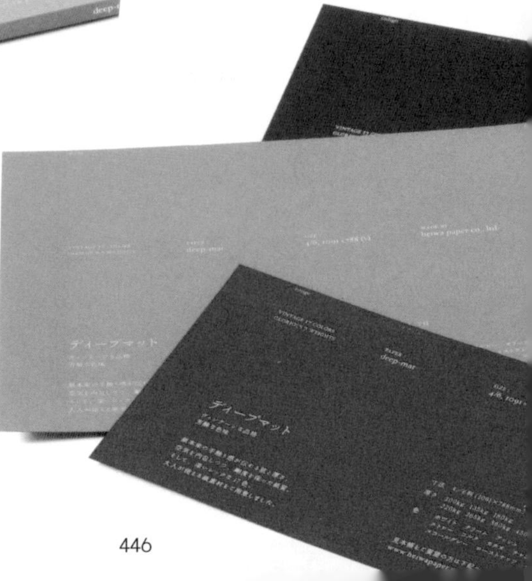
ディープマット
deep-mat

deep-mat
heiwa paper co., ltd.

MADE BY
heiwa paper co., ltd.
DESIGN BY
artless Inc.
MADE BY
heiwa paper co., ltd.
DESIGN BY
artless Inc.

a
high-quality
premium paper
deep-mat
ディープマット

deep-mat
ディープマット

high-quality
premium paper
deep-mat
VINTAGE 17 COLORS
GLORIOUS 7 WEIGHTS
PAPER :
deep-mat
mulberry
ディープマット
ヴィンテージな品格
芳醇な色味
紙本来の手触り感が伝わる肌と厚さ。
空気を内包しつつ、剛度を保った紙質。
として、深いシックな17色。
大人が使える紙素材をご用意しました。
deep-mat
deep-mat
ローストナッツ
roast nuts
VINTAGE 17 COLORS
GLORIOUS 7 WEIGHTS

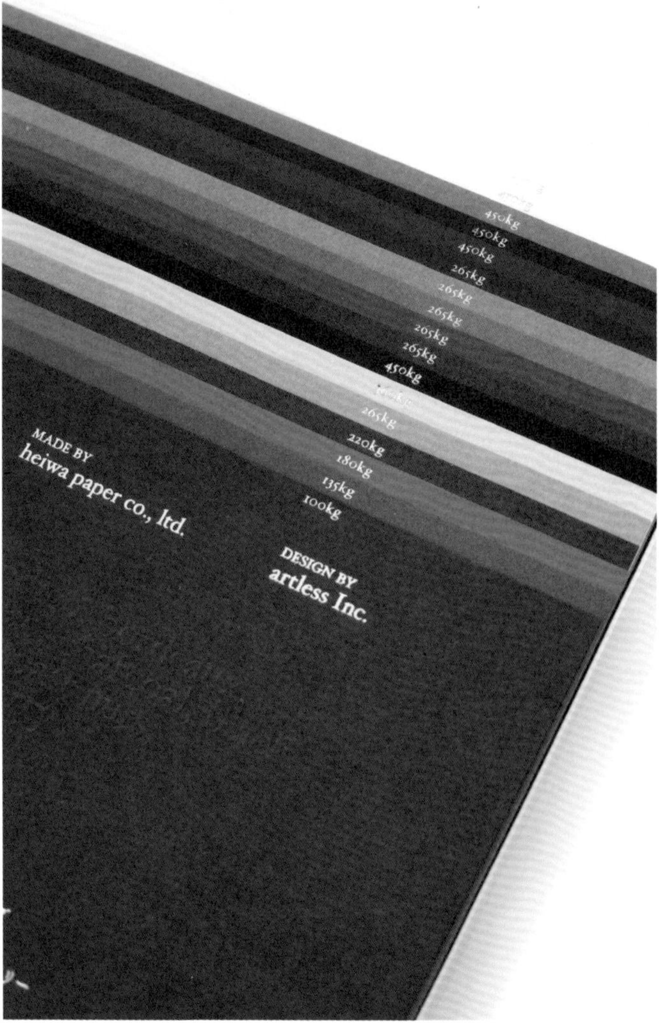
450kg
450kg
450kg
265kg
265kg
265kg
205kg
265kg
450kg
265kg
220kg
180kg
135kg
100kg
MADE BY
heiwa paper co., ltd.
DESIGN BY
artless Inc.

melez.
melez.
melez.
melez.

DAY TO NIGHT PACK
N°01
WAKE UP
N°02
SLEEP
N°03
BALANCE
MELEZ LATTE PACK
N°09
INDULGE
N°10
SPICE
N°12
MATCHA
FALL/WINTER PACK
N°01
WAKE UP
N°06
BOLD
N°10
SPICE
elez.

melez
LIFESTYLE
TEA
FALL/WINTER PACK
WAKE UP
BOLD
SPICE
BALANCE

BALANCE
BEAUTY
PURE
ICED TEA PACK
Nº07 REFRESH
Nº08 HAPPY
Nº09 INDULGE
DAY TO NIGHT PACK
Nº01 WAKE UP
Nº02 SLEEP
Nº03 BALANCE
Nº04 BEAUTY
Nº05 PURE
Nº09 INDULGE
Nº02 SLEEP
Nº03 BALANCE

melez.
MELEZ LATTE PA
Nº09
INDULGE
bourbon vanilla rooibos
25 gr
Nº10
SPICE
melez masala chai
25 gr

melez.
ICED TEA PACK
Nº07
REFRESH
citrus pineapple melange
25 gr
Nº08
HAPPY
strawberry mint tisane
25 gr
Nº09
INDULGE
bourbon vanilla rooibos
25 gr

Oh!
Teatre
CCCB
Un nou escenari
per a la cultura i les arts

Uau!
Teatre
CCCB
Un nou escenari
per a la cultura i les arts
Oh!
Teatre
CCCB
Shhh!
Teatre
CCCB
Uau!
Teatre
CCCB

Shhh!
Teatre
CCCB
Un nou escenari
per a la cultura i les arts
Oh!
Teatre
CCCB
Un nou escenari
per a la cultura i les arts
Shhh!
Teatre
CCCB
Un nou escenari
per a la cultura i les arts

Oh!
Teatre
CCCB
Un nou escenari
per a la cultura i les arts
Shhh!
Teatre
CCCB
Un nou escenari
per a la cultura i les arts
Oh!
Teatre
CCCB
Un nou escenari
per a la cultura i les arts
Uau!

Shhh!
Teatre
CCCB
Un nou escenari
per a la cultura i les arts.

Shhh!
Teatre
CCCB
Un nou escenari
per a la cultura i les arts.

Oh!
Teatre
CCCB
Un nou escenari
per a la cultura i les arts.

Shhh!
Teatre
CCCB
Un nou escenari
per a la cultura i les arts.

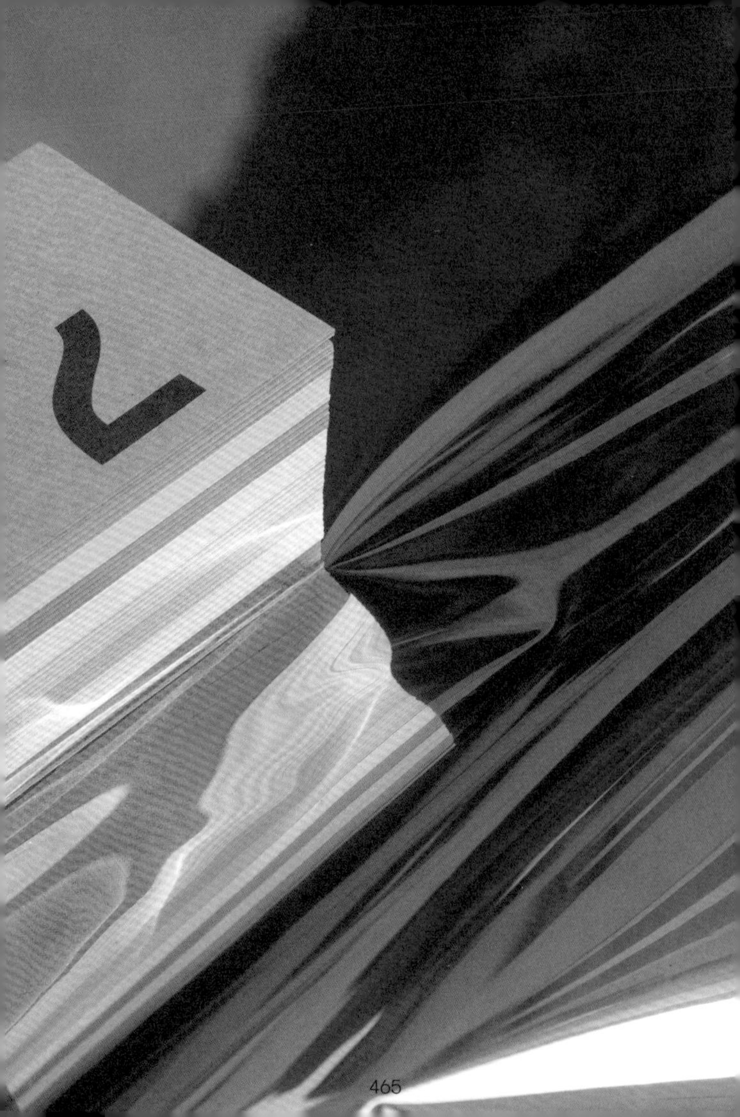

Frédéric Breyss
architecte associé
f.breysse@huitetdemi.fr
+33 (0)6 10 82 13 56
+33 (0)4 91 68 00 26
21, place Alexandre Labadié
13001 Marseille — France
huitetdemi.fr
huit et demi
architectes associés

huitetdemi.fr
Frédéric Breysse
architecte associé
f.breysse@huitetdemi.fr
+33 (0)6 10 82 13 56
+33 (0)4 91 68 00 26
21, place Alexandre Labadié
13001 Marseille — France

8½
huit et demi
architectes associés
huitetdemi.fr
contact@huite

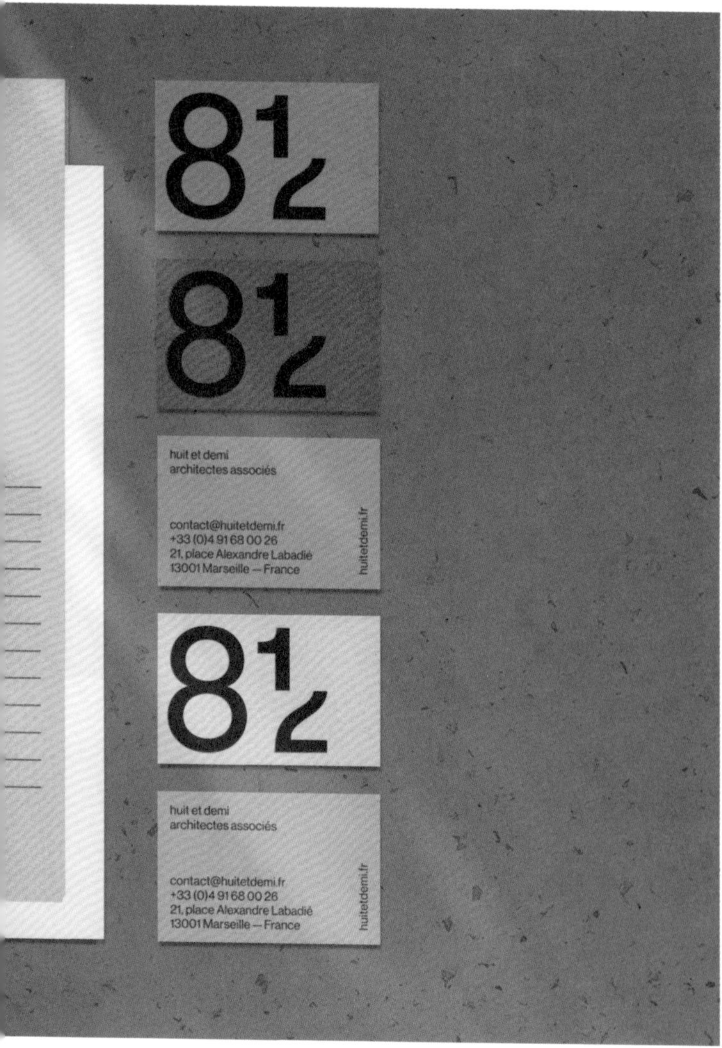
huit et demi
architectes associés
contact@huitetdemi.fr
+33 (0)4 91 68 00 26
21, place Alexandre Labadié
13001 Marseille — France
huitetdemi.fr
huit et demi
architectes associés
contact@huitetdemi.fr
+33 (0)4 91 68 00 26
21, place Alexandre Labadié
13001 Marseille — France
huitetdemi.fr

images3

images3
PHOTOLITHO
RETOUCHE
PRÉPRESSE
Karine Rochat
Images 3 SA
Avenue de France 23bis
Case postale
CH-1000 Lausanne 7
T +41 21 621 89 89
M +41 79 438 61 45
karine@images3.ch
www.images3.ch
images3
PHOTOLITHO
RETOUCHE
PRÉPRESSE
Denis Hauswirth
Images 3 SA
Avenue de France 23bis
Case postale
CH-1000 Lausanne 7
T +41 21 621 89 89
M +41 79 438 61 45
denis@images3.ch
www.images3.ch
images3
PHOTOLITHO
RETOUCHE
PRÉPRESSE
Matthieu Csakodi
Images 3 SA
Avenue de France 23bis
Case postale
CH-1000 Lausanne 7
T +41 21 621 89 89
M +41 79 438 61 45
matthieu@images3.ch
www.images3.ch
images3
PHOTOLITHO
RETOUCHE
PRÉPRESSE
Natalie Bossy
Images 3 SA
Avenue de France 23bis
Case postale
CH-1000 Lausanne 7
T +41 21 621 89 89
M +41 79 438 61 45
nathalie@images3.ch
www.images3.ch

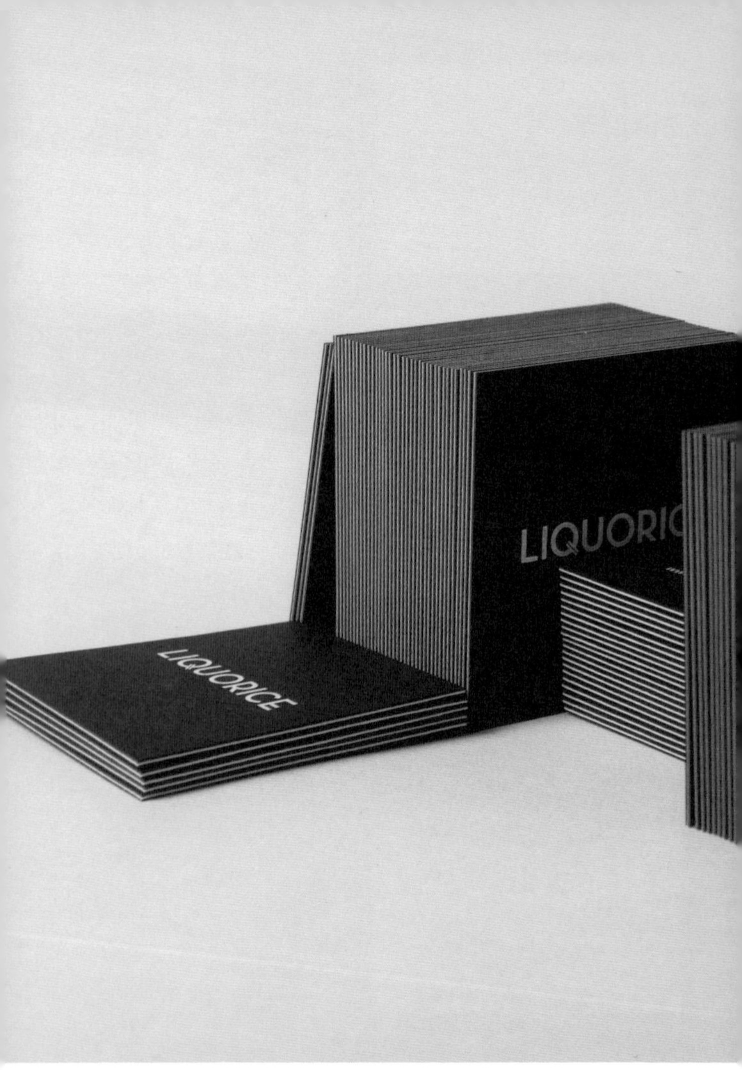
LIQUORICE
LIQUORIC

Scott Bonanno
Director
Liquorice Studio
Level 1, 184 Brunswick Street
Fitzroy, Victoria 3065
Phone +61 3 9023 5767
Mobile +61 402 442 939
scott@liquoricestudio.com
www.liquoricestudio.com
LIQUORICE

Lubomír Typlt
Mobilizace
22 04 —
05 06 2011
Bohuslava Olešová
Princip neurčitosti
20 09 —
06 11 2011
Pavel Baňka
Nejen Marginálie
20 09 —
06 11 2011
Dirk Brömmel
Vila Tugendhat
16 11 2011 —
29 01 2012

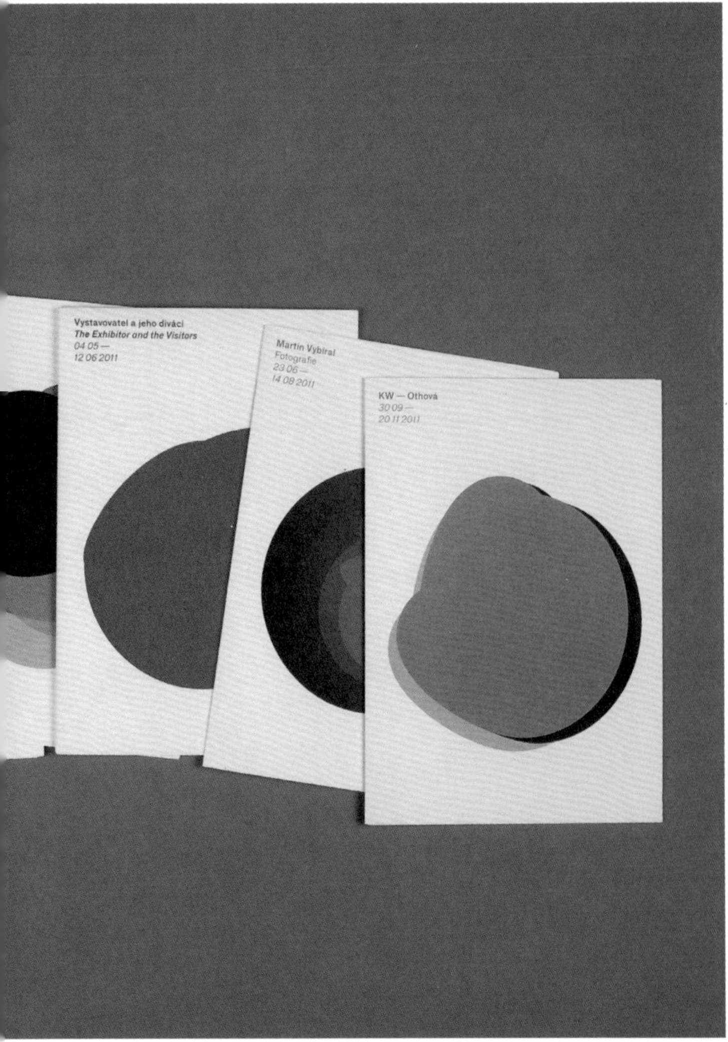
Vystavovatel a jeho diváci
The Exhibitor and the Visitors
04 05 —
12 06 2011
Martin Vybíral
Fotografie
23 06 —
14 08 2011
KW — Othová
30 09 —
20 11 2011

www.dum-umeni.cz
www.dum-umeni.cz
www.dum-umeni.cz

www.dum-umeni.cz
www.dum-umeni.cz
www.dum-umeni.cz
www.dum-umeni.cz

Studio-mw / PORTFOLIO /
www.studio-mw.fr

Le Père
Lachaise
Studio-mu / PORTFOLIO / Le Père Lachaise
www.studio-mu.fr

NEONKĖS
ALL NIGHT LONG
CULTURE
WHATEVER
KANDY KILLERS
RIEŠUTINĖS
BERNELIŲ MIŠIOS
THE DEW
UNTITLED

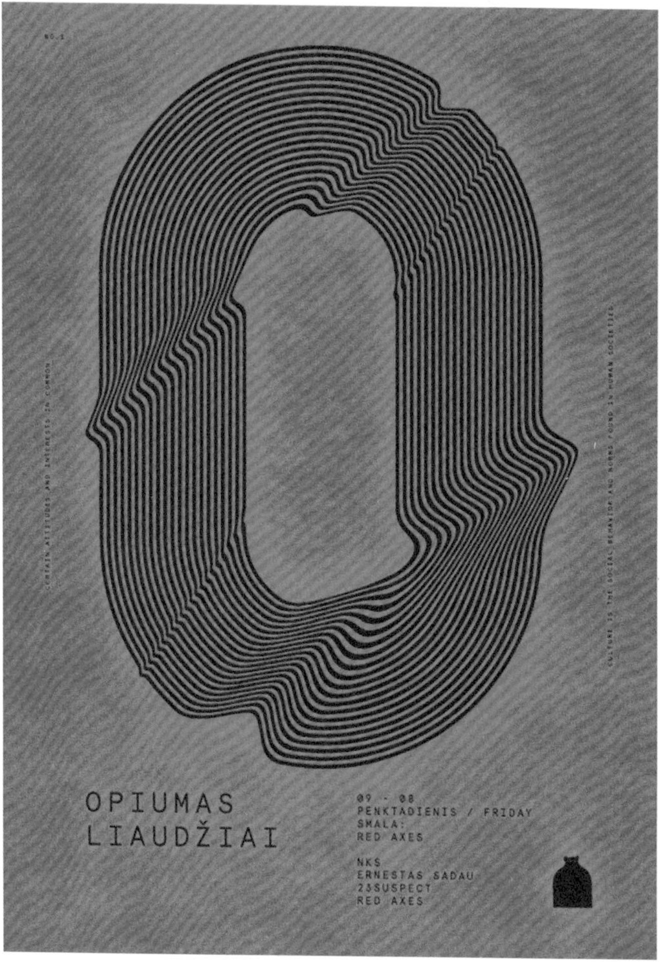
CERTAIN ATTITUDES AND INTERESTS IN COMMON
CULTURE IS THE SOCIAL BEHAVIOR AND NORMS FOUND IN HUMAN SOCIETIES.
OPIUMAS
LIAUDŽIAI
09 - 08
PENKTADIENIS / FRIDAY
SMALA:
RED AXES
NKS
ERNESTAS SADAU
23SUSPECT
RED AXES

NO.1
CERTAIN ATTITUDES AND INTERESTS IN COMMON
CULTURE IS THE SOCIAL BEHAVIOR AND NORMS FOUND IN HUMAN SOCIETIES.
DYNAMO
09 - 08
PENKTADIENIS / FRIDAY
SMALA:
RED AXES
NKS
ERNESTAS SADAU
23SUSPECT
RED AXES

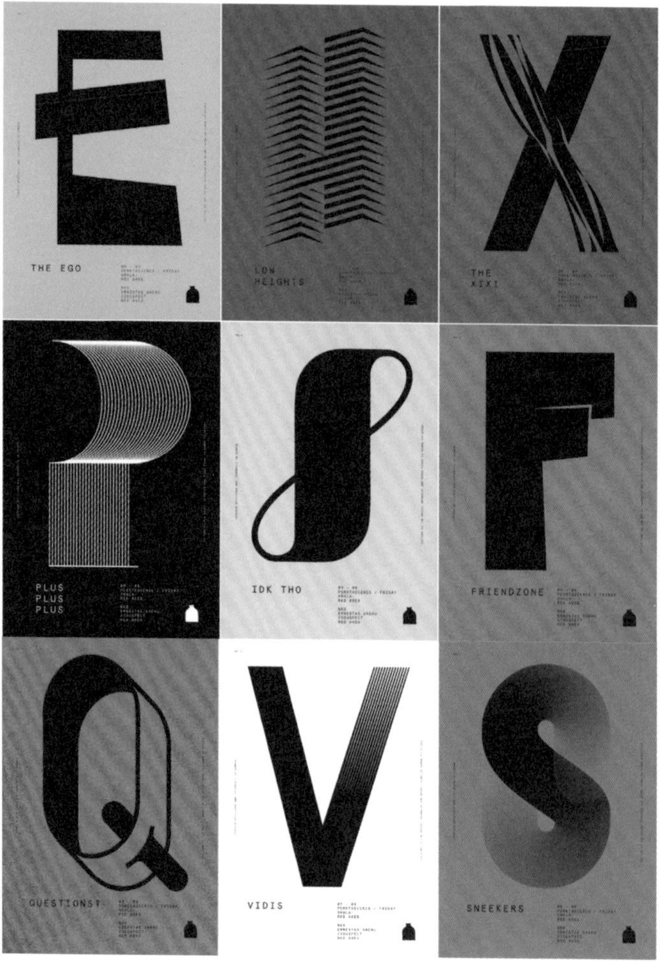
THE EGO
LOW HEIGHTS
THE XIXI
PLUS PLUS PLUS
IDK THO
FRIENDZONE
QUESTIONS?
VIDIS
SNEEKERS

WHATEVER
UNTITLED
09 . 08
PENKTADIENIS / FRIDAY
SMALA:
RED AXES
NKS
ERNESTAS SADAU
23SUSPECT
RED AXES
CERTAIN ATTITUDES AND INTERESTS IN COMMON

DC
CULTURE
RIEŠUTINĖS

BERNELIŲ
MIŠIOS
XIXI

OPIUM
012053

OPIUM
LIAUDŽIAI

BERNELIŲ
MIŠIOS

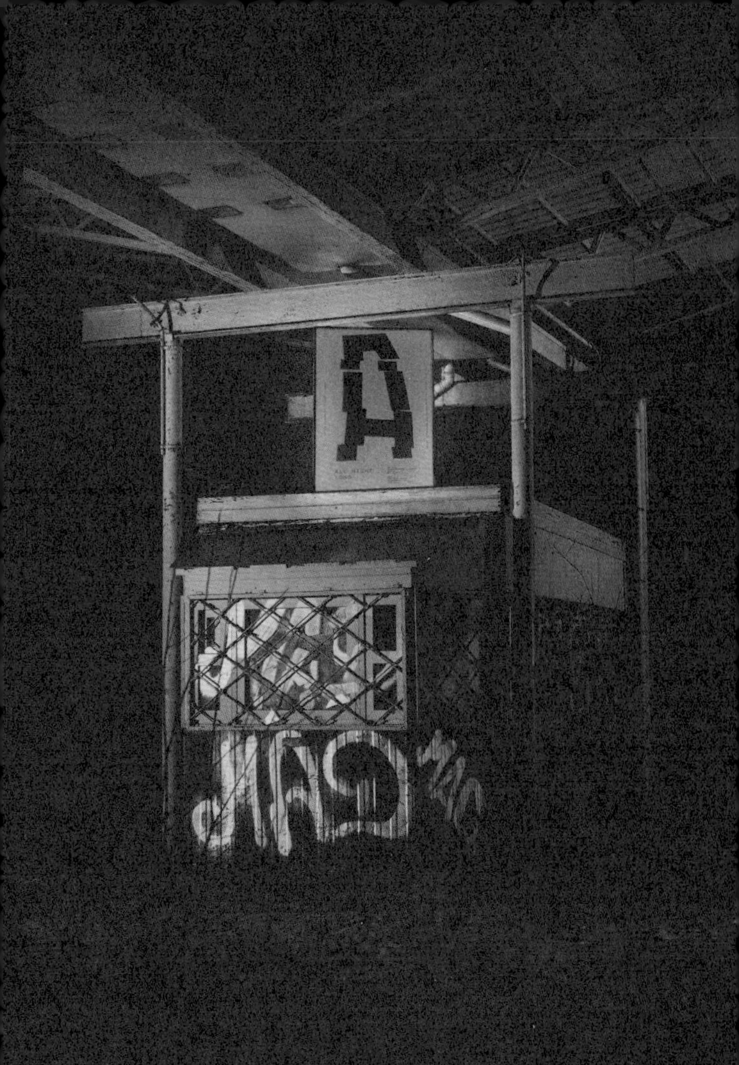

"Colour is an incredible tool because it can exist everywhere."

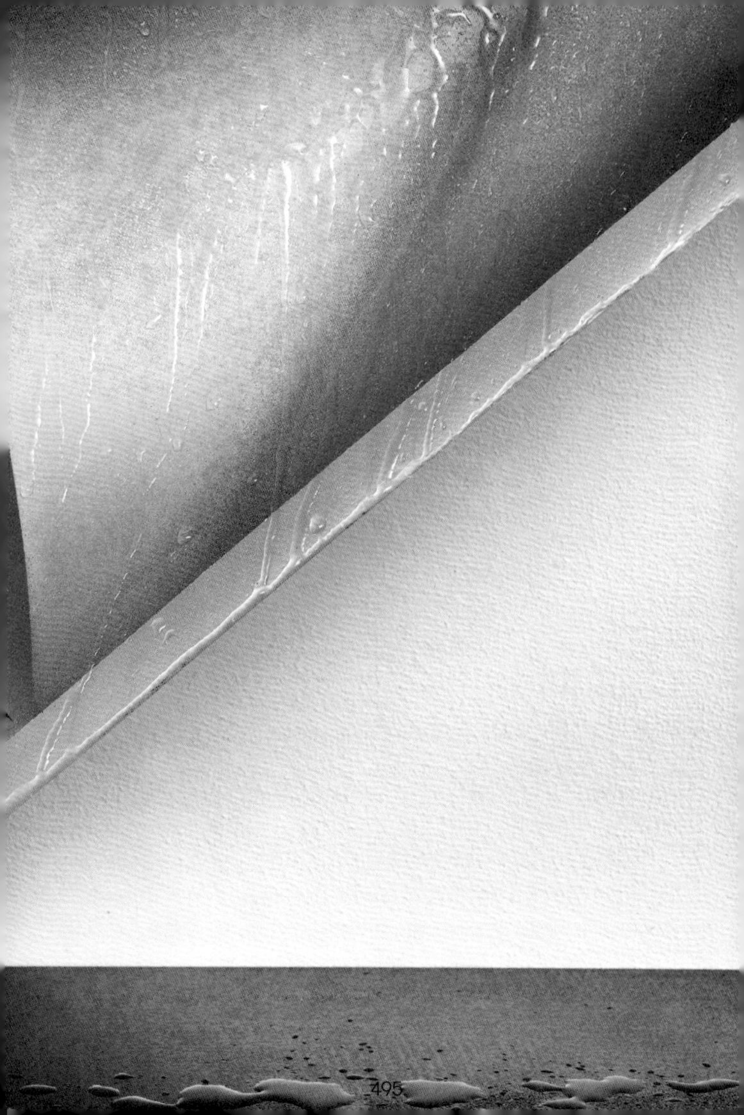

SURF. A DISTURBANCE OF
A MOVING SWELL TO THE JOY OF THE CITY

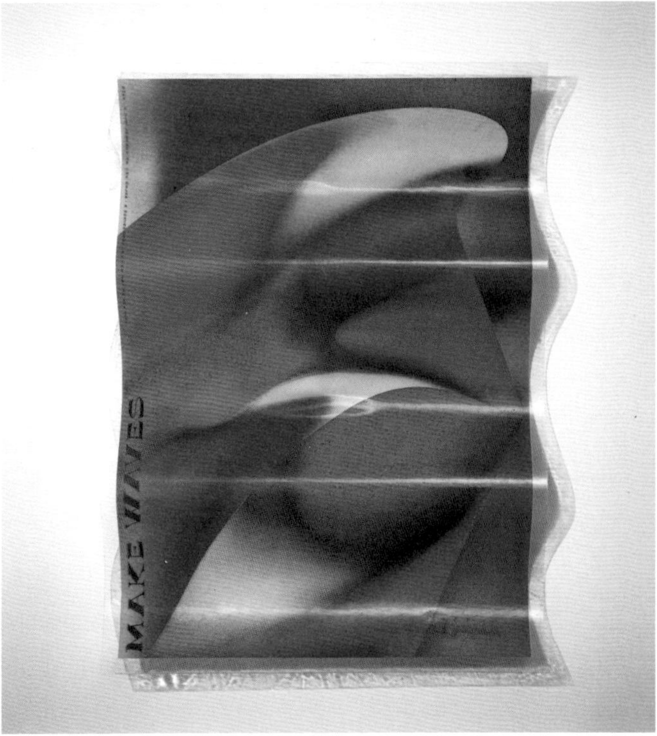
MAKE WAVES

GREEN
SPACE
IS
DESIGNED
SPACE

THE
MUSEUM
OF
MOUTH-
FEEL

M

GREEN
SPACE
IS
DESIGNED
SPACE
YOU
ARE
WHAT
YOU EAT

LTURE:
TIC
THE MECHANICAL POETRY OF FEEDING THE MASSES
GROWING FOOD ON THE DRAWING BOARD

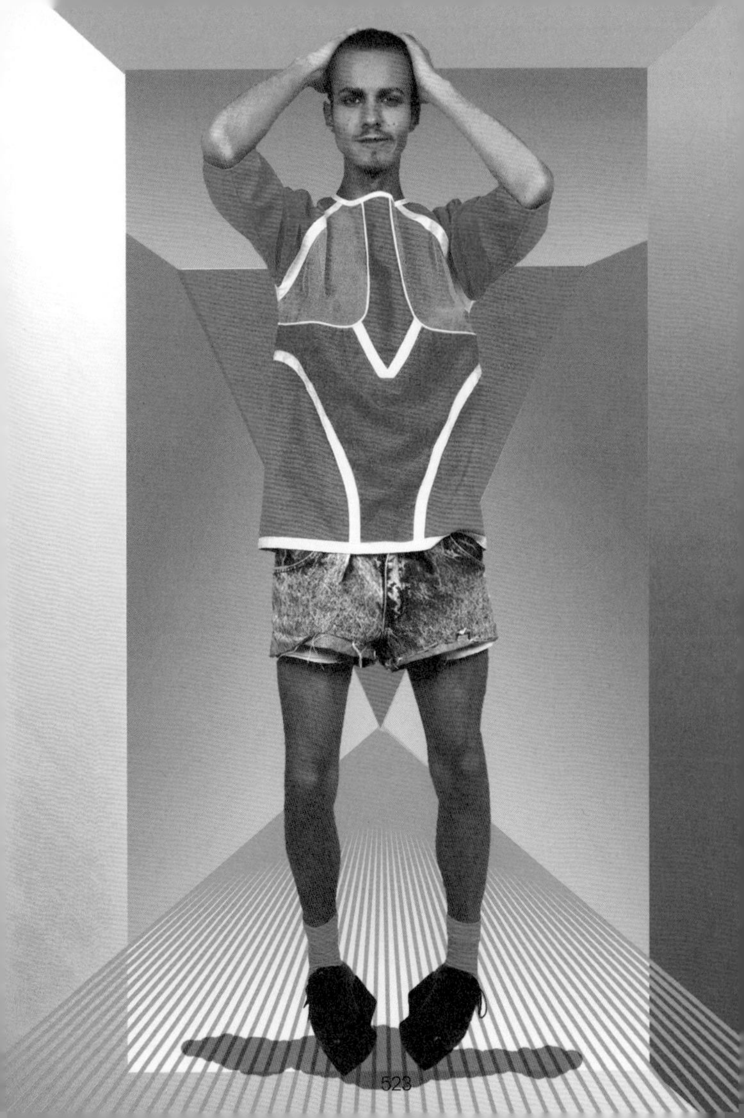

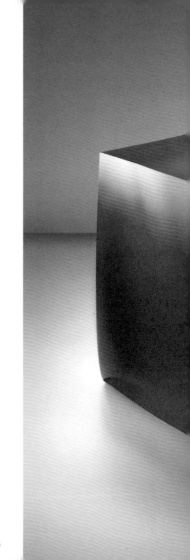

SHOW
ARENA
536

BREAD
BUTTER
by Zalando

NOW IN
FASHION
NOW IN
MUSIC
NOW IN
TREND SHOW
EVERYONE
BREAD
BUTTER
by Zalando
BREADANDBUTTER.COM

SPLICE

SECOM

HUSH
黑沙海灘/PRAIA DE HAC SA/HAC SA BEACH
沙灘音樂會/CONCERT
恭碩良 / 盧凱彤 /
KINOCO HOTEL /
SUPPER MOMENT /
BREAK THE RULES /
DE-AQUA/ ACHUN /
FORGET THE G /
SCAMPER /
80&TAL / 草莓皇國 /
WHYOCEANS /

SH
/FULL MUSIC/2017
ELLO NICO /
/ STREETGUNS /
BOMBEIROS /
YSER/CROSSLINE /
SUMMER /
E CASTE / 六道母 /
AO + VJ MIGUEL /
E FUNK /
hush!
HUSH
黑沙海灘/PRAIA DE HAC-SÁ/HAC SA BEACH 30/4-01/5
hush!

HUSH
CONCERTO NA PRAIA / FULL MUSIC / 2017
HUSH
CONCERTO NA PRAIA / FULL MUSIC / 2017
13:00-14:30
BREAK THE RULES (珠海)
DE-AQUA (澳門)
其他體驗

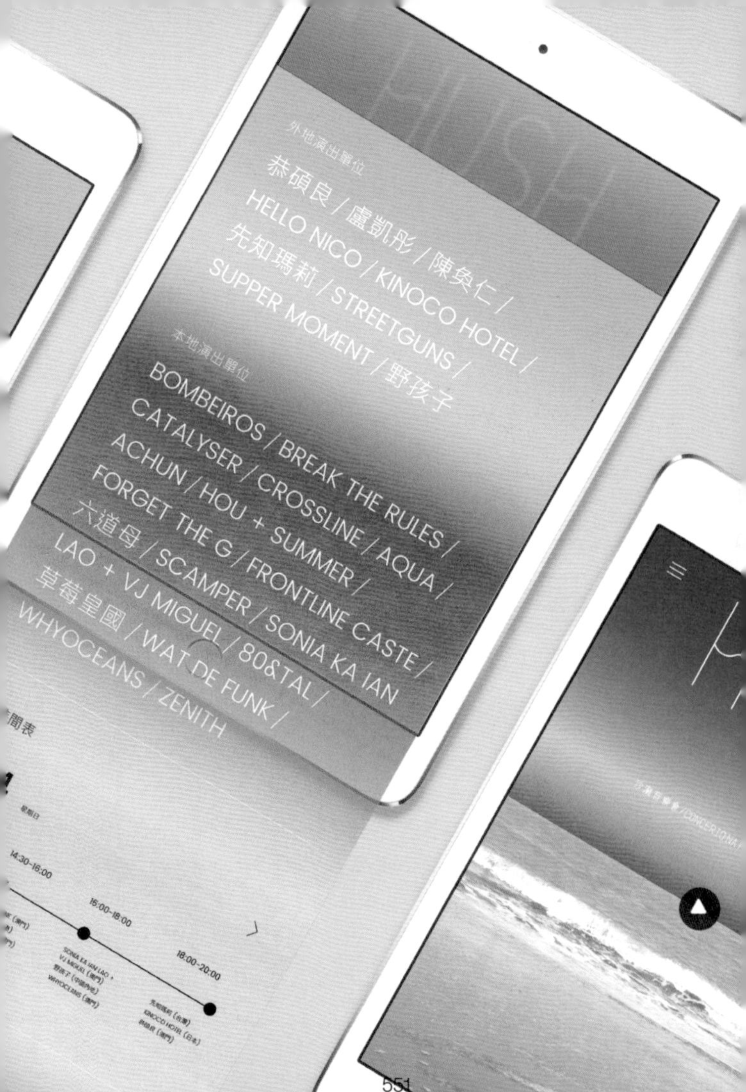
外地演出單位
恭碩良 / 盧凱彤 / 陳奐仁 /
HELLO NICO / KINOCO HOTEL /
先知瑪莉 / STREETGUNS /
SUPPER MOMENT / 野孩子
本地演出單位
BOMBEIROS / BREAK THE RULES /
CATALYSER / CROSSLINE / AQUA /
ACHUN / HOU + SUMMER /
FORGET THE G / FRONTLINE CASTE /
六道母 / SCAMPER / SONIA KA IAN
LAO + VJ MIGUEL / 80&TAL /
草莓皇國 / WAT DE FUNK /
WHYOCEANS / ZENITH
14:30-16:00
16:00-18:00
18:00-20:00

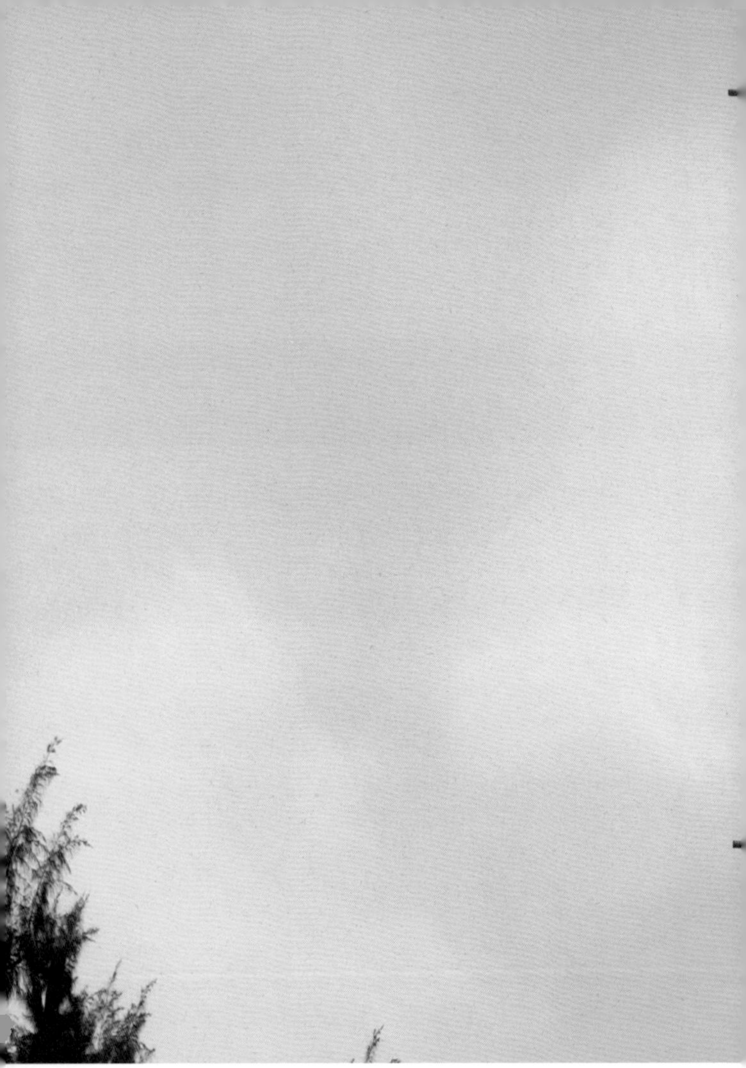

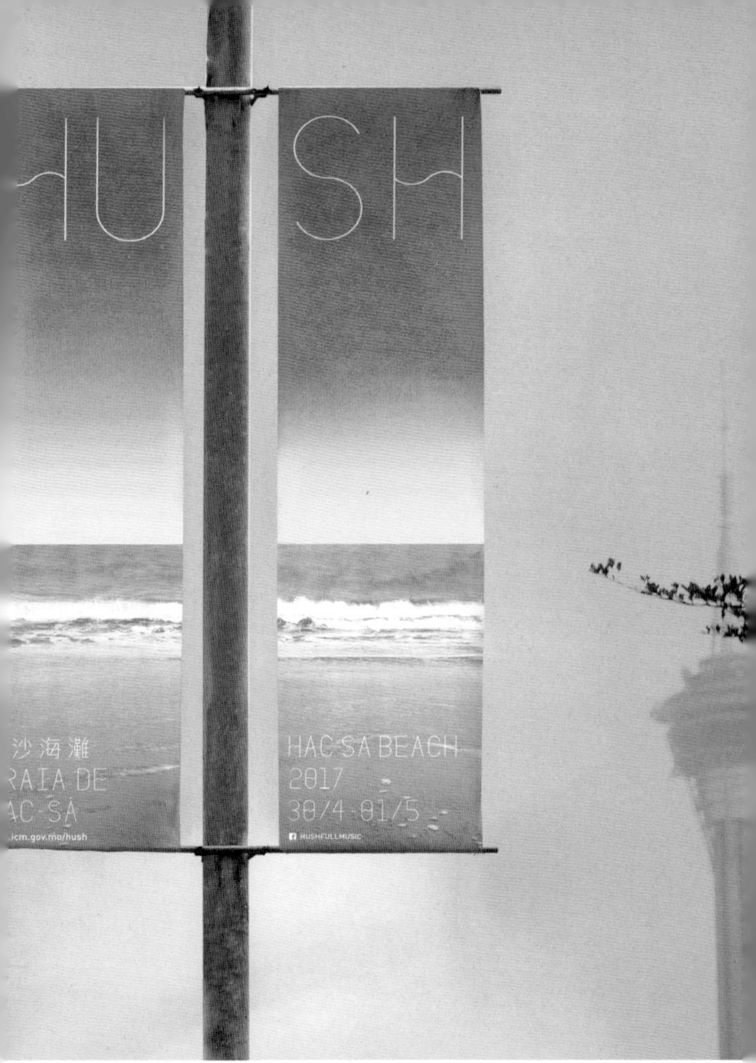
HU
SH
沙海灘
RAIA DE
AC-SÁ
.icm.gov.mo/hush
HAC SA BEACH
2017
30/4-01/5
HUSHFULLMUSIC

HUS

KINOCO
PER MOMENT
六道母 L
SCAM
JUN KUNG

WAT DE FUN
TOMO
CATALYSER

Mobilier
Art de la table
Food equipment
pour l'événement
aktuel.fr
AKTUEL
Comptoir
des bons espaces
Mobilier
Art de la table
Food equipment
pour l'événement
aktuel.fr
AK
TU
EL
Comptoir
des bons espaces
Mobilier
Art de la table
Food equipment
pour l'événement
aktuel.fr
A
KTU
EL
Comptoir
des bons espaces
Mobilier
Art de la table
Food equipment
pour l'événement
aktuel.fr
AKTUEL
Comptoir
des bons espaces

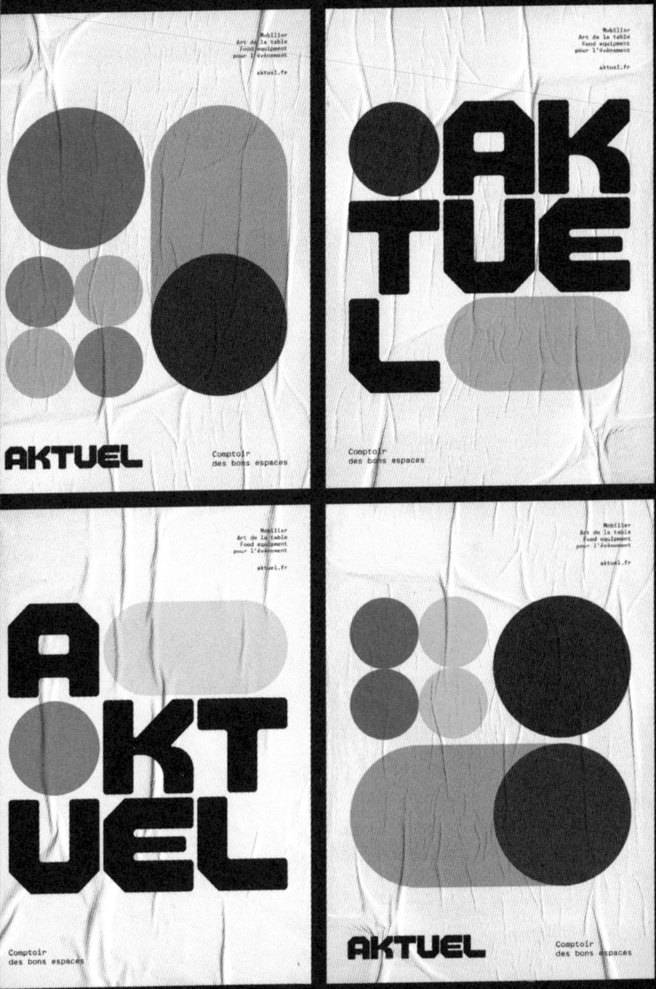
Mobilier
Art de la table
Food equipment
pour l'événement
aktuel.fr
AKTUEL
Comptoir
des bons espaces
Mobilier
Art de la table
Food equipment
pour l'événement
aktuel.fr
AK
TUE
L
Comptoir
des bons espaces
Mobilier
Art de la table
Food equipment
pour l'événement
aktuel.fr
A
KT
UEL
Comptoir
des bons espaces
Mobilier
Art de la table
Food equipment
pour l'événement
aktuel.fr
AKTUEL
Comptoir
des bons espaces

AKTUEL
AKTUEL
Comptoir
des bons espaces.

Mai – ZA les Glaises
Cedex
9 30 30
2 30 30
aktuel.fr
SAS Aktuel · Capital : 1 614 300€
RCS : Evry 444 507 506 – APE : 77297
FR 41 444 507 506 – SIRET 444 507 506 00022
Palaiseau, le 14 décembre 2018
bone de nos prestation : ensemble, des pistes
l, on est fier de notre style : coup d'oeil
s mobiliers, grand choix de coloris, look
prit chaleureux, toujours actuels...
mobilier qui se passe de déco! Chez Aktuel on
ne. On concoit nos mobilier de manière à ce
ent le plus léger possible afin de ne pas
santé de nos équipes ou de nos clients qui
le matériel. Cela contribue à réduire
arbone de toutes les livraisons.
, on a de l'expérience. On veille donc à
et vous proposer des produits robustes
ous offrons une seconde vie lorsque nous
s nos gammes. Et c'est vous qui en tirez le
l, on a à coeur de proposer le meilleur
meilleur prix. C'est pour cela que l'on
s mobiliers empilables afin de gagner de la
les camions et ainsi réduire vos coûts de
et l'impact carbone en livraison et en
notre bonus écologique déduit de votre facture
e livraison et reprise. Contactez nous pour en
s.
Marc Dupuis,
Directeur des Opérations
A
K
T
U
A
U
KT
E
AKTUEL
Mobilier
Art de la table
Food equipment
pour l'évènement
Comptoir
des bons espaces.
aktuel.fr

AKTUEL
Comptoir
des bons espaces
Mobilier
Art de la table
Food equipment
pour l'évènement
AKTUEL
Comptoir
des bons espaces
Mobilier
Art de la table
Food equipment
pour l'évènement

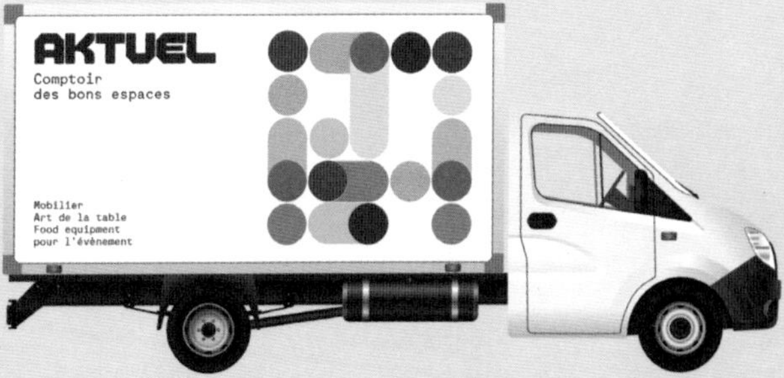
AKTUEL
Comptoir
des bons espaces
Mobilier
Art de la table
Food equipment
pour l'évènement

U
A
KT
E
L
AKTUEL

quila
Alex

AKTUEL
Comptoir
des bons espaces

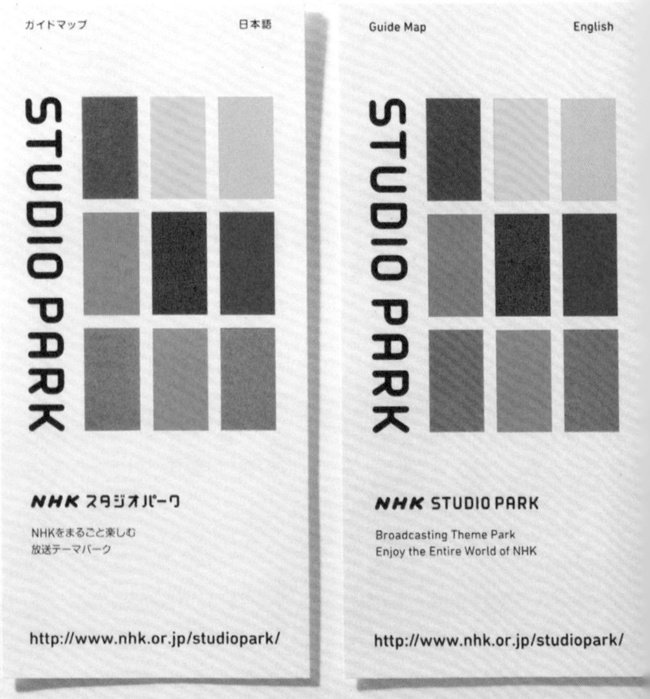
ガイドマップ
日本語
STUDIO PARK
NHK スタジオパーク
NHKをまるごと楽しむ
放送テーマパーク
http://www.nhk.or.jp/studiopark/
Guide Map
English
STUDIO PARK
NHK STUDIO PARK
Broadcasting Theme Park
Enjoy the Entire World of NHK
http://www.nhk.or.jp/studiopark/

导游图
中文
STUDIO PARK
NHK STUDIO PARK
享受NHK的全部
放送主题公园
http://www.nhk.or.jp/studiopark/
가이드맵
한국어
STUDIO PARK
NHK STUDIO PARK
NHK를 마음껏 즐길 수 있는
방송 테마 파크
http://www.nhk.or.jp/studiopark/

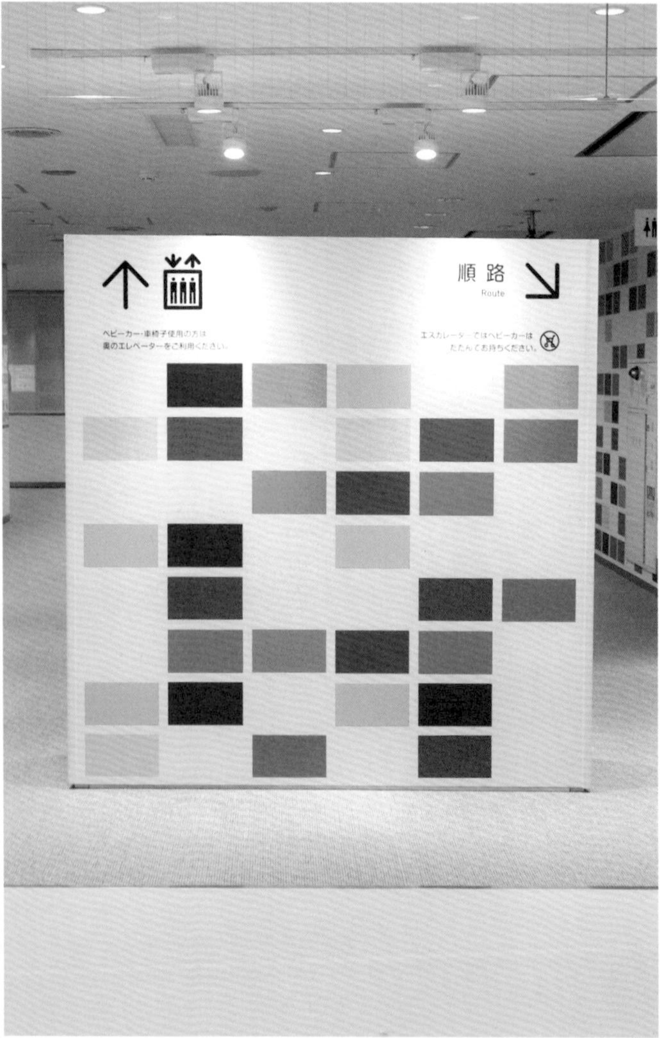

ベビーカー・車椅子使用の方は
奥のエレベーターをご利用ください。
順 路
Route
エスカレーターではベビーカーは
たたんでお持ちください。

天に舞
Dance
of
STUDIO PARK

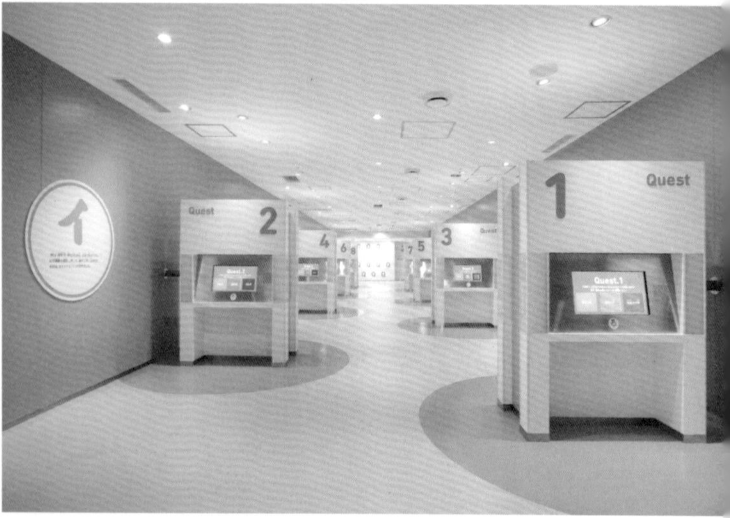
イ
Quest
2
Quest.2
4
6
8
7
5
3
Quest
1
Quest
Quest.1

から!を探してみよう
09
21
13
08

STUDIO PARK NEWS
10
スタジオパークNEWS
STUDIO PARK NEWS
あなたも番組スタッフに！
報道スタジオでニュースを作ってみよう

アフレコスタジオ
REC
STUDIO B
STUDIO C
STUDIO A
STUDIO B
STUDIO C

Triennale Design Museum
Triennale Design Museum
TDM 5:
GRAFICA
ITALIANA

eriodici
/ Magazines
il manifesto
il manifesto

Gariba
Dow Jo
Budej
Zukun
menti di
ialità compositiva

Pubblicità
Sicilia avanti
con i comunisti
e con l'unità
della sinistra
POLITICA 1

I GIOVANI REPUBBLICANI
CONTRO IL CONCORDATO
per la pace contro il terrorismo

Il prodotto
in scena
Packaging alimentare:
sistema ed emozione
/ Food packaging:

/ Packaging
Imballaggi
Carta per imballaggio: texture e invenzione
Packaging: modularità visiva e branding

the
gourmet
tea
QUICHE de
ALHO PORO
SALADA

the
gourmet
tea
QUICHE de
SALADA

"Colour is the ground base of our work. From all possible points of view — scientific, aesthetic, physiologic — it is either the medium or the message of our work."

WINES
WHITE WINES
LAVIÑA CATALUÑA
CHARDONNAY SOUTH AFRICA
SAVIGNON BLANK CHILE
PINOT GRIGIO ITALY 5,00£ 7,00£ 19,00£
SAVIGNON BLANK N. ZEALAND
CHABLIS FRANCE 6,50£ 8,00£
RED WINES
LAVIÑA CATALUÑA
SHIRAZ SOUTH AFRICA
MERLOT CHILE
MALBEC MERLOT
CHIANTI ITALY 6,00£ 7,50£ 22,00£
RIOJA SPAIN 6,00£ 7,50£ 22,00£
ROSE WINES
DUDLEY'S STONE
SPARKLING AND CHAMPAGNES
PROSECCO
PERRIER JOUET
SHOTS OF SPIRITS ARE 25 ml
no-one.co.uk

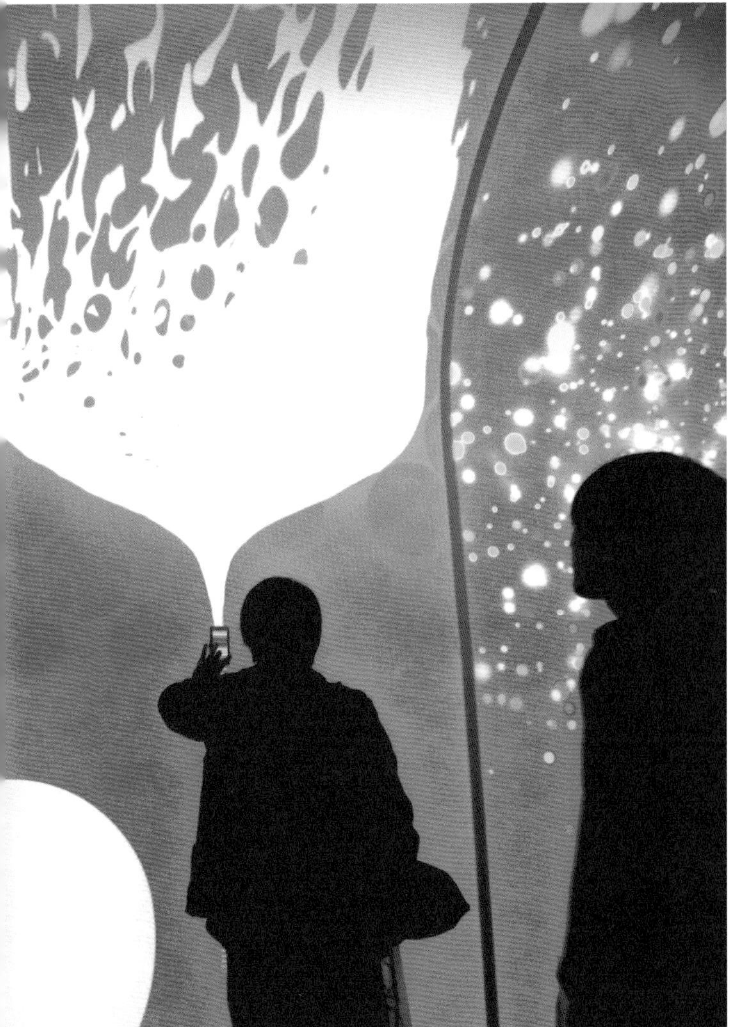

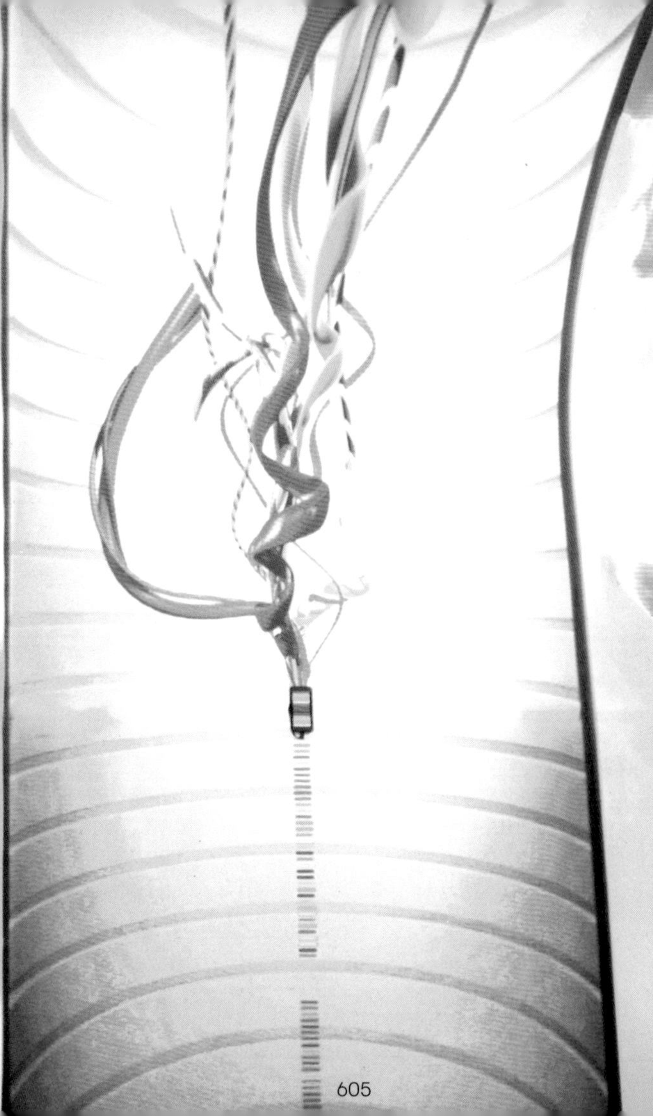

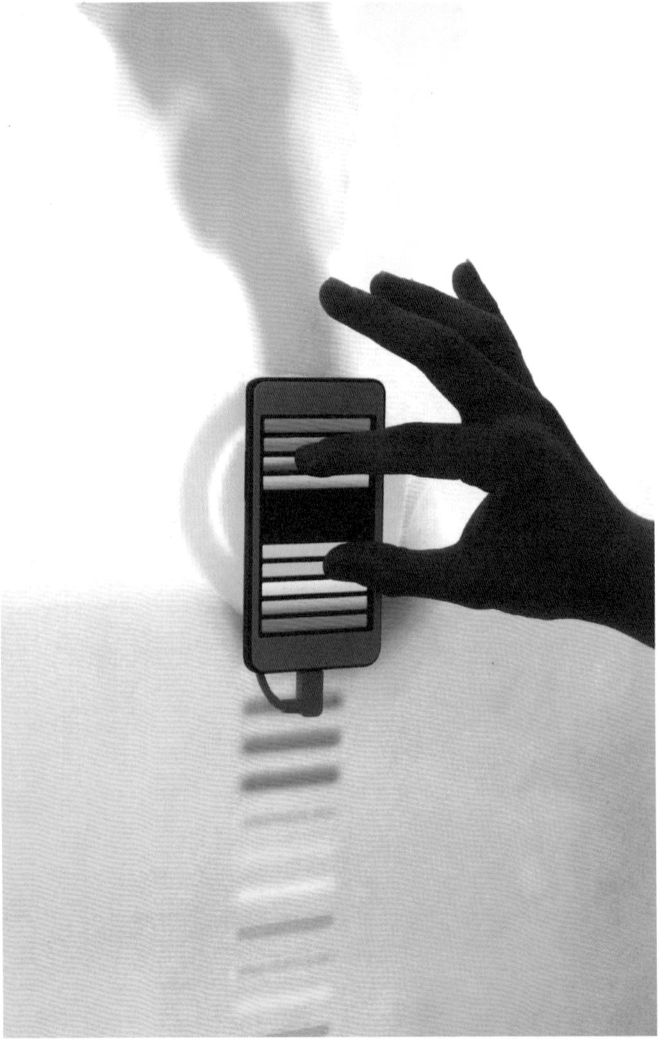

INDEX

010–013

Vrrb
FRVR

Client: Vrrb Interactive

014–019

Charitea
Susanna Nygren Barrett

Design & Art Direction: The Studio
Still Life Photography: Erik Lefvander
Product Photography: Patrik Lindell

020–023

Toscatti
Anagrama

Client: Wagner Brands
Photography: Carogafoto

024–029

Jack Kerouac Book Covers
Torsten Lindsø Andersen

030

Beyond Blue
Holt

Client: Beyond Blue

031

Polaroid Exhibition Collateral
Holt

Client: Centre for Contemporary Photography (CCP) Melbourne

276–283

Let It Blow 2019

Hey

Client: Hey
Photography: Enric Badrinas

284–289

NY FASHION WEEK

Paul Sangwoo Kim

Client: Art Center College of Design
Special Credits: Clive Piercy

290–299

Pride Toronto

Bruce Mau Design

Client: Pride Toronto
Agency: Bruce Mau Design
Managing Director: Tom Keogh
Creative Director: Luis Coderque
Associate Creative Director: Michael Mavian
Senior Designer: Sebastian Rodriguez
Senior Production Designer: Steven McLellan
Designer: Brooke Mackey, Davis Scherer
Account Manager: Lauren Grudzinski
Account Coordinator: Karan Singh
Animator 'Launch Video': Demmy Kyoung
Animator 'Programming Video': By The Booth

300–305

GF Smith

SEA

Client: GF Smith
Illustration: FIELD

380–383 **PANTONE® PLUS SERIES Posters**
Base Design

Client: PANTONE®
Photography / Props: Maurice Scheltens, Liesbeth Abbens

384–387 **Ink Films Identity**
R.I.S. Projects

Client: Ink Films

388–391 **Vicente Aleixandre Library Visual Identity & Signage System**
Txell Gràcia Design Studio

Client: Badia del Vallès City Council

392–397 **Inna Art Space 10**
Transwhite Studio

398–403 **Pony Bar Monthly Programme**
La Tigre

Client: Pony Bar

404–409 **The Beardshop**
I LIKE BIRDS

Client: The Beardshop
Website Coding: Thomas Lempa

480–489

Opium Visual Language
Andstudio

Photography: Martyna Jovaisaite, Vismante Ruzgaite

491–499

Make Waves
This is Pacifica

PRO Shaper: Pedro Vieira / Feelflows
Video Director: Le-Joy
Surfer Photography: Le-Joy
Gallery Photography: NUMO / Nuno Moreira

500–505

Eating by Design
Raw Color

Client: Premsela
Curation: Marije Vogelzang, Koos Flinterman
Project Management: Floor van Ast

506–511

On Strike
Raw Color

Client: Ontour

512–513

The Moment in A Springs
Daisy Balloon

Client: Osaka Takashimaya
Photography: Hiroshi Manaka
Retouching: Yoshiaki Sakurai
Make-up: Ken Nakano
Hair: Koji Ichikawa
Styling: Koji Oyamada

514–517

Wear(e) the Future

Zim&Zou

Client: FRAC Nord-Pas-de-Calais

518–523

COLORPLANE

Midnight Rendez-Vous

Graphic Design: Alexandre Delo Rivière
Photography: Jules Faure

524–527

Jelly & Light

Le Creative

Photography: Fabrice Fouillet
Lighting: Nessimo by Artémide
Special Credits: Artémide (Castore), Ionna Vautrin (Binic)

528–533

The Rainbow Thieves

Fabio Novembre, Dino Cicchetti, Giuseppe Modeo

Client: ARTCOM Media Group
Production: Driade
Photography: Pasquale Formisano

534–539

Bread & Butter NOW

Craig & Karl

Client: Zalando

540–543 **Colourful Crossing**
Camille Walala

Client: Better Bankside, Transport for London

---

544 **Camille Walala x Industry City**
Camille Walala

Client: WantedDesign Brooklyn
Photography: Courtesy of Image City

545–547 **Dream Come True**
Camille Walala

Client: Splice

548–557 **HUSH FULL MUSIC 2017**
untitledmacao

558–565 **Aktuel**
Brand Brothers

566–573 **NHK Studio Park**
ujidesign

Client: Japan Broadcasting Corporation (NHK)
Direction: NHK Enterprise Inc.
Architecture: Takashi Nakahara, Tsuyoshi Tanio
Photography: ©NHK

574–585

TDM5: GRAFICA ITALIANA

Fabio Novembre, Dino Cicchetti,
Patrizio Mozzicafreddo, Giorgio Terraneo

Client: Triennale di Milano
Graphic Design: Leftloft
Photography: Pasquale Formisano

586–591

The Gourmet Tea — Cidade Jardim

Alan Chu

Client: The Gourmet Tea
Team: Thiago Moretti
Photography: Djan Chu

592–595

DreamBox

carnovsky

Client: Elisabeth Leriche

596–599

La Selva – RGB: The Black Series

carnovsky

Client: Jaguarshoes Collective
Photography: Jeff Metal

600–607

docomo Palette UI 2011

TORAFU ARCHITECTS, WOW

Client: docomo
Production: Taiyo Kogyo, DENTSU
Programming: RaNa design, WOW
Sound & Lighting: Prism
Sound Source: WOW, Masato Hatanaka
Photography: WOW

BIOGRAPHY

Anagrama

www.anagrama.com

With a strong focus in brand development and positioning, Anagrama's services span across the entire branding spectrum from strategic consulting to logotype and peripheral design. Based in Monterrey, Mexico City, Tokyo, and the US, its multidisciplinary team also creates objects, spaces, and multimedia experiences.

PP. 020–023, 242, 332–337

Andersen, Torsten Lindsø

instagram.com/torsten.rasmus

Torsten Lindsø Andersen was a student at The Royal Danish Academy of Fine Arts before growing his career as a designer within the branding and visual communication industry. Led by his passion in typography, he currently heads the type design department at Kontrapunkt.

PP. 024–029

Andstudio

andstudio.lt

Based in Vilnius, Andstudio is a branding studio that specialises in visual identities, graphic systems, printed materials, and web design. It is driven in its search for originality and meaningful connections between strategy and design, design and business, and business and customer.

PP. 192–205, 480–489

Anymade Studio

anymadestudio.com

Set up in 2009 by Petr Cabalka and Filip Nerad who are based in Prague, Anymade Studio specialises in visual communication inspired by music, contemporary fashion, and the visual arts. Each project is approached playfully with an eye for originality and detail as well as an emphasis on individuaity, function, and quality.

PP. 422–423, 474–477

---

artless Inc.

www.artless.co.jp

Establised in 2000 by Shun Kawakami, artless Inc. is a global branding agency that conducts design with architecture. Working across a variety of touchpoints, the Tokyo-based studio has won several awards from prestigious design organisations along the way, including Cannes and D&AD.

PP. 446–451

Ascend Studio

www.ascendstudio.co.uk

An independent full-service branding and design agency based in London, Ascend Studio adopts a thoughtful and methodical approach in research, positioning, strategy, and graphic communication. Its work is defined by a clear vision expressed through concepts that are strategically led and objectively measured against business goals.

PP. 156–159

Ataz, Andrea

andreaataz.com

A graphic design graduate from Murcia, Andrea Ataz received the Leonardo da Vinci scholarship for an internship in Belgium. Growing her career both as a freelancer and an employee over the years, her work has since been published by notable annual design publications.

PP. 238–241

Atelier Neşe Nogay

ateliernesenogay.com

Atelier Neşe Nogay is an Istanbul-based creative studio that was formed in 2010. It adopts a passionate approach across a wide range of sectors that include art, culture, fashion, food, and beauty. The studio stands out with its simple yet sophisticated visual aesthetics – collaborating with a variety of local and international clients.

PP. 452–457

Atipus

www.atipus.com

Barcelona-based graphic communication studio Atipus specialises in corporate identities, art direction, packaging design, editorial design, and web development. Built in 1998, it has since been awarded by several national and European design organisations due to its creative and conceptual work.

PP. 416–421

ATMO Designstudio & FELD | studio for digital crafts

atmodesign.de / www.feld.studio

ATMO and FELD are design studios that leverage on relentless, precise, and high-speed computational processes or custom machinery to create memorable work. Both studios believe in the power of collaboration and specialise in thought-provoking ideas that are also aesthetically pleasing.

PP. 122–129

Avant Post

www.avantpost.fr

Avant Post is an art direction studio based in Paris. Founded by Quentin Berthelot, Johan Mossé, and Adrien Weibel, it specialises in images for printed and digital media. Its portfolio features thoughtful type design and colour combinations.

PP. 464–469

Balancer Production

facebook.com/balancerproduction

Balancer Production is a design brand and collective set up by a group of graduates from the National Taiwan University of Science and Technology. It seeks to find the balance between reality and one's dreams by creating products with aesthetic and commercial value – making life more fun in the process.

PP. 344–351

Barrett, Susanna Nygren

the-studio.se

Susanna Nygren Barrett is the creative director and co-founder of The Studio in Stockholm with Mattias Börjesson. Besides leading strategic design and branding assignments for local and international clients, she is also a guest lecturer and holds workshops at various design schools.

PP. 014–019

Base Design

www.basedesign.com

Base is an international network of studios led by creatives in Brussels, New York, Geneva, and Melbourne. It works with clients on 360° branding solutions that encompass the traditional, physical, and digital worlds – building iconic brands by communicating purpose, value, and vision.

PP. 132–139, 380–383

Błażewicz, David

www.davidblazewicz.com

David Błażewicz is a graphic designer based in Warsaw who specialises in visual identities, editorial design, and print. He focuses on working with typography in most of his projects as he considers it to be one of the most important basic elements of visual design.

PP. 206–209

Bleed

www.bleed.no

With offices in Oslo and Vienna, Bleed is an independent design consultancy that creates brands and experiences through concept development, art direction, graphic design, and service design. By questioning the definition of design, it aims to challenge today's conventions around art, visual language, media, and identity.

PP. 220–227

Bræstrup, Thomas

www.thomasbraestrup.com

Thomas Bræstrup is a graphic designer who graduated from the Royal Danish Academy of Fine Arts. Currently offering his expertise at Twentyten Studio in Copenhagen, he designs posters, visual identities, publications, websites, and packaging with a passion for typography and a simple yet conceptual approach.

PP. 228–231

Brand Brothers

www.brandbrothers.fr

Brand Brothers specialises in brand strategy and visual identities. Working from Paris and Toulouse for emerging startups and established companies, it is driven by curiosity, transmission, reflection, and new challenges to produce useful, intelligible, and beautiful designs for the people.

PP. 062–067, 558–565

Brighten the Corners

brightenthecorners.com

Known for its simple but concept-driven work, Brighten the Corners is an award-winning design studio in London and Aschaffenburg run by Frank Philippin and Billy Kiosoglou. It happily switches between public, corporate, and cultural environments in offering its graphic design services across a variety of platforms.

PP. 260–263

Browns

www.brownsdesign.com

Since its inception in 1998, Browns has been producing thoughtful work with a purity of form for esteemed clients all around the world. The studio has received notable awards and recognition along the way, including Creative Review magazine's 'Design Studio of the Year 2011' title.

PP. 161–163

Bruce Mau Design

www.brucemaudesign.com

Based in Toronto, Bruce Mau Design is a multidisciplinary design firm that works with organisations shaping the future of their respective industries worldwide. It seeks to identify the purpose behind a company to create a generative and sustainable brand narrative – bringing compelling ideas to life to help businesses grow.

PP. 290–299

Bureau Collective

www.bureaucollective.ch

Bureau Collective is a multidisciplinary creative studio founded by Ollie Schaich and Ruedi Zürcher in 2009. Based in St.Gallen, the team works with a wide range of clients through the spectrum of graphic design, mainly focusing on projects within the cultural fields.

PP. 118–121

Carl Nas Associates

carlnas.com

Using design as a global language that can communicate needs instantly, Carl Nas Associates is a London-based consultancy that believes in the idea that 80 percent of all sensory impressions are visual. Through its digital, motion, spatial, and print work, it creates outcomes that are bespoke and impossible to copy across different mediums and industries.

PP. 432–435

---

carnovsky

www.carnovsky.com

carnovsky is an artist and designer duo based in Milan comprising Francesco Rugi and Silvia Quintanilla. Besides conceptualising and designing experimental exhibitiions, they also create relevant products that breathe life into their ideas.

PP. 592–599

Chu, Alan

www.chu.arq.br

Alan Chu is an architect and urbanist who graduated from Mackenzie Presbyterian University. He was a partner at Chu & Kato Architects from 2004 to 2010 when he joined Isay Weinfeld's office design team. His work has been recognised and awarded in Brazil and abroad.

PP. 586–591

---

communion w

www.communion-w.com

communion w actively analyses and strategises for ever-changing market situations. With originality and market insights being its strengths, the Hong Kong-based company owns a remarkable portfolio of advertising and graphic design work. For the projects featured, it collaborated with designer Gertrude Wong, who currently leads Studio Bien Bien.

PP. 102–111

Craig & Karl

www.craigandkarl.com

Craig & Karl live in different parts of the world but collaborate to create bold work that is often filled with simple messages executed in a thoughtful and humorous way. Besides working with major international brands, they have also had their projects exhibited in renowned institutions like the Musée de la Publicité and the Museum of the Moving Image.

PP. 534–539, 608–613

Daikoku Design Institute

daikoku.ndc.co.jp

Formed in 2011 by Daigo Daikoku, the award-winning Daikoku Design Institute excels at simple, clear, and bold concept ideations as well as design executions. It focuses on art, style, and technology while collaborating with socially-conscious entities to create new value.

PP. 036–043

Daisy Balloon

daisyballoon.com

Daisy Balloon is the collaborative effort between artist Rie Hosokai and art director/graphic designer Takashi Kawada. Since forming in 2008, they have produced many balloon artworks based on ideas of perception — fascinating audiences through the intricacy of detail that suggests architectural qualities. The duo sets out to achieve harmony with its surroundings through its projects.

PP. 512–513

Edgar Bąk Studio

www.edgarbak.info

Edgar Bąk is a Polish visual communication designer who avoids big gestures. By orienting himself to the tools at hand and their specificity, he focuses on the visual grammar and project brief – working towards the final outcome as if solving a mathematical equation. His eponymous studio focuses primarily on visual identity design.

PP. 048–053

ENZED

www.enzed.ch

ENZED is a design consultancy in Lausanne that specialises in print, corporate identities, and editorial design. Founded in 2001 and currently run by Nicolas and Mélanie Zentner, the team is driven by a passion for typography and minimal Swiss design.

PP. 470–471

Established

www.establishednyc.com

Established was founded in 2007 by Sam O'Donahue and Rebecca Jones. A full-service boutique agency, it offers graphic design, branding, art direction, and package design services backed by a track record of creating highly successful, award-winning global brands for a wide range of clients.

PP. 254–259

FRVR

Set up in Prague, FRVR was a multidisciplinary graphic studio that specialised in brand creation, visual identities, custom typography, iconography, and character design. Founded by Jan Vranovský and Dan Friedlaender, its approach was rooted in the strict, simple, and rational style of 1960s and 1970s graphic design.

PP. 010–013

Fundamental

www.fundamental-studio.com

Fundamental is a Hong Kong-based creative studio. Its team and core philosophy is driven by the belief that substantial communication is the key to creating and providing the best design solutions for clients across the art, cultural, F&B, and entertainment sectors.

PP. 436–445

Golden, Chris

thestudiogold.net

Chris Golden is a multidisciplinary designer who utilises illustration, collage, and mixed media to create contextual pieces. Currently based in Melbourne, he founded The Studio Gold, a client-based 3D content studio that has collaborated with brands such as Nike, Adult Swim, Dolby, and Puma to produce creative multimedia installations.

PP. 172, 338–339

Grandpeople

Located in Bergen, Grandpeople was a multidisciplinary design studio established by Christian Bergheim, Magnus Voll Mathiassen, and Magnus Helgesen. It offered services in graphic design, art direction, and illustration for clients across various industries such as Nike, Converse, and Microsoft.

PP. 310–311

Helmo

helmo.fr

Founded in Montreuil by Thomas Couderc and Clément Vauchez who first met in 1997, Helmo specialises in graphic design for cultural institutions and festivals in France. It is driven by 'the ability to draw strong and coherent universes while preserving a place for permanent variations or escapements'.

PP. 272–275

Hey

heystudio.es

A multidisciplinary design studio based in Barcelona, Hey works on graphic design and illustration projects for clients around the world. It is driven by the profound conviction that good design means combining content, functionality, graphical expression, and strategy.

PP. 188–191, 276–283, 458–463

Heydays

heydays.no

In shaping what is next, Heydays helps to launch and grow meaningful companies through brand strategy and development as well as digital product design. In every one of its projects, the Norwegian studio strives to find balance between the idea, function, and aesthetics.

PP. 366–369

Holt

holtdesign.com.au

Holt is a Sydney-based design practice with an established philosophy and fundamental belief in the role that design plays in communication within modern society. It offers brand-building services and award-winning design expertise that are matched to the individual requirements of each client.

PP. 030–031, 264–268

HUMAN

www.byhuman.mx

Founded by Alejandro Flores in 2016, HUMAN is an independent design firm based in Mexico City. It offers a wide spectrum of branding services, in which all aspects are carefully optimised to deliver a project that effectively establishes its clients' desired positioning and increases their brand value.

PP. 152–155

Hybrid Design

hybrid-design.com

Hybrid Design in San Francisco is a collection of people who love intersections in cultures, genres, tastes, industries, techniques, forms, materials, personalities, and ideas. Its team members liken themselves to problem solvers, improvisors, artists, craftspeople, thinkers, adventurers, and doers who are completely in love with the minutia of typography, materials, and experience.

PP. 074–081

I LIKE BIRDS

www.ilikebirds.de

Located in Hamburg, I LIKE BIRDS is a creative studio run by designers André Gröger and Susanne Kehrer. The team enjoys experimenting with mediums to develop customised solutions and transform various types of information into a visual language that conveys the content in a fluid, effective manner.

PP. 404–409

Ibanyez, Albert

www.dosgrapas.com

Albert Ibanyez is a graphic designer who is passionate about colours and typography. He runs Barcelona-based studio DosGrapas to help clients improve their way of communicating with efficient, fun, and unique projects in the form of editorial design, web design, and spaces.

PP. 340–343

JJAAKK

JJAAKK was the work alias of Jesse Kirsch, the middle sibling of three brothers who all share the same initials. A School of Visual Arts graduate, the Portland-based award-winning designer was known to work on packaging, posters, and visual identities – creating bold and fun design solutions.

PP. 032–035, 068–071

Kim, Derek

www.approvedsf.com

Derek Kim is a designer based in San Francisco who specialises in identity, typography, and poster design for cultural establishments and small startup companies. He also initiates personal projects that allow his creativity to expand into different sectors besides design.

P. 269

Kim, Paul Sangwoo

A graduate in branding and motion graphics, Los Angeles-based Paul Sangwoo Kim designs for television, film, UI, branding, commercials, and documentaries. After starting his career at Prologue Films under Kyle Cooper, he has since built his portfolio and skills at a variety of studios.

PP. 284–289

Kitty McCall

www.kittymccall.com

Kitty McCall is a design label focused on joyful patterns. It all started in 2011 when founder Catherine Nice began creating unique fabric and art prints that would inject interest and intrigue to the home. Her work is inspired by abstraction, asymmetry, strong shapes, geometric detailing, and bold colours.

PP. 306–309

Kurppa Hosk

kurppahosk.com

Kurppa Hosk is a diverse team of design thinkers and doers in Stockholm and New York. It collaborates with brave organisations by using business, brand, and experience design to inform and inspire meaningful progression. Its business artistry combines commercial and behavioral research, insights, and analyses with boldness, beauty, technology, and craft.

PP. 312, 318–323

La Tigre

latigre.net

La Tigre is an independent studio based in Milan that believes in timeless ideas. Founded in 2009, it specialises in refined visual design solutions and data visualisation for local and global clients. Its team converts ideas, visions, and inspirations into a system of visual expressions that elevate brands.

PP. 398–403

Laliberté, Simon

behance.net/slaliberte / bangbang.ca

Simon Laliberté set up Montreal-based studio BangBang in 2012 to unite graphic design and screen-printing in the same entrepreneurial structure. More than just a workshop for paper and textiles, it is also a design agency that specialises in visual identities, packaging, and publishing for a mixed clientele.

PP. 232–235

Le Creative

lecreative.paris

Dedicated to art direction, photography, and design, Le Creative is a Paris-based studio that was built by Mathieu Missiaen and Julien Morin. With a focus on fashion, design, contemporary art, and architecture, the team is committed to originality, quality, and hand-crafted work that is fundamentally multidisciplinary and driven by research.

PP. 524–527

Lee, Ken-tsai

behance.net/kentsailee

Ken-tsai Lee has earned an international reputation as a designer, educator, and curator in his role as an assistant professor at Taiwan TECH, a representative of Type Directors Club and Art Directors Club New York. His work has been recognised by numerous leading design organisations and publications.

PP. 094–101

Liefhebber, Nick

www.liefhebber.biz

Nick Liefhebber is a Dutch graphic designer who believes in solving problems with creative ideas and design. By distilling the essence of the message, his work reflects the fact that every story is unique. Inspired by patterns and rhythms, Nick also uses the associative powers of shapes and materials to communicate at an intuitive level through his illustrations.

PP. 140–143

Liquorice Studio

liquorice.com.au

Formed in 2008 by Scott Bonanno, Liquorice is a team of talented individuals whose vast collective experience covers just about every type of communication design service. Currently a partner of global creative agency Iris, the Melbourne-based studio specialises in brand and identity design for print and the web for clients in various sectors.

PP. 472–473

Midnight Rendez-Vous

Midnight Rendez-Vous was a fashion label known for its eccentric pieces. Its 'wild and crazy' creator/designer, Renaud Duc, drew inspiration from the clash between materials to delight club kids. Each outfit exuded a unique, cool, and extravagant vibe for 'quirky and stylish' nights.

PP. 518–523

Mind Design

www.minddesign.co.uk

Established in 1999, Mind Design is a design consultancy in London that specialises in the development of visual identities. Run by Holger Jacobs and Virgile Janssen, it works with start-ups and established international companies by combining hands-on craftsmanship, conceptual thinking, and intuition.

PP. 352–355

My Wet Calvin

mywetcalvin.com / soundcloud.com/mywebcalvin

Comprising architect-designer Leonidas Ikonomou and pre-school educator Aris Nikolopoulos, My Wet Calvin is a noise-pop duo from Greece. Besides taking part in music-related visual and design projects, they have also been involved in commercial work that has earned them recognition.

PP. 072–073

Novembre, Fabio

www.novembre.it

Born in 1966 with a background in movie direction and architecture, Fabio Novembre founded his own studio in 1994. Besides exhibiting his work at numerous international platforms like the Triennale Design Museum and the Italian Pavillion at the 2009 Shanghai Expo on behalf of the Commune of Milan, he also designs products inspired by his passions.

PP. 528–533, 574–585

Palatre et Leclere Architectes

Led by Olivier Palatre and Tiphaine Leclere in 2006, Paris-based Palatre et Leclere Architectes were involved in projects of varying natures for public and private clients. The duo were recognised by Le Moniteur in 2011 for their work on the Second Chance school.

PP. 614–619

Peltan-Brosz

peltan-brosz.com

Founded in 2011, Budapest-based Peltan-Brosz has grown into a reputable studio by defining unique visions and developing a trademark style through intensive visual research, experimentation, and teamwork. Always hungry for new ideas, the team's goal is to deliver progressive and tailored solutions by gaining maximum insights into every assignment.

PP. 356–365

Pentagram

www.pentagram.com

The world's largest independent design consultancy as of 2019, Pentagram was set up in 1972. The firm specialises in graphic design, industrial design, and architecture – producing printed materials, environments, products, and interactive media for a wide range of international clients.

PP. 166–171, 176–181

Podhajsky, Leif

leifpodhajsky.com

Leif Podhajský is a multidisciplinary creative studio that produces cutting-edge imagery, artwork, and creative direction. It aims to push boundaries and communicate engaging ideas based on the exchange between organic systems and new technologies that inspire and stimulate thought.

PP. 112–117

POST

www.deliveredbypost.com

POST is all about creating work that is thoughtful, responsible, and relevant. An agile design and branding studio based in London, it is driven to help businesses with well-crafted answers and intelligent strategic thoughts. The team works collaboratively with clients to communicate each story while consciously applying practices that encourage positive change.

PP. 424–431

Post Projects

postprojects.com

Driven to evolve its craft and honour the legacy of contemporary design, Post Projects is a graphic design and consulting studio located in Vancouver. It believes in the ability of design to tell a story, stir an emotional response, and communicate with a clarity that is more than the sum of its parts.

PP. 182–187, 490

Present & Correct

www.presentandcorrect.com

Since 2009, Present & Correct has been a haven for stationery, paper, and office objects. Its product range is sourced from all over the world, and is mostly inspired by homework, post offices, schools, and vintage collectibles. Through its online shop, it also offers original designs by international designers.

PP. 216–219

R.I.S. Projects

R.I.S. Projects or Revenge is Sweet was a creative studio based in Paris and London. Set up by Lee Owens and Angelique Piliere in 2006, its services included art direction, design, illustration, and consultation across a broad range of applications and mediums.

PP. 384–387

Raw Color

www.rawcolor.nl

Raw Color's work showcases thoughtful treatments of material and colour by mixing graphic design with photography. Headed by Daniera ter Haar and Christoph Brach, research and experiments form the basis of the Eindhoven-based studio's visual language.

PP. 500–511

Resort Studio

resortstudio.ch

Founded in 2012 by Michael Häne and Dieter Glauser who both studied at the Zürich University of the Arts, Resort Studio is a visual communication and graphic design entity that develops sophisticated design solutions with a clear visual language and high standards of design, originality, and precision in execution.

PP. 328–331

Reynolds & Reyner

reynoldsandreyner.com

As one of the most experienced branding agencies in Eastern Europe, Kiev-based Reynolds & Reyner is an authority on what constitutes quality design. With most of its clients being based overseas, the studio knows what it takes to overcome challenges and make a lasting impact from strategy to execution.

PP. 370–379

RISOTTO

www.risottostudio.com

RISOTTO is a riso-print specialist and stationery company led by designer Gabriella Marcella based in Glasgow. Masters of the A3, it produces work for a range of clients – quickly, creatively, and sustainably. The house style is wonderfully playful, as seen across its limited edition products.

PP. 144–151

SEA

www.seadesign.com

SEA is an award-winning brand communications agency working across all media and disciplines based in London. By harnessing creativity and intelligent design to solve complex issues and communicate powerful ideas, it develops compelling visual identities for some of the world's most influential brands and transforms businesses.

PP. 130–131, 300–305

Studio 5•5

www.5-5.paris

Founded by Vincent Baranger, Jean-Sébastien Blanc, Anthony Lebossé, and Claire Renard, 5•5 is an award-winning global design collective based in Paris. It brings together creative collaborators with multidisciplinary backgrounds who follow a comprehensive design approach to offer useful and aspirational objects for as wide an audience as possible.

PP. 054–059

STUDIO BENS

studio-bens.com

STUDIO BENS is an office for graphic design in Berlin that was set up by Jens Ludewig and Benjamin Rheinwald in 2015. With context always being at the foreground of the creative process, it focuses on the cultural and lifestyle sectors to produce a wide range of work.

PP. 164–165

Studio Brave

studiobrave.com.au

Based in Melbourne, Studio Brave builds brands of influence by helping businesses transform and grow. Propelled by a determination to differentiate as well as combine passion with purpose, its guiding vision comes from the studio's name itself, where brave thinking leads to unexpected outcomes.

PP. 313–317

Studio Dumbar

studiodumbar.com

With an innate drive to create outstanding work, Studio Dumbar builds meaningful brands by bringing them from strategy to reality. Part of Dept, an international digital network, its approach is based on pure, simple, and powerful concepts. The award-winning studio in Rotterdam aims to help its clients be seen and appreciated in a cluttered market landscape.

PP. 324–327

Studio Mad Keen

www.mad-keen.co.uk

Founded by designer Ryan Dixon, Studio Mad Keen (formerly Mad Keen Design & Art Direction) is a brand and identity design consultancy based in Surrey. It sets out to convey the true personality of the brands it partners with, backed by over 20 years of industry experience.

PP. 173–175, 270–271

Studio mw

studio-mw.fr

With a focus on original and contemporary solutions, Studio mw is a visual communication and graphic design studio in Paris. Founded and run by Jeanne Moinon, it specialises in printed designs, in addition to artistic collaborations and experimental research.

PP. 478–479

This is Pacifica

www.thisispacifica.com

Pacifica is an independent studio based in Porto. Established in 2007 by Pedro Serrão, Pedro Mesquita, and Filipe Mesquita, it focuses on branding, graphic design, interactive design, packaging, space design, and motion graphics work. The team believes in ideas, solving problems, and embracing opportunities online, offline, and everything else in between.

PP. 491–499

Toormix

www.toormix.com

Toormix is a Barcelona-based studio that seeks to create transversal brand experiences to help businesses connect better with their customers. Using a strategic approach focused on communication, user experience, and innovation, it believes that design goes beyond mere aesthetic value and should be infused into a company's DNA.

PP. 410–415

TORAFU ARCHITECTS

torafu.com

Founded in 2004 by Koichi Suzuno and Shinya Kamuro, TORAFU ARCHITECTS has been involved in a diverse range of projects that cover architectural design, interior design, product design, spatial installations, and filmmaking. Based in Tokyo, the team has received multiple awards including the Design for Asia Grand Award.

PP. 600–607

Transwhite Studio

transwhite.cn

Transwhite Studio was set up in Hangzhou in 2011. A multi-faceted design studio that dabbles in experimental design as well as new communication ideas, its primary focus lies in graphic design. The team's diverse portfolio includes art exhibitions, social events, and cross-disciplinary collaborations.

PP. 044–047, 392–397

Txell Gràcia Design Studio

www.txellgracia.com

After years of experience in Amsterdam, Berlin, and Barcelona, Meritxell Gràcia moved to New Zealand to grow her career and set up her own design studio. She has worked across a wide variety of projects, from corporate identities to packaging and web design to motion and environmental graphics.

PP. 388–391

---

ujidesign

ujidesign.com

Established in 2005 by award-winning art director Yutaka Maeda, ujidesign is a creative studio based in Tokyo. Its range of services span across graphic design, packaging, way-finding, and book design as well as web design and development.

PP. 566–573

untitledmacao

untitledmacao.com

untitledmacao is an award-winning design studio built by two Macao-based designers who specialise in visual identities, web design, as well as wayfinding and signage design. It seeks to impart energy and creativity in all its work through innovation, aesthetics, and the practicality associated with communication, analysis, and positioning.

PP. 082–093, 243–253, 548–557

Walala, Camille

camillewalala.com

Camille Walala is a London-based artist who is also known as a purveyor of positivity, as expressed through the vibrant colours and bold patterns in her work. From the micro to the macro, each piece harnesses optimistic typography and exuberant geometries to create environments that stimulate the senses and inspire joy.

PP. 540–547

Wan, Tim

studiowan.uk

A Best New Blood award-winner at the D&AD in 2011, Tim Wan focuses on information and typographic-driven design solutions. In 2014, he founded Studio Wan, a London-based graphic design studio working on cultural, creative, and commercial projects including visual identities, magazines, books, and other printed matter.

PP. 060–061

yeye weller
yeyeweller.de

An award-winning illustrator based in Munster, yeye weller loves soccer, the rain, and sarcasm. As much as he has always wanted to draw like Caspar David Friedrich, he has so far failed to do so — which is why he 'combines bad jokes with nice colours' in his work.

PP. 210–215

Your Friends

Your Friends was a graphic design studio in Oslo run by Carl Gürgens and Henrik Fjeldberg. It offered innovative solutions for print, digital, and environmental media for a diverse range of clients from the public, cultural, and commercial sectors.

PP. 236–237

Zim&Zou
www.zimandzou.fr

Driven by their love for creating real objects from paper and taking photos of the outcomes, Lucie Thomas and Thibault Zimmermann set up Zim&Zou studio in Nancy to explore the material further. Anchored in craftsmanship, they create all the elements by hand as they explore different fields including paper sculptures, installations, graphic design, and illustration.

PP. 514–517

Acknowledgements

We would like to specially thank all the designers and studios who are featured in this book for their significant contribution towards its compilation. We would also like to express our deepest gratitude to our producers for their invaluable advice and assistance throughout this project, as well as the many professionals in the creative industry who were generous with their insights, feedback, and time. To those whose input was not specifically credited or mentioned here, we truly appreciate your support.

Future Editions

If you wish to participate in viction:ary's future projects and publications, please send your portfolio to: we@victionary.com